Realism Reconsidered

The Legacy of Hans Morgenthau in Inter

Realism Reconsidered

The Legacy of Hans Morgenthau in
International Relations

Edited by

Michael C. Williams

OXFORD
UNIVERSITY PRESS

OXFORD
UNIVERSITY PRESS

Great Clarendon Street, Oxford ox2 6DP

Oxford University Press is a department of the University of Oxford.
It furthers the University's objective of excellence in research, scholarship,
and education by publishing worldwide in

Oxford New York

Auckland Cape Town Dar es Salaam Hong Kong Karachi
Kuala Lumpur Madrid Melbourne Mexico City Nairobi
New Delhi Shanghai Taipei Toronto

With offices in

Argentina Austria Brazil Chile Czech Republic France Greece
Guatemala Hungary Italy Japan Poland Portugal Singapore
South Korea Switzerland Thailand Turkey Ukraine Vietnam

Oxford is a registered trade mark of Oxford University Press
in the UK and in certain other countries

Published in the United States
by Oxford University Press Inc., New York

British Library Cataloguing in Publication Data
Data available

Library of Congress Cataloging in Publication Data
Data available

Typeset by SPI Publisher Services, Pondicherry, India
Printed in Great Britain
on acid-free paper by
Biddles Ltd., King's Lynn, Norfolk

ISBN 978–0–19–928861–8 (Hbk.)
ISBN 978–0–19–928862–5 (Pbk.)

1 3 5 7 9 10 8 6 4 2

☐ ACKNOWLEDGEMENTS

This volume was inspired by the centenary of Hans Morgenthau's birth in 2004. Many of the papers were first presented at a conference in November of that year at Gregynog Hall outside Newtown in Wales, where Morgenthau had himself in 1969 attended the conference marking the fiftieth anniversary of the Department of International Politics in Aberystwyth. I would like to thank the University of Wales, Aberystwyth and the Department of International Politics for their support for the conference. I am also extremely grateful to Joel Rosenthal, President of the Carnegie Council on Ethics and International Affairs for his encouragement and support for the project, and to the Carnegie Council for its financial assistance. Financial support was also provided by the British Academy through its international conference fund, and I would like to thank the Academy.

A number of individuals were crucial at various stages in the project. Richard Wyn Jones, and particularly Rita Abrahamsen, provided key encouragement at the outset and support throughout. Toni Erskine graciously lent her intellectual and organizational skills. Her contribution was invaluable. For lively debate at the Gregynog meeting, I am grateful also to colleagues and friends who attended and whose comments and criticisms played an important role in developing the final versions of the chapters in this volume.

☐ CONTENTS

☐ ABOUT THE CONTRIBUTORS

Chris Brown is Professor of International Relations and Head of the Department of International Relations at the London School of Economics. He is the author of numerous articles in international political theory and of, among others, *Understanding International Relations* (Palgrave, 3rd edn. 2005 with Kirsten Ainley), *Sovereignty, Rights and Justice* (Polity, 2002) and co-editor (with Terry Nardin and N. J. Rengger) of *International Relations in Political Thought: Texts from the Greeks to the First World War* (Cambridge University Press, 2002). He is a former Chair of the British International Studies Association.

Professor Michael Cox teaches in the Department of International Relations at the London School of Economics (LSE) where he is also Chair of the Cold War Studies Centre. The author and editor of over a dozen books, his most recent publication is an eight-volume edited study, *Twentieth Century International Relations* (Sage, 2007). In 2002 he was appointed Chair of the United States Discussion Group at Chatham House. In 2006 he was elected Chair of the European Consortium for Political Research (ECPR); and in 2007 he will be a visiting Fellow in the Nobel Institute in Oslo. He is currently editor of the journal *International Politics* and sits on the editorial board of *Cold War History*. He is currently completing a volume on US foreign policy for Oxford University Press.

Campbell Craig is Professor of International Relations at the University of Southampton, where he lectures in American foreign policy, Cold War and nuclear history, and International Relations theory. He is the author of several books and articles on these topics, including (with Fredrik Logevall) *America and the Cold War: A New History*, forthcoming from Harvard University Press.

Oliver Jütersonke is Research Coordinator for the Programme for Strategic and International Security Studies (PSIS) at the Graduate Institute of International Studies in Geneva, Switzerland. He also holds a post-doctoral position in the Graduate Programme for Interdisciplinary Research in Ethics at the University of Zurich. He has written extensively on Morganthau since 2002. Recent publications include 'Hans J. Morgenthau on the Limits of Justiciability in International Law', *Journal of the History of International Law*, 8: 2 (2006); with Keith Krause, 'Peace, Security, and Development in Post-Conflict Environments',

Security Dialogue, 36: 4 (2005); and with Rolf Schwarz, 'Divisible Sovereignty and the Reconstruction of Iraq', *Third World Quarterly*, 26: 4–5 (2005).

Anthony F. Lang, Jr. is a Senior Lecturer in the School of International Relations at the University of St Andrews. He writes and teaches on international political theory, US Foreign Policy, and Middle East politics. He is the author of *Agency and Ethics: The Politics of Miiltary Intervention* (2002), editor of *Just Intervention* (2003) and an edited version of Hans J. Morgenthau's lectures on Aristotle (2004), and co-editor of *Ethics and the Future of Conflict* (2003) and *Hannah Arendt and International Relations* (2005), along with various chapters and articles.

Richard Ned Lebow is the James O. Freedman Presidential Professor of Government at Dartmouth College and a fellow of the Centre of International Studies at the University of Cambridge. His most recent single-authored book is *The Tragic Vision of Politics: Ethics, Interests and Orders* (Cambridge University Press, 2003). Recent co-edited volumes include *Ending the Cold War* (Palgrave, 2004), *Unmaking the West: 'What-If' Scenarios that Rewrite World History* (Michigan, 2006), and *The Politics of Memory in Postwar Europe* (Duke, 2006).

Richard Little is Professor of International Politics at Bristol University. He is a former editor of the *Review of International Studies* and a past chair and president of the British International Studies Association. His most recent book, written with Barry Buzan is *International Systems in World History*. He is currently completing a book on the balance of power and editing a book with Stuart Kaufman and William Wohlforth on *The Balance of Power in World History*.

Nicholas Rengger is Professor of Political Theory and International Relations at St Andrews University. He has published in many areas of contemporary political and international theory and intellectual history. Most recently he has completed a book to be called *The Judgment of War: Political Theory and the Uncivil Condition* (forthcoming, 2007) and is currently working on defending a sceptical, anti-perfectionist political philosophy and its implications for both politics in general and international relations in particular.

William E. Scheuerman is Professor of Political Science and West European Studies at Indiana University (Bloomington). He is author of *Between the Norm and the Exception: The Frankfurt School and the Rule of Law* (MIT Press, 1994), and *Carl Schmitt: The End of Law* (Roman and Littlefield, 1999), and *Liberal Democracy and the Social Acceleration of Time* (Johns Hopkins, 2004), as well as editor of other volumes. He is presently writing an intellectual biography of Hans J. Morgenthau.

Michael C. Williams is Professor in the Department of International Politics at the University of Wales, Aberystwyth. His publications include *The Realist Tradition and the Limits of International Relations* (2005) and *Culture and Security: Symbolic Power and the Politics of International Security* (2007). He is currently completing a book (with Rita Abrahamsen) entitled *Security Beyond the State: Transnational Security Networks in International Politics.*

Introduction

Michael C. Williams

'What would Hans Morgenthau say?' This question occurs naturally, sooner or later, to those with an interest in realism and world politics. But to a degree, of course, it is a question that the field of International Relations (IR) has been asking itself for over half a century, and it continues to do so today.[1] Morgenthau remains a—perhaps the—founding figure in the study of IR, and his influence continues to be felt in contemporary controversies over how best to understand international politics. Debates over the place of realism in foreign policy, over what it means to be a 'realist', or whether it makes any sense to be one, almost inevitably include some reference to Morgenthau. And since realism remains a key fulcrum around which debates over international politics continue to turn, questions about its nature and adequacy—and Morgenthau's formulation of it—have remained central to the study of IR.

For many years references to Morgenthau in debates over realism and IR were increasingly rhetorical. As the field of IR became increasingly dominated by the neorealism advocated by Kenneth Waltz, Morgenthau's realism came to be seen as ever more anachronistic—an interesting and important episode in the history of thinking about the subject, no doubt, but one scarcely to be seen as a serious contribution to the construction of the rigorously parsimonious scientific theory that was (and to some extent still is) the goal of this mode of thinking about world politics. However, the last half decade has seen a marked recovery of interest in Morgenthau's thinking, and indeed a renewed interest in 'classical' realism as a whole. Rather than seeing Morgenthau as simply an historical placeholder in disciplinary narratives about great debates between idealists and realists, or as representing a pre-scientific form of realist 'thought' superceded by neorealist 'theory',[2] there has been a notable re-engagement with the substance of Morgenthau's thinking, an engagement often allied to the claim that his realism is not only more complex than we have often been led to believe, but of considerably greater contemporary relevance than we have imagined.

The essays in this book seek to contribute to this broad re-engagement. They are united by the conviction that Morgenthau has more to tell IR today than has generally been recognized, and that to engage with his thinking raises a set of issues much broader than those usually considered under the rubric of realism today. There is little chance of any Introduction managing to convey the breadth of issues raised by the prospect of 'reconsidering' realism, and I will not succumb to the temptation here. What may be useful to do, however, is to examine briefly the intellectual context against which the revival of interest in Morgenthau's thinking has been taking place.

Morgenthau past and present

For much of the period since his death in 1980, interpretations of Morgenthau followed three trajectories that had already become well defined during his lifetime. One strand has remained essentially laudatory, though increasingly at the level of broad statements of principle rather than precise analysis. Here, Morgenthau's insistence on 'power politics' and his attack on the liberal idealism of interwar thinking and policy was (and is) seen as a bracing and essential contribution to a re-orientation of the study of world politics, and as a key and continuing element in the sound foundation and intellectual consolidation of the field of IR. His pointed critique of legalism and warnings about the limited potential of international organizations continue to capture the concerns of those whose faith in such remedies to the problems of war and peace had been badly shaken in the twenty years crisis of the interwar period. His core concept of 'interest defined as power' appeared not only to provide, as he had claimed, an enduringly relevant map for making sense of the terrain of international politics, but also a particularly useful tool for thinking about the role of the United States in the world. Perhaps almost as importantly, it seemed to provide a bulwark against what was perceived as America's tendency towards an ineffective and imprudent vacillation between universalism and isolationism.[3]

Even at the height of his stature, however, Morgenthau's thinking was always subject to sustained and telling criticism, and this did not change. Philosophically, his view of 'human nature' was attacked as at the very least reductionist and unduly pessimistic, and at worst as indefensibly deterministic. Theoretically, his core concepts of power and the national interest were attacked as too vaguely formulated to be analytically useful. Practically, the focus on the centrality of power politics was viewed by critics as exactly the kind of 'realism' that the world in general and US policy in particular did *not* need, contributing to development and continuation of the Cold War and leading (despite Morgenthau's disavowals) to disastrous policies pursued in the name of the international balance of power, such as those in South-East Asia.

As I will discuss a little later, these views have by no means vanished; indeed they have remained remarkably resilient over the decades. Yet it is important to note another view of Morgenthau's thinking that had a fundamental impact on his legacy, and indeed on his standing in IR today. This views his thinking as basically *obsolete*. Apart from those who had long believed that Morgenthau's state-centred realism was by definition obsolete in a world of nuclear weapons and increasing interdependence, perhaps the most notable early manifestation of this charge came from the nascent behavioural movement in political science that took hold in the mid-1960s. As is well known, Morgenthau was unremittingly hostile to behaviouralism and its vision of a 'science' of politics, whether domestic or international—a position he advanced in *Scientific Man versus Power Politics*,[4] and from which he never fundamentally wavered. Yet the core methodological arguments advanced within the behavioural movement, if not its model of scientific knowledge per se, had a profound impact on the stature of Morgenthau's form of realism in IR. The demand for specific kinds of conceptual and causal precision sat ill with the forms of thinking and expression that Morgenthau saw as appropriate for the study of politics; and as the claims of science advanced in the field, so too his thinking became cast as increasingly 'pre-scientific'— inspirational perhaps, but scarcely proper social science. Perhaps even more importantly, even if the more sweeping claims of the behavioural movement failed to gain the predominance its proponents had hoped for (though its influence should by no means be underestimated), they spurred and legitimized a broader trend towards rationalism in political science that did have a broader impact, an impact that continues to this day.

The most influential expression of this rationalist turn in IR was of course the neorealism developed by Kenneth Waltz. Within the categories defined by Waltz, Morgenthau was cast as an unsystematic thinker (in every sense of the word). In the classification set out in *Man, the State, and War*, Waltz saw Morgenthau's concern with human nature as an indication of his status as a 'first image' thinker concerned with 'man', while his concern with questions of domestic politics was characteristic of a 'second image' theorist interested in the nature of 'the state'. What Morgenthau was not, damningly in Waltz's view, was a 'third image' theorist of the impact and determinations of the international system, the theme that he famously developed in later years and that for over a decade cast the debate over realism in tones distinctly uncongenial, and often hostile, to those set out by Morgenthau.[5]

Waltz was hardly alone in seeing Morgenthau's thinking about international politics as one whose time had passed. From the mid-1970s, rationalist liberalism argued that even if one accepted his focus on interest and power, Morgenthau's realist conclusions did not follow. All of this gave rise to the so-called 'neo-neo debate' that dominated the 1980s, lasted well into the 1990s, and continues to cast a shadow over contemporary IR theory.[6] Within this debate, Morgenthau's brand of realism had little place.

A similar conclusion was advanced by those who reacted against the rationalist confines of the neo-neo debate. While thinkers such as Richard Ashley evinced an early respect for Morgenthau,[7] the broader Critical movement that emerged in the 1980s and gathered pace over the next ten years was cast largely in opposition to realism. Even those currents that found value in realist thinking as a means of countering the dominance of rationalism often defined this in opposition to Morgenthau. In Robert Cox's influential formulation, for example, Morgenthau was cast as a part of the problem with IR: a proponent of 'problem-solving' theory, and a key figure in the movement away from the historically sensitive and intellectually fertile forms of realism that Cox associated with Friedrich Meinecke and E. H. Carr.[8]

By the early 1990s, in sum, while Morgenthau remained a key point of reference in IR, these allusions became increasingly off-hand and sketchy. He continued to be cited as a key historical figure in the evolution of the study of world politics, and to be summarily praised, condemned, or dismissed along the lines suggested above. Yet there was little sustained interest in his work and little sense that any was likely to emerge, or to be worth engaging in. Over the past decade, and particularly over the last five years, this trend has seen a substantial and in many ways startling reversal. Both Morgenthau and classical realism have become subjects of increasingly wide and sophisticated engagement. Indeed it might not be too much to say that interest in both is at a point not seen since Morgenthau's death. Books and articles examining Morgenthau's realism have begun appearing with greater frequency in IR theory than they have in several decades.[9] More broadly, key figures within the 'realist' canon have been brought together in attempts to provide new contributions to contemporary theorizing.[10]

This book is a reflection and contribution to this movement, but before discussing its contribution, it is useful to reflect briefly on some of the reasons behind this revival of interest. The interpretation and use of 'classical' thinkers in intellectual and political debate is never a wholly innocent process. It always reflects its historical genesis and context of current concerns. As Ned Lebow argues in his conclusion to this volume, this contemporary context is inextricable from broader controversies over both the current intellectual status of the discipline of IR, and broader developments in world politics today. And, as many of the essays in this volume attest, debates about the meaning and relevance of realism have been given added impetus by the evolution of US foreign policy over the past six years. These pressing political concerns have, however, also been bolstered by intellectual and analytic trends, and in the next few pages I would like to examine some of the specific disciplinary dynamics contributing to the emergence of a renewed substantive engagement with Morgenthau and classical realism.

Broadly speaking, this new-found interest stems from three disciplinary sources. The first is an increasing and increasingly sophisticated awareness of the disciplinary history of IR. Spurred by the conviction that accounts that disciplines give of their history have important implications for current analysis and future trajectories, and by a sense that conventional accounts of the evolution of the field of IR bear little resemblance to its actual development, disciplinary historians have begun to make serious and sustained enquiries into this evolution.[11] Inevitably, this means that key historical figures take on renewed significance and are subject to detailed analysis, and interest in Morgenthau is in part a consequence of this trend. Equally importantly, while different disciplinary histories may focus on 'internal' or 'external' approaches to their fields of study, they almost unavoidably question and unsettle prevailing disciplinary narratives about clear theoretical 'traditions' and founding debates. In IR, for example, this has involved challenges to notions of a unified 'realist tradition' standing in opposition to 'idealism', while at the same time providing interpretations of canonical thinkers that challenge their place within the stories that the field tells about its intellectual progenitors.

This increased interest in disciplinary history has corresponded with a renewed attention to the relationship between IR and political theory, and with the broader domain of international *political* theory as opposed to international *relations* theory associated with the neo-neo debate.[12] Here, interrogations of classical figures in political and international thought have provided means of both challenging appropriations of these thinkers into undifferentiated traditions or hackneyed accounts, as well as widening the conceptual concerns and lineages of thinking about international politics. The range of such engagements is extensive and, it seems, expanding: Thucydides, Machiavelli, Hobbes, Clausewitz, and a host of others have become subject to re-examination as a means of challenging prevailing uses of their legacies and exploring different philosophical lineages and orientations in IR.[13]

Part of Morgenthau's current popularity arises from his undergoing a similar process of reinterpretation and recovery, but it is also a consequence of his position as a focal point where a number of diverse but interconnected themes in these reinterpretive endeavours intersect. This has generated both considerable interest in his international political theory in its own right, and in its relationship to overlooked or underappreciated links between realism and diverse lineages in philosophy, social and political thought, and legal theory. Philosophically, much of the attention has focused on Morgenthau's relationship to Nietzsche. Morgenthau's espousal of a 'will to power' in human nature has long been seen (and often criticized) as a crudely 'Darwinian' or 'biological' strain in his thinking.[14] Locating the concept of the will to power against the backdrop of Nietzsche's analysis highlights instead its potential links to much more complex notions concerning the construction of subjectivity and its collective formation and expression under modern social and political conditions.[15] This is not only historically informative, but also potentially connects aspects of Morgenthau's realism to complex and interesting themes in post-Nietzschean philosophy and social analysis.[16]

Perhaps most strikingly in this regard, and explored in far greater depth, is how a serious engagement with Morgenthau's intellectual background connects his realism to important strands of post-Nietzschean German thought, particularly those associated with Max Weber and Carl Schmitt. While Morgenthau's connections to Weber have long been noted, more recent analyses have sought to demonstrate that the issues at stake in this connection go far beyond the familiar story of Weber's advocacy of an ethics and politics of responsibility as opposed to an ethic of absolute ends, to explore how this lineage is connected to some of the broadest questions surrounding the nature of politics in modernity, and how Morgenthau's realism stands clearly within such an engagement.[17]

Similarly, after having long been almost completely ignored or overlooked, the connections between Morgenthau's thinking and that of the controversial Weimar jurist Carl Schmitt are now finally coming clearly to light and being explored in their numerous implications.[18] Whether in terms of Morgenthau's engagement with Schmitt's controversial 'concept of the political', or with the related questions of the politics of exception, decision, and sovereignty, these studies not only broaden our understanding of Morgenthau's realism—they also connect it to some of the most significant and hotly contested issues in contemporary politics and political thought.[19]

The connection to Schmitt has also been part of a broader desire to show how Morgenthau's thinking needs to be seen in the context of the philosophy and politics of law.[20] It is well known that Morgenthau's initial academic training was in law, and that his early work focused on international legal questions. What more recent analyses have made clear, however, is how deeply his engagement with questions of law, and with the relationship between law and politics as a whole, contributed to his understanding of IR and the development of his realism. In the Weimar intellectual and political context from which Morgenthau emerged, the most crucial political debates often had an explicitly legal cast. Questions of the relationship between the legal and the political spheres, the conceptual and social foundations of legal and political order (both domestic and international), and the nature of sovereignty were all part of complex and highly politicized controversies that went far beyond the rather narrow remit that legal issues have often come to occupy in studies of international law in IR today. Morgenthau's struggle with these issues, often implicit in his later works and only clearly evident in his earlier and largely unexplored texts, has become a point of entry where legal thinkers and social and political theorists have been able to shed important light on one of IR's most prominent thinkers, and have been able to reintroduce themes largely absent from the field of IR in recent years.

Lastly, there is a nascent interest in the relationship between Morgenthau's 'European' roots and his 'American' thinking. The relationship between these two has long been contested. To some, Morgenthau was a classic figure in the European tradition of *realpolitik*, and his importance lies primarily in conveying the truths of power politics to a naïve America that in the wake of the Second World War found itself a global power. To others, there are two Morgenthaus: an 'early' European, steeped in law and political philosophy, and a 'later' American thinker who (whether out of cynical calculation or genuine conversion) became a chief proponent of the social 'science' of realism. Important epistemological and methodological issues are highlighted by this distinction, but arguably more interesting questions have recently been raised by examining Morgenthau's more overarching concern with the fate of republican forms of government and American democracy in the light of his evaluation of the experience of Weimar Germany. Here, the question is not a clear distinction between the American and European thinker, but rather one of a complex and by no means successful attempt—shared with thinkers as diverse as Reinhold Niebuhr and Hanna Arendt—to wrestle with some of the broadest problems of political life as a whole, not just a theory of IR.[21] Once again, these are issues that make Morgenthau's thinking of interest and relevance to an audience far wider than just historians of IR theory.

A third set of reasons for the renewed engagement with Morgenthau and classical realism arises from within trajectories of IR theory itself. As criticisms of Waltzian neorealism have gained increasing traction, an interest in re-examining realism has come from a variety of sources. From one direction, neoclassical realists, while retaining an attachment to Waltz's stress on systemic pressures, have argued that it is necessary to reopen questions of foreign policy and the domestic sources of state action. As a consequence, the divide between second and third image theorizing that marginalized forms of realism such as Morgenthau's is showing signs of eroding. Similarly, as social constructivist theorizing has gained an increasing presence and acceptance in the field, self-identified realists have sought to incorporate questions of identity into their theories, opening up connections to broadened understandings of the place of such issues in classical realism.[22] Finally, amongst those critical of the (neo)realist and rationalist orthodoxy of the 1980s and 1990s, a renewed sense of engagement and even appreciation for classical realism can be discerned. The broader roots of Morgenthau's thinking and its relationship to wider and more diverse traditions of political thought and social analysis discussed above have been both an outcome and an inspiration for a reconsideration of the relationship between realism and its critics.

In all these senses, just as claims about Morgenthau and realism arguably served to narrow the intellectual purview of IR at a certain point in its history, they are now—ironically perhaps—being used to open it back up. There are no doubt dangers in this, and potential distortions. Interpretive treatments are always in danger of 'presentism', of reading their own concerns, inclinations, and theoretical orientation too easily onto past thinkers. The specific political questions that exercised Morgenthau, it is obvious to say, but probably worth saying anyway, were not directly the same as our own—though his concerns with the question of nuclear weapons, with the fate of democracy under the intense pressures of international events, not to mention his reflections on the nature of political judgement, are far from irrelevant today. Moreover, as the chapters collected here show, in addition to bringing to light the breadth of the thinking of one of the field's most influential figures, a reconsideration of Morgenthau's legacy may well provide a set of openings and inspirations that can help contemporary thinking come to terms with the challenges of a theory of international politics in the world today.

The plan of the book

This volume does not seek to find 'the' Morgenthau, to settle once and for all the nature of his realism, or to discover the essence of realism itself. In line with the diversity of reasons behind the renewed interest in Morgenthau today, the contributors explore a wide range of issues, intellectual lineages, and questions of contemporary significance.[23] In the first chapter, Anthony F. Lang, Jr. draws upon recently published material to re-establish a seldom discussed and often overlooked ethical and political perspective in Morgenthau's realism: the influence of Aristotle. As Lang demonstrates, Morgenthau's thinking exhibits a deep engagement with Aristotelian thinking and themes, particularly the virtue of prudence. In fact, he argues, prudence is not simply cautious calculation in Morgenthau's vision of power politics, it is part of a much broader set of concerns that extend to questions of ethics, judgement, and the nature of the good life. In Lang's view, recognizing these concerns not only demonstrates that the roots of Morgenthau's thinking are broader than generally recognized; it also provides important contributions to contemporary debates in which realists have been engaged, such as those surrounding the conflict in Iraq.

If the Aristotelian dimension of Morgenthau's thinking has been generally overlooked, placing his thinking in a German context has become the focus of considerable recent attention. Nowhere has this been more evident than in discussions of Morgenthau's relationship to the controversial Weimar jurist Carl Schmitt. The next two chapters address this crucial issue. Chris Brown argues that Schmitt's analysis of the shift away from the classical European order provides an essential clue in appreciating Morgenthau's own understanding of the development of the modern state system and its contemporary dynamics. Comparing Schmitt's important work, *The Nomos of the Earth* with Morgenthau's early essay 'The Twilight of International Morality', he argues that both share a nostalgia for the absolutist state system that is grounded in a specific philosophical understanding of politics. The evolution of modern international politics is, accordingly, not just the tale of continually shifting power relations: it represents fundamental transformations in the foundations of political order as a whole—transformations that both thinkers viewed with considerable foreboding as the violent but nevertheless limited political aspirations and conflicts of the early modern era gave way to a world of crusading universalisms that was infinitely more dangerous. Morgenthau, Brown argues, shared much of Schmitt's theoretical appraisal of this shift and its importance, but he nonetheless possessed a commitment to democratic politics that Schmitt lacked and, as a consequence, represents a forward-looking political realism rather than a reactionary conservatism.

William Scheuerman, one of the first and most astute analysts of the 'hidden dialogue' between Schmitt and Morgenthau, argues in Chapter 3 that this lineage underpins Morgenthau's thinking about US foreign policy and his appraisal of the rise of American power as exemplified in the

Monroe Doctrine. Scheuerman holds that the lessons in political realism that Morgenthau self-consciously sought to teach Americans grew directly out of his engagement with Schmitt, even if for both personal and political reasons Morgenthau rarely made this connection explicit and never explored it in detail in his English-language writings. As well as illustrating some of the sources of Morgenthau's thinking, Scheuerman argues, this lineage is also the source of some of its most striking weaknesses and tensions, particularly in his contributions to debates on American foreign policy and his attempts to deal with growing transnational complexity and the implications of nuclear weapons.

In Chapter 4, Oliver Jütersonke takes the focus on law in a rather different direction. While acknowledging that the connection to Schmitt is important, he cautions against seeing Morgenthau's realism as a simple replication of Schmitt's politics of friend and enemy, arguing that this is only part of the broader array of equally important juridico-political debates against which Morgenthau's thinking needs to be understood. Key in this regard are Morgenthau's connections to some of the most prominent names in the evolution of international law, such as Lauterpacht and Kelsen, and their shared concern with the question of the nature and limits of legal mechanisms for the settlement of international disputes. While Morgenthau's realism is conventionally seen as standing in opposition to international law, Jütersonke argues that it emerges recognizably from his early engagement with the relationship between law and politics—a legacy that continued to structure his thinking about international politics in his most well-known work, *Politics Among Nations*.

Morgenthau did not accept a categorical divide between domestic and international politics. Nor, accordingly, did he view theories of international politics as distinct from broader traditions of political philosophy, and he drew extensively upon not only Aristotle, but also figures including Burke, the Federalists, and contemporary thinkers such as Hanna Arendt. Nicholas Rengger's contribution unearths one of the most intriguing and yet overlooked aspects of this broader dialogue—Morgenthau's exchange with Michael Oakeshott on the meaning of tragedy and its place in politics. Tragedy is of course often associated with realism in IR,[24] but as Rengger argues describing the international sphere as tragic has implications that go well beyond a simple recognition of the often terrible events that punctuate world politics, raising questions about the nature of politics as a whole—and whether tragedy is an appropriate or revealing foundation for international political theory, and an appropriate attitude when judging policies and events.

If few figures are as closely associated with realism as Morgenthau, then few concepts are so closely tied to it as the balance of power. In Chapter 6, Richard Little brings the two together in a detailed examination of Morgenthau's view of the balance of power and its changing historical structure and significance. In Little's account, Morgenthau's understanding of the balance of power is not, as Stanley Hoffmann once charged, a 'timeless monotony', but a complex and contemporarily resonant view of the relationship between social structures, states, and the European state system. Most importantly, the emergence of the balance of power as a conscious principle of statecraft in seventeenth century Europe, Little argues, was crucial for Morgenthau, demonstrating the important link between theory and practice, and showing that far from holding a purely structuralist or materialist understanding of the balance of power, Morgenthau actually advanced a nuanced and complex view of its functioning that included a stress on the role of ideas with important affinities to contemporary social constructivist thinking about the constitution of international orders.

The question of the balance of power was obviously not just an historical concern for Morgenthau, he saw it as crucial to the great geopolitical confrontation of his times: the Cold War. In fact, realism is frequently identified with the confrontational policies of the Cold War, and is sometimes even seen as one of the causes of that protracted and often dangerous confrontation. In his contribution, Michael Cox shows that Morgenthau was far from a crusading Cold Warrior. Although he felt it was vital to grasp the conflictual and competitive nature of US–Soviet relations, Morgenthau was equally (if sometimes rather inconsistently) convinced of the need to avoid casting this struggle in Manichean terms. Perhaps most significantly, he recognized that the political struggle in and for the developing world did not fit comfortably onto a simplistic template of balance of power politics and domino theories. He presciently argued that it was vital to recognize the importance and legitimacy of national struggles in colonial and post-colonial states, a stance that underpinned his early, prescient, and outspoken criticisms of US policy in Vietnam. Morgenthau's critique, Cox holds, is far from irrelevant for thinking about American foreign policy today.

Few transformations have had so great an impact on ideas about the balance of power, the nature of realism, and the politics of the Cold War as the advent of nuclear weapons. Campbell Craig's contribution examines the fundamental tensions in Morgenthau's realism brought about by his attempts to think through the implications of this novel and fearsome destructive capability. Gradually becoming aware that nuclear weapons made great power war unsurvivable, and thus traditional understandings of realism unviable, Morgenthau was spurred to a renewed engagement with the logic of a world state that he had previously rejected. Tracing this dilemma through Morgenthau's shifting views on nuclear strategy and limited war, Craig argues that he sought a merging of realist and utopian views as the basis for a new international order, at the same time that his philosophical position precluded achieving such a vision.

In Chapter 9, I seek to show how a broader understanding of the 'roots'[25] of Morgenthau's realism can shed light on some of the most intense recent debates over foreign policy, those between realists and neoconservatives. While neoconservatism is sometimes seen as a form of realism, or as implacably opposed to realism, I argue that a fuller grasp of the roots of neoconservatism reveals a more complex relationship. Like neoconservatism, Morgenthau's thinking reflects a continuing concern with the fate of liberal modernity, and in many ways his diagnosis of the pathologies of modern politics is quite similar to that found within strands of neoconservatism. However, the implications that Morgenthau drew from this situation were in many ways deeply opposed to those advocated by contemporary theorists of American 'national greatness'. When seen in this light, Morgenthau's realism actually speaks to contemporary concerns in a way that many contemporary formulations of realism cannot.

The conclusion to the volume is provided by Richard Ned Lebow. Whereas this Introduction earlier focused on the largely disciplinary context against which the revival of interest in Morgenthau can be seen, Lebow casts his net wider, taking in the political context of the end of the Cold War and the relationship between ideas and political action. Analysing the multiple relationships between processes of interpretation and structures of influence, he shows that current interest in classical political thinkers (and classical realism) is linked to broader questions about how best to understand and react to developments in world politics, and to concerns about the ability of the field of IR to do so effectively.

As contributions to disciplinary history, as appreciations of Morgenthau as a political thinker of no mean consequence, and as contributions towards debate about the current status and future development of the study of international politics and its relationship to political practice, the chapters in this book seek to show how an engagement with one of IR's most oft-cited but arguably least understood thinkers can enrich not only our understanding of the evolution of thinking about world politics, but also our ability to address today's concerns.

NOTES

1. As is conventional, the field of International Relations as a scholarly discipline will hereafter be abbreviated as IR. 'Realism' as a school of thought is uncapitalized throughout for aesthetic reasons.
2. Kenneth Waltz, 'Realist Thought and Neorealist Theory', in Robert L. Rothstein (ed.), *The Evolution of Theory in International Relations* (Columbia: University of South Carolina Press, 1991), 21–37.
3. For a pointed recent argument in these terms, see John Mearsheimer: 'Hans Morgenthau and the Iraq war: realism versus neoconservatism', http://www.opendemocracy
4. Hans J. Morgenthau, *Scientific Man versus Power Politics* (Chicago, IL: University of Chicago Press, 1946).
5. Kenneth Waltz, *Theory of International Politics* (Boston, MA: Addison-Wesley, 1979). Important exceptions include Joel Rosenthal, *Righteous Realists: Political Realism, Responsible Power, and American Culture in the Nuclear Age* (Baton Rouge, LA: Louisiana State University Press, 1991), and Michael J. Smith, *Realist thought from Weber to Kissinger* (Baton Rouge, LA: Louisiana State University Press, 1986).
6. Ole Waever, 'The Rise and Fall of the Inter-Paradigm Debate', in Steve Smith, Ken Booth and Marysia Zalewski (eds.), *International Theory: Positivism and Beyond* (Cambridge: Cambridge University Press, 1996), 149–85. See also, Jeffrey W. Legro and Andrew Moravcsik, 'Is Anybody Still a Realist?', *International Security*, 24: 2 (1999), 5–55; and the responses in 'Brother Can You Spare a Paradigm (Or Was Anybody Ever a Realist?)', *International Security*, 24: 3 (1999), 165–93.
7. See particularly his 'Political Realism and Human Interests', *International Studies Quarterly*, 25: 2 (1981), 533–68.
8. Robert W. Cox, 'Social Forces, States and World Orders: Beyond International Relations Theory', in Robert Keohane (ed.), *Neorealism and its Critics* (New York: Columbia University Press, 1986), 204–54.
9. Since much of this literature is covered in detail in the following chapters, I will not try to canvass it here; but see, for example, Benjamin Mollov, *Power and*

Transcendence: Hans J. Morgenthau and the Jewish Experience (Lanham, MD: Lexington, 2002); William Bain, 'Deconfusing Morgenthau: Moral Inquiry and Classical Realism Reconsidered', *Review of International Studies*, 26: 3 (2000), 445–64; Sean Molloy, 'Truth, Power, Theory: Hans Morgenthau's Formulation of Realism', *Diplomacy and Statecraft*, 15: 1 (2004), 1–34; Veronique Pin-Fat, 'The Metaphysics of the National Interest and the "Mysticism" of the State: Reading Hans J. Morgenthau', *Review of International Studies*, 31: 3 (2005), 217–36; Robert Shilliam, 'Tragedy in Context: "German Backwardness", Hans Morgenthau, and the Fate of a Liberal Tradition', *European Journal of International Relations* (forthcoming); Michael C. Williams, 'Why Ideas Matter in IR: Hans Morgenthau, Classical Realism and the Moral Construction of Power Politics', *International Organization*, 58: 4 (2004), 633–65.

10. Again, a sampling might include Campbell Craig, *Glimmer of a New Leviathan: Total War in the Realism of Niebuhr, Morgenthau, and Waltz* (New York: Columbia University Press, 2003); Stefano Guzzini, *Realism in International Relations and International Political Economy* (London: Routledge, 1998); Johnathan Haslam, *No Virtue Like Necessity: Realist Thought in International Relations* (New Haven, CT: Yale University Press, 2002); Richard Ned Lebow, *The Tragic Vision of Politics* (Cambridge: Cambridge University Press, 2004); Sean Molloy, *The Hidden History of Realism: A Genealogy of Power Politics* (London: Palgrave, 2005); Alastair Murray, *Reconstructing Realism* (Edinburgh: Keele University Press, 1997); Michael C. Williams, *The Realist Tradition and the Limits of International Relations* (Cambridge: Cambridge University Press, 2005).

11. See particularly, Brian Schmitt, *The Political Discourse of Anarchy* (Albany, NY: State University of New York, 1998), and 'Anarchy, World Politics and the Birth of a Discipline: American International Relations, Pluralist Theory and the Myth of Interwar Idealism', *International Relations*, 16 (2002), 9–31; Duncan Bell, 'Political Theory and the Functions of Intellectual History: A Response to Emmanuel Navon', *Review of International Studies*, 29: 1 (2003), 151–60.

12. A selection in a well-developed and expanding literature might here include Charles Beitz, *Political Theory and International Relations* (Princeton, NJ: Princeton University Press, 1979); Andrew Linklater, *Men and Citizens in the Theory of International Relations* (London: Macmillan, 1982), R. B. J. Walker, *Inside/Outside: International Relations as Political Theory* (Cambridge: Cambridge University Press, 1993); Nicholas Rengger, *International Relations, Political Theory, and the Problem of Order* (London: Routlege, 1999); Chris Brown, Terry Nardin, and Nicholas Rengger (eds.), *International Relations in Political Thought* (Cambridge: Cambridge University Press, 2002).

13. Amongst a now extensive literature, a broad survey can be found in Beate Jahn (ed.), *Classical Theory in International Relations* (Cambridge; Cambridge University Press, 2006).

14. See, for example, Jack Donnelly, *Realism in International Relations* (Cambridge; Cambridge University Press 2000); Annette Freyberg-Inan, *What Moves Man: The*

Realist Theory of International Relation and its Judgement of Human Nature (Albany, NY: SUNY Press, 2004); Bradley Thayer, 'Bringing in Darwin: Evolutionary Theory, Realism and International Politics', *International Security*, 25: 2 (2000), 124–51.

15. See Ulrik Enemark Peterson, 'Breathing Nietzsche's Air: New Reflections On Morgenthau's Concepts of Power and Human Nature', *Alternatives*, 24: 1 (1999), 83–118; as well as the discussion in Christophe Frei, *Hans Morgenthau: An Intellectual Biography* (Baton Rouge, LA: University of Louisiana Press, 2001); for interesting assessments of Nietzche's will to power see Mark Warren, *Nietzsche and Political Thought* (Cambridge, MA: MIT Press, 1991); and David Owen, *Maturity and Modernity: Nietzsche, Weber, Foucault and the Ambivalence of Reason* (London: Routledge, 1997).

16. For a rare and insightful discussion of this lineage in realism, albeit without reference to Morgenthau, see James Der Derian, 'A Reinterpretation of Realism', in Francis A. Beer and Robert Harriman (eds.), *Post-Realism: The Rhetorical Turn in International Relations* (East Lansing, MI: University of Michigan Press, 1996), 277–304.

17. For example, Tarak Barkawi, 'Strategy as a Vocation: Weber, Morgenthau and Modern Strategic Studies', *Review of International Studies*, 24: 2 (1998), 159–84; and Stephen Turner, 'Morgenthau as a Weberian', in G. O. Mazur (ed.), *One Hundred Year Commemoration to the Life of Hans J. Morgenthau, 1904–2004* (New York: Semenenko Foundation, 2004), 88–114.

18. Especially William Scheuerman, 'Another Hidden Dialogue' in his *Carl Schmitt: The End of Law* (New York: Rowan and Littlefield, 1999), 225–51; see also John McCormick, *Carl Schmitt: Against Politics as Technology* (Cambridge: Cambridge University Press), 302–14. In IR, see Hans-Karl Pichler, 'The Godfathers of "Truth": Max Weber and Carl Schmitt in Morgenthau's Theory of Power Politics', *Review of International Studies*, 24: 2 (1998), 185–200; and the rejoinder by Jef Huysmans, 'Know your Schmitt: A Godfather of Truth and the Spectre of Nazism', *Review of International Studies*, 25: 2 (1999), 323–8; broader still is Huysmans, 'The Question of the Limit: Desecuritization and the Aesthetics of Horror in Political Realism', *Millennium: Journal of International Studies*, 27: 3 (1998), 569–89.

19. For a series of analyses of the concept of exception in the context of the war on terror see the Special Section of *Security Dialogue*, 37: 1 (2006), 7–82.

20. See especially Martti Koskenniemi, *The Gentle Civilizer of Nations: The Rise and Fall of International Law, 1870–1960* (Cambridge: Cambridge University Press, 2002), and Koskenniemi, 'Carl Schmitt, Hans Morgenthau, and the Image of Law in International Relations', in Michael Byers (ed.), *The Role of Law in International Politics* (Oxford: Oxford University Press, 2000), as well as the work of William Scheuerman cited above.

21. See especially Vibeke Schou Tjalve, *American Jerimiahs?: Reinhold Niebuhr, Hans J. Morgenthau, and the Realist Recovery of a Republican Peace* (Copenhagen: Copenhagen Political Studies Press, 2004).

22. For instance, Johnathan Mercer, 'Anarchy and Identity', *International Organization*, 49: 2 (1995), 229–52, and Williams, 'Why Ideas Matter in IR'.
23. Inevitably, of course, there are many connections or themes—whether to other thinkers (such as Marx, Weber, Niebuhr, or Kennan) or schools of thought (feminism, political economy) that might have been explored but that are left aside here.
24. As evidenced in the title of John Mearsheimer's *The Tragedy of Great Power Politics* (New York: Norton, 2002), and Lebow's *Tragic Vision of Politics*.
25. See Benjamin Frankel (ed.), *Roots of Realism* (London: Frank Cass, 1996).

1 Morgenthau, agency, and Aristotle

Anthony F. Lang, Jr.

Realists are either amoral analysts of the international system who focus only on power or immoral Machiavellians who see nothing wrong with using violence and deception to advance the national interest. This, at least, is the caricature often found in critical and even some sympathetic accounts of the realist tradition. Indeed, it does apply to some theorists especially those writing from a neorealist or structural framework. If this caricature of realism is correct, then realists have nothing to say about some of the most pressing problems of the twenty-first century—humanitarian intervention, clashing civilizations, and promoting democracy, to name just a few that surround the conflict between the United States and Iraq at the time of this writing. Realists reduce all these dilemmas to states pursuing power in accordance with their national interest. For theorists, this means avoiding normative conflicts and for policymakers it means building up and using power to smash those who attack you and change regimes when necessary.

Thankfully, the idea that realists cannot speak to normative theoretical debate or policy dilemmas that require moral choice is false. In this chapter, I find in one of the founders of the realist tradition—Hans J. Morgenthau—a nuanced understanding of the relationship between ethics and politics. Morgenthau's ethical framework has recently come under investigation by various writers, who see him as drawing from Nietzsche, the American founders, and even Judaism. One influence that has not been explored at great depth, but which I argue is central to grasping Morgenthau's understanding of ethics, is the political philosophy of Aristotle. In particular, Morgenthau drew from Aristotle an appreciation of the virtue of prudence and its role in negotiating the complexities of human existence.

Based in part on his recently published lectures,[1] this chapter suggests that Morgenthau drew from Aristotle a conception of agency more attuned to the normative dimensions of politics. Human persons are not simply self-seeking, power hungry egoists, but intellectual, moral, and spiritual beings who understand their obligations in relation to the community. At the same time, they are often frustrated in attempting to pursue those obligations. This idea of the human person is mirrored in Morgenthau's conception of the state pursuing its interests in the international realm. Rather than self-seeking, power hungry agents, states can also embody norms of prudence and justice, but only contingently and in relation to their historical experience. How states and persons can act in pursuit of their interests yet also respect moral standards is explored throughout Morgenthau's works and finds echoes in Aristotle's *Nichomachean Ethics* and *The Politics*.

This Aristotelian conception of agency allows Morgenthau to retain the principle that persons and states pursue their interests, but in pursuing those interests they might well be acting in accordance with normative standards. The virtue of prudence, which Morgenthau locates in the practice of diplomacy, provides the tool by which interests and principles can be brought into alignment. The privileging of prudence suggests new ways of understanding the American 'war on terror' by demonstrating its failure to appreciate how in pursuing political actions—in this case seeking to make the world safe from terrorism—the agent undertaking such a task cannot see itself as the paragon of virtue. Instead, the prudent actor will be attentive to the ways in which his own political community results from a complex political history, a recognition that allows for a more balanced and less 'moralistic' foreign policy.

The chapter proceeds as follows: In the first section, I examine agency as a concept and point towards how Aristotle provides a fuller picture of human life than the dominant sociological accounts currently occupying scholars of IR. I then turn to a brief overview of Morgenthau's perspective on ethics. Most readings of his work locate Morgenthau's conception of ethics as outside of the political sphere, such as from a divine command perspective. I suggest that this reading of him (while true in part) fails to account for the sophisticated way in which he understood the relationship between politics and ethics, a relationship that appears closer to Aristotle. From here, I propose how Aristotle's philosophy provides an account of agency for Morgenthau that influenced his theory of IR. In the final section, I use this interpretation of Morgenthau to critique the US war on terror. In so doing, I hope to demonstrate the continuing relevance of Morgenthau's approach to IR. Understanding his perspective on the nexus of politics and ethics at the international level is not simply a matter of intellectual history; rather, it can continue to generate important insights on the politics of American empire.

1.1. **Aristotle and agency**

Realism—in both its classical and structural varieties—assumes a theory of agency. At the individual level, realists see human behaviour as resulting from either fear or aggression. At the state level, realists see foreign policy as a product of the same fear and aggression, characteristics that are heightened by the condition of anarchy.[2] As constructivists have pointed out, realists have not developed these assumptions at any length, creating a theory that does not account for the impact of ideas on international affairs.[3] For those interested in international ethics, a lack of attention to agency creates a theoretical framework in which agents cannot be held responsible for their actions, that is, a world in which moral judgments play no role.[4]

But this fear-based explanation of human behaviour can only take us so far. A more sophisticated conception of agency is necessary to understand and evaluate how individuals and states act in the political sphere. At its core, agency is the capacity to change the world. This capacity, however, is not simply a physical characteristic; a hurricane changes the world, but we do not conventionally describe it as having agency. Rather, agency connects the physical capacity to change with either an analytical or evaluative dimension. The predominant understandings of agency in the discipline of IR are analytical, borrowed from sociology, and generally tied to debates about the relationship between agents and structures. The question driving these debates is whether or not behaviour can be explained as the result of properties internal to the units within a system or the properties of the system as a whole. For neorealists, behaviour is best explained on the basis of the system as a whole. The fault of classical realists, according to this view, is that they look primarily to the internal characteristics of the agent for explanations rather than to the structure of the system.[5] Constructivist theorists, still focused on this relationship between agents and structures, have argued that neorealists fail to provide a theory that fully appreciates the interactions that occur between agents and the structures within which they operate. Constructivists have argued that agents do exist independently of structures in which they operate, but that they are partly constituted by those structures.[6]

While useful in understanding how the interests of states arise from factors both internal and external, these constructivist insights do not fully appreciate how a theory of agency has relevance not only for explaining behaviour but for grasping the role of rules, norms, and evaluations of the international system. Indeed, the sociologically derived debates about agents and structures have relevance primarily in so far as they provide some taxonomic rigor to theoretical explanations. Ethical, legal, and political conceptions of agency, however, have a far more useful purpose. These conceptions of agency—which remain largely absent from IR debates—provide important insights on how to evaluate IR and foreign policy. Attributing agency to an entity results in certain rights and responsibilities being granted to that entity. For instance, if states are agents in the international system, they can be said to have a right to be free from interference (the traditional notion of sovereignty). More controversially, they might also be held responsible for outcomes in legal and even moral terms. The idea of state agency and responsibility has been the subject of numerous legal debates, some of which culminated in the passage of the Articles on State Responsibility by the International Law Commission in 2001.[7] These Articles have contributed to international law such that states can now be considered liable for countermeasures, including financial countermeasures, for violations of international legal norms. Various international and national courts have begun to draw upon these provisions in their judgments.[8]

Yet another way to conceptualize agency comes from moral philosophers whose work, naturally, focuses on the individual person rather than corporate entities such as the state. But, while their focus is on the person, insights derived from these philosophical debates can be applied to how states act at the global level. One division among ethicists is between those who focus upon acts versus those who focus on agents. The former would include utilitarian and deontological ethical theories. These theories evaluate actions and provide rules or criteria for right action. The latter includes virtue ethics or what some call agent-centred morality. This form of moral philosophy evaluates the agent, with particular attention paid to that agent's character (or soul in older versions). A central concern of these theories is that a moral theory should not be a set of rules imposed upon persons that they have to struggle to fulfil against their wishes. Rather, ethics should provide us with an understanding of why the human person acts in the way she does, and, in so doing, incorporate that understanding into our forms of evaluation and judgment. Such an understanding of ethics, then, would include an explanatory element in that it would help us to explain why people act the way they do, along with an evaluation of that action.

Aristotle is often seen as the first agent-centred ethicist in that his understanding of right behaviour was premised upon a set of assumptions about why the human person acts the way he does. In the *Nichomachean Ethics*, Aristotle argues that all things tend towards an end, a *telos*. In terms of human actions, Aristotle reviews a range of different ends towards which humans tend, including honour, money, pleasure, and even happiness. But, since to claim that happiness is the end of all action is a platitude, there must be a better way to describe the human good. For Aristotle, that ultimate description is 'human good turns out to be activity of soul in accordance with virtue, and if there are more than one virtue, in accordance with the best and most complete'.[9] Such a description requires a greater appreciation of what Aristotle means by virtue, which is not simply good behaviour. Rather, virtue is the pursuit of excellence in a certain field of activity. This pursuit is not a goal to be achieved, but a continued action that each time it is performed gives a sense of attainment and satisfaction to the agent.

At first glance, such a theory of ethics does not provide much explanation for why people act. Yet this simple structure allows us to construct a theory that both explains human behaviour and also allows us to evaluate it. For Aristotle, this theory involves acting in ways that conform to excellence for Athenian gentlemen at a particular time in history, although he believes he is providing a more universal theory based on human biology. We need not agree with his more universal conception of human agency to see that the framework he provides allows one to construct a theory of behaviour that can be both explanatory and evaluative.

One of the virtues developed by Aristotle, however, need not remain confined to his time and place bound notion of the human person. The virtue of prudence, or *phronesis* in the Greek, is intimately connected to the very nature of virtue and Aristotle's teleological project for it is the ability to reason about how to obtain the good. It is the ability to know what is good and to act upon it, thus combining the intellectual with the moral realms. *Phronesis* does not arise from the mere accumulation of factual knowledge, but comes from a life lived in a community in which individuals must negotiate their differences and come to some common standards of behaviour.

As a result, human action arises from both right reason about proper behaviour and also from habits acquired through education and life in a civic community. Aristotle concludes the *Nichomachean Ethics* by pointing to the importance of legislation and actually conceives of the study of ethics as a branch of the study of politics. Education into the virtues is a central part of Aristotelian theory, and this education only takes place in a civic community that values the correct things. This puts particular importance on political structure as the means to produce good political leaders and arenas in which human flourishing can take place.

Aristotle, then, provides three central insights about agency:

- The human person acts in pursuit of a *telos*, an end towards which persons naturally tend. The virtues provide a means by which to evaluate how the person pursues those ends.

- *Phronesis*, or prudence, is one of the most important virtues. It is the ability to reason about the human good. It derives from both factual knowledge and historical experiences.

- Training in this and the other virtues results from living in a community that is well governed and which allows individuals to both rule and be ruled. This suggests it is a community where individuals need to take into account the agency and interests of their fellow citizens.

These insights provide a conception of agency that is richer than the standard IR theory debates. It does relate to those debates, however, in that Aristotle provides an understanding of the agent as living in a community that shapes his or her interests and knowledge. As the next section demonstrates, Morgenthau does not completely adopt this Aristotelian framework, but he does, nevertheless, draw heavily on it in understanding why humans and the states in which they live act in certain ways.

1.2. **Morgenthau and morality**

In order to locate Morgenthau's understanding of agency, it is essential to take his thought beyond the standard realpolitik with which he is often associated. Indeed, appreciating Morgenthau's ideas about the relationship between ethics and politics demonstrates how his conception of agency mirrors the Aristotelian project.

Although he claimed 'I have always maintained that the actions of states are subject to universal moral principles',[10] locating the ethical in Morgenthau's thought is not easy. In *Politics Among Nations*, the book for which he is best known, he seems to place morality outside the practice of international politics, conceptualizing it as a 'constraint' upon the pursuit of power. He also argues that in spite of the hopes of liberals, there is no agreed upon ethic, but only ethical frameworks that arise from specific contexts. Even more problematic, those ethical frameworks are yoked to nationalist ideologies, making them part of the international contest for power and interest.[11]

So, while he claimed an interest in ethics, Morgenthau did not seem to centrally incorporate such themes into his analyses of international affairs. Reinterpretations of his work have struggled with this impression, both drawing attention to his interests in ethics but also appearing to reinforce the idea that they stand outside the central concerns of a political analyst. Greg Russell and Joel Rosenthal were two of the first theorists to demonstrate that the picture of Morgenthau as an amoral theorist of power politics fails to appreciate his interest in and attention to the normative element of international affairs.[12] Russell examined how Morgenthau moved away from his 'European' background of *realpolitik* and was influenced by the American context with its often-moralistic foreign policy discourse. Rosenthal explores how the dilemma of living in a world of nuclear power prompted not only Morgenthau but also other realists to confront central questions of ethics and responsible uses of power. For both theorists, however, Morgenthau was arguing against an American tendency to moralize political practices and, while he himself believed morality had a role to play, he sought to downplay that tendency in order to convince Americans of their responsibility to understand power.

Other scholars have looked to Morgenthau's formative educational experiences in Germany as a source for his views on ethics and politics. Christoph Frei locates Morgenthau in a Nietzschean tradition, focusing primarily on his education and early career in Germany and Spain. Frei sees Nietzsche as an early influence on Morgenthau, but one whose impact became progressively less pronounced; 'While Morgenthau remains attached to the analyst, he refuses to follow the prophet.'[13] According to Frei, Nietzsche revealed to Morgenthau the importance of power along with a healthy intellectual scepticism when confronting legal and moral interpretations of politics. But Morgenthau did not adopt Nietzsche's 'transvaluation of values', instead hoping for a more secure normative grounding for politics. Frei argues that Morgenthau found in the 'classical humanist tradition' a moral basis that informed his own life, making him 'sensitive to issues concerning freedom, the right to self-determination, and the dignity of each and every human being'.[14]

For Benjamin Mollov, that grounding can be found in Morgenthau's Judaism.[15] While he does not appear to have been a practising Jew, Morgenthau's political activities and social interactions suggest a strong identification with Judaism. For Mollov, these activities establish the importance of Judaism in Morgenthau's thought. Mollov argues that Reinhold Niebuhr—who Morgenthau called 'the father of us all'— connected Morgenthau to his Jewish roots, an ironic link in that Niebuhr was a Christian pastor. A. J. H. Murray also argues that Morgenthau drew on a distinctly Judeo-Christian moral framework, one that he struggled to connect to his theories about power politics.[16]

Yet, Morgenthau's own statements and these sympathetic readings of his work reinforce the idea that ethics stands outside of the political sphere. Rather than being motivated by the desire to pursue the good and manifest it in the political community, the Morgenthauian political actor pursues power and only later seeks to reinterpret his actions through the lens of a transcendent moral code. In so doing, the political remains a world apart, one in which power remains the central currency. The image of the prophet chastising the king, a common theme in the Jewish scriptures, seems most appropriate here. Rather than being concerned with ethics himself, the king is forced to act morally by the prophet who demands justice while the king pursues power.

1.3. **Morgenthau, Aristotle, and agency**

Although Morgenthau drew upon this Judeo-Christian heritage in his understanding of ethics, he also drew upon the classical account offered by Aristotle. For Aristotle, all activities seek a good, and the highest good is to be found in the construction of the political space in which citizens would be trained to understand the good and its relation to the community. The ideal person was one who could both rule and be ruled. Unlike the conflicted relationship between the Ancient Hebraic king and prophet, the Aristotelian ruler was one who knew the good and made it concrete in the construction of the political sphere.

To argue that Morgenthau was influenced by Aristotle, however, is a difficult prospect. Especially if one reads through his major works on international politics, there appears very little that would link the two. Even in the reinterpretations of his work, hardly any explore an Aristotelian link. But Morgenthau knew Aristotle's work well; when asked to list the ten most influential books he had read, Aristotle's *The Politics* made the list.[17] Morgenthau engaged Aristotle's work throughout his career, especially as a teacher. In his unpublished papers, there exists a transcript of notes for lectures on Aristotle's *The Politics* dating from 1947 while he taught at the University of Chicago.[18] In another set of typed lectures from his papers, he begins a historical survey of political thought by comparing Aristotle with Machiavelli. In those same lectures, he cites the famous assertion that the study of politics is simply a footnote to Aristotle and Plato.[19] Kenneth Thompson noted that Morgenthau taught a seminar on *The Politics* from 1956 through 1966.[20]

Morgenthau had a version of these lectures, or more accurately seminars, recorded and transcribed from the early 1970s. He intended to publish them himself, but was not able to return to them before he died in 1980.[21] After editing and revising, they have now been published as *Political Theory and International Affairs: Hans J. Morgenthau on Aristotle's The Politics*.[22] In these seminars, Morgenthau progresses through *The Politics*, addressing the Aristotelian themes of methodology, the state, equality, comparative government, and revolutionary change. But the seminars were not simple descriptions of Aristotle's thought; rather, Morgenthau engaged Aristotle, sometimes agreeing with his interpretations, other times using him as a foil against which he could present alternative notions of politics.

Because of this engagement with Aristotle rather than a direct incorporation of his ideas into Morgenthau's work, it is difficult to claim that Morgenthau was an Aristotelian. Rather, Morgenthau drew from Aristotle a framework for approaching the political. Within that framework, he incorporated his own insights on politics, challenging, for example, Aristotle's ideas of the common good and his inability to appreciate the importance of power. Thus, Morgenthau can write in *Scientific Man and Power Politics* 'The Aristotelian truth that man is a political animal is true forever' without adopting Aristotle's ideas about the value of a political community being oriented towards the good.[23]

Morgenthau's conception of agency arises from Aristotle's theories of the relationship between the *vita activia* and the *vita contempletiva,* a relationship that informs Aristotle's ideas about *phronesis* as described above.[24] For Morgenthau, the danger of the contemplative life was that it could produce a Hamlet who agonizes over decisions and thus fails to act. In two articles, one published in 1945 and the other in 1971, Morgenthau developed the relationship between thought and action. In exploring that relationship, it becomes clearer that he saw ethics not as an outside discipline on power hungry persons, but as an integral part of the human person's approach to political life.

In 1945, Morgenthau published a short article with the provocative title 'The Evil of Politics and the Ethics of Evil'. The article is part of his project to refute the assumptions of interwar liberalism.[25] He begins by noting that 'Man is a political animal by nature...he is a moralist because he is a man.'[26] Like Aristotle, Morgenthau recognizes that the human person cannot escape the ethical and political elements of existence. By nature, we live in community and by nature, we evaluate our actions in terms of some standards. A dilemma arises, however, because ethical standards and good intentions cannot match the fact of living in community. Morgenthau identifies various attempts to surmount this dilemma, with particular attention paid to efforts to distinguish personal from political morality. Both advocates of realpolitik and liberal utopians commit this fallacy; the former uses this to justify whatever actions he wishes in the political sphere, while the latter seeks, like Woodrow Wilson, to castigate nations that violate personal Judeo-Christian norms.

For Morgenthau, neither of these two positions appreciates the problems that arise from two other elements of the human condition. Two sets of problems actually exist, one arising from the person as an individual, and the second from the person living in community. Individuals fail to live up to ethical standards because they are unable to predict the outcome of their actions, what Morgenthau calls 'the natural limitations of the human intellect'. Being unable to predict the consequences of actions means that good intentions will, inevitably, go awry as a single action travels an unpredictable course. The second problem for the individual is that each person seeks a vast array of goals, most of which cannot be pursued simultaneously.[27] These two problems mean that the individual can never really escape the ethical dilemmas of action.

The second set of problems arises from the fact that people live and act in the context of a community. First, in a world of scarcity, competition for resources (on both the personal and international level) will lead to compromises of good intentions. The second, better known to students of realism, is that the human person seeks power, or what Morgenthau calls the *animus dominandi*. While the first could, conceivably, be resolved by ensuring the just distribution of resources in a community, the second can never be resolved.

Here then we have Morgenthau's schematic of human agency. Individuals act in the political realm, but they also judge their political actions according to moral standards. Yet they never live up to those standards because of both failings of the human condition qua individuals and qua members of a political community. For Morgenthau, however, this situation does not lead to an abandonment of morality or a perfectionist moral standard. Indeed, these are the two extremes against which he seems to be positioning himself. He concludes that morally informed political action is possible, but only if one acts in accordance with a set of standards that look strikingly like the Aristotelian virtue of prudence:

Neither science nor ethics nor politics can resolve the conflict between politics and the ethics of harmony. We have no choice between power and common good. To act successfully, that is, according to the rules of the political art, is political wisdom. To know with despair that the political act is inevitably evil, and to act nevertheless, is moral courage. To choose among several expedient actions the least evil one is moral judgment. In combination of political wisdom, moral courage, and moral judgment man reconciles his political nature with his moral destiny.[28]

The combination of judgment, courage, and knowledge is the definition of the prudent person, the ideal of a virtuous individual that Aristotle identifies in both the *Nichomachean Ethics* and *The Politics.*

This theme of political virtue appears in a second article devoted to the question of political agency. In his 1971 article, 'Thought and Action in Politics', Morgenthau begins by arguing that the human person wishes to change the world around her through political action. But, because individuals face so many obstacles to true political action, they will resort to political thought in hopes of changing the world. While this has been true of all political theory, according to Morgenthau recent political science has taken this desire to change the world through analysis to its extreme. Political scientists seek primarily to accumulate knowledge and facts in order to guide political decisions.

For Morgenthau, however, this approach fails to appreciate what the political actor really needs. Rather than an accumulation of facts, political actors need a combination of knowledge, courage, and skill. These three elements of action, mirrored in Aristotle's ideal political actor, culminate for Morgenthau in the idea of political wisdom:

Wisdom is the gift of intuition, and political wisdom is the gift to grasp intuitively the quality of diverse interests and of power in the present and future and the impact of different actions upon them. Political wisdom, understood as sound political judgment, cannot be learned; it is a gift of nature, like the gift of artistic creative or literary style or eloquence of force of personality. As such, it can be deepened and developed by example, experience and study. But it cannot be acquired through deliberate effort by those from whom nature has withheld it.[29]

Again, Morgenthau finds in an Aristotelian conception of political virtue the answer to the existential crisis of the human condition. This political actor must embody prudence, the ideal of Aristotelian politics.

Aristotelian themes thus appear in these two articles. But what of Morgenthau's larger corpus of works? Do these same themes appear in *Politics Among Nations*, for example? In his lament about the failure of nationalistic ethics to constrain the pursuit of power in the international system, we find a nostalgia for a different, aristocratic morality. This moral framework arose from the diplomatic traditions of nineteenth century Europe, in which individual leaders knew the 'rules of the game' and were loathe to violate them. In briefly explaining this ideal, Morgenthau describes the moral ideal of the nineteenth century diplomat in Aristotelian terms:

The moral standards of conduct with which the international aristocracy complied were of necessity of a supranational character. They applied not to all Prussians, Austrians, or Frenchman, but to all men who by virtue of their birth and education were able to comprehend them and to act in accordance with them. It was in the concept and the rules of natural law that this cosmopolitan society found the source of its precepts of morality. The individual members of this society, therefore, felt themselves to be personally responsible for compliance with these moral rules of conduct; for it was to them as rational human beings, as individuals, that this moral code was addressed.[30]

Certainly an atavistic conception of international affairs—one premised upon the idea of an enlightened diplomat adhering to moral standards that the demos could not comprehend much less act upon—this idea of morality and the practice of politics does indicate that Morgenthau conceptualized ethics in terms of what is today sometimes called virtue ethics, a tradition that draws upon Aristotle as one of its originators.[31]

This interpretation of Morgenthau is reinforced in his lectures on Aristotle. In examining Book II of *The Politics*, Morgenthau assesses Aristotle's views on slavery. Rather than condemn them outright (which he eventually does), Morgenthau uses these passages to explore the issue of equality. He understands Aristotle to be arguing that equality among a group of people does not always apply, for equality should be judged on the basis of whatever task has brought those persons together. This leads Aristotle, and Morgenthau, to ask if everyone is equal in their ability to rule. The answer, for both, is no. As Morgenthau states:

Another way to think about this same issue of equality is to think about political judgment. Most of the people I know who deal with foreign policy are devoid of political judgment. It is a very rare quality. So, I would not exclude *a priori* the proposition that people are different by nature in different respects, and that they are also different with regard to politics. . . . I'm convinced that only a small minority is capable of governing. Most of the people who govern are unqualified to govern.[32]

Along these same lines, in *The Purpose of American Politics*, Morgenthau lamented the decline of 'objective standards of excellence' in the American public, linking this to the collapse of a public realm.[33] The use of that phrase, 'standards of excellence' is sometimes used as a translation of Aristotle's concept of *arête*, the Greek word for virtue.

This virtue ethic can be found, perhaps, in Morgenthau's understanding of diplomacy, which leads to his theory of state agency. While *Politics Among Nations* is remembered for many things, few recall that it concludes on the importance of diplomacy as the only way to moderate power and pursue peace. After stipulating that power is what states pursue and that nationalism has prevented ethics from moderating that power, few options are left to create a peaceful world order. Dismissive of liberal and idealist schemes for world order—in part because of their failure to articulate a global ethic—Morgenthau concludes that patient and prudent practice of diplomacy is humanity's only hope. His review of what diplomacy requires has, again, an Aristotelian echo; it must combine knowledge (intellectual virtue) with the ability to act in moments of crisis (moral virtue). Indeed, the first 'rule' of successful diplomacy is the elimination of the 'crusading spirit', a rule that conforms well to the Aristotelian idea of virtue as being about moderation between extremes.[34]

One could take Morgenthau's emphasis on the diplomat and aristocratic leadership in matters of foreign policy as the foundation for a theory of state agency. As I have argued elsewhere, Morgenthau's focus on the prudent individual as the representative of the political community is an important part of how he conceptualizes the power of the state. Diplomacy does not appear merely at the end of *Politics Among Nations* as the only possible means to constrain the excesses of nationalism. It is the final, and most important, element of national power:

Of all the factors which make for the power of a nation, the most important, and of the more unstable, is the quality of diplomacy. All the other factors which determine national power are, as it were, the raw material out of which the power of a nation is fashioned. The quality of a nation's diplomacy combines those different factors into an integrated whole, gives them direction and weight, and awakens their slumbering potentialities by giving them the breath of actual power. The conduct of a nation's foreign affairs by its diplomats is for national power in peace what military strategy and tactics by its military leaders are for national power in war. It is the art of bringing these different elements of national power to bear with maximum effect upon those points in the international situation which concern the national interest most directly.[35]

The state cannot act, even with the material elements of power, without the ability of the diplomat to bring those factors to bear in interactions with other leaders. The state, in other words, is embodied by the diplomat/leader who must turn potential into actual power and influence.

Some constructivist theorists have argued that the state is a 'person' and should be seen as such when providing explanations and evaluations of international politics. This debate, however, has focused primarily on using sociological categories to demonstrate the 'reality' and unity of the state.[36] Rarely have these questions about the agency of the state focused on the normative consequences of these assumptions.[37] Morgenthau's focus on the individual leader as the embodiment of the state, a leader who in the pursuit of the good of the political community can be seen as an Aristotelian political agent, provides a theory of personal and state agency that can be simultaneously explanatory and evaluative.

Morgenthau's theory of agency can be summarized as follows: The human person acts in pursuit of certain goods but in the context of an existential crisis. That crisis is defined by the scarcity of resources and the existence of conflicting aims, aims that the actor seeks to overcome through the pursuit of power. But the need to evaluate actions through ethical standards ensures that the political agent does not engage in actions with no constraints. When representing the political sphere in the age of the sovereign nation state, the political leader could be unconstrained in his actions as he seeks to protect himself and the community at all costs. But the political representative will act more in accordance with a moderate and morally sensitive conception of the good if he sees himself in the context of a community of other representatives who must accommodate their own interests and needs. Acting in the international community of global diplomacy, the political actor will seek the interests of his state but do so in a way that respects the interests of other states.

We have then a theory of agency, both personal and state, that mirrors in some respects the Aristotelian conception identified above. Like Aristotle, Morgenthau finds that agents pursue certain ends. But in pursuing those ends, they need the virtue of prudence to truly know their interests and to act upon them. Moreover, those interests and ends arise not from a simple accumulation of facts but from a set of life (for the person) or historical (for the state) experiences. A prudent agent will also understand that he or she lives in a community with others, a community that both shapes his or her interests (as constructivist IR theory suggests) but also forces the agent to accommodate his or her interests in interactions with others. Being a virtuous person and state, in other words, is not simply a matter of conforming to certain ideals; it is a matter of acting in ways that combine self-interested goals with an appreciation and understanding of others.

1.4. **Morgenthau and the war on terror**

Can this theory of political agency speak to current dilemmas in the international system today? Classical realists like Morgenthau and Kennan were well known for their chastisements of American foreign policy during the Cold War. Those critiques examined the inability of the American political leadership to understand the limits on its power. While representing ideals that the realists supported, they argued that American foreign policy took those ideals to a messianic extreme, ignoring the interests of other states.[38]

Recent works on the classical realist tradition have used it in much the same way as a critique of the policies of the Bush administration.[39] Michael Williams' critique of the neoconservatives through his articulation of a 'wilful realism', of which Morgenthau is an exemplar, relates to the ideas of agency I have developed here. In particular, Williams argues that Morgenthau and the realist tradition does not present a unified agent who clearly pursues interest through the accumulation of power, but instead proposes a political project in which the agent must continually be constructed. This resonates with the Aristotelian inspired notion of agency described above. In his treatment of Morgenthau's idea of the national interest, Williams points to the inherent contestability of the concept, something too many other commentators on realism have missed. More importantly for my purposes, Williams notes that the construction of the national interest, that which motivates the agency of the state, is an ongoing practice, one that links history with moral purpose.[40] An ethic focused on practice and the accumulation of knowledge through historical experience reflects the influence of an Aristotelian sensitivity to how habits and ongoing practices construct the human agent in the moral and political realm.

Williams uses his reinterpretation of Morgenthau to critique the neo-conservative project, arguing that the neoconservative insistence on the need for a heroic return to American values in foreign policy ignores the ongoing practice oriented construction of American ideals. The Aristotelian inspired conception of agency I have provided here takes this critique even further. Aristotelian philosophy, because of its teleological character, is sometimes assumed to put ends before means. In fact, however, Aristotle's notions of political and moral action do not separate means and ends. Instead, the means one carries out are just as much actions as the ends one is pursuing. In other words, one cannot justify immoral means through virtuous ends because acting in the public sphere is a continuous project which does not have a beginning or ending. This ongoing practice leads to a politics that must always have in sight the good for the human person and the political community but can never sacrifice persons or ideals in pursuit of longer-term trends. Morgenthau makes this point in his 1945 article:

All action is therefore at the same time means and ends, and it is only by an arbitrary separation of a certain chain of actions from what precedes and follows it, that we can attribute to certain actions the exclusive quality of means and ends. Actually, however, the totality of human actions presents itself as a hierarchy of actions each of which is the end of the preceding and a means for the following. This hierarchy culminates in the ultimate goal of all human activity which is identical with the absolute good, be it God, humanity, the state or the individual himself. This is the only end that is nothing but end and hence does not serve as a means to a further end. Viewed from it, all human activity appears as a means to the ultimate goal. In the last analysis, then, the doctrine that the ethical end justifies unethical means leads to the negation of absolute ethical judgments altogether.[41]

Morgenthau's emphasis on the ongoing character of political action, basically that it cannot be judged on the basis of ends alone, provides an entry into how these insights can help critique the American led 'war on terror'. In response to the attacks of September 11, 2001, the Bush administration launched a campaign to rid the world of terrorism. Many across the American, and indeed international, political spectrum, accepted that initial campaign as a justifiable project. The ensuing war against Iraq undermined many of those justifications, leading many to believe that the larger war on terrorism is actually a means to advance traditional economic and security interests of the United States. Nevertheless, it is that initial acceptance and embrace of the American mission to which Morgenthau's critical views on agency speak. To see how, let me briefly turn to one defender of the war on terror, Jean Bethke Elshtain.

Elshtain, along with a number of other scholars and activists, drafted a public statement in the wake of the attacks of September 11, entitled 'What We're Fighting For'. That letter, signed by a range of Americans across the political and intellectual spectrum, defended the attacks on Afghanistan as a just war as a response to an attack on 'American values'. Elshtain went on to defend the letter and American policy in her book, *Just War Against Terror*.[42] In both the letter and, to a greater extent, the book, Elshtain argues that the attacks of September 11 were an attack on American values. This corresponds with arguments of those who claimed that the cause of the attacks could not be found in past US foreign policies, but in the very essence of what constitutes the United States—the privileging of individual freedom, equal treatment of women, and freedom of religion being central to that essence. As she states: 'That is why I argue that such persons [terrorists] hate us for what we are and what we represent and not for anything in particular that we have done. How are we to respond to their demands? By refusing to educate girls and women? By repealing the franchise? By establishing a theocracy run by radicals?'[43]

This foundation for her argument moves Elshtain into a defence of the attacks on Afghanistan and a critical engagement with those in the scholarly and activist world who argued that the use of force by the United States was not just. In places, her argument corresponds well to the Just War tradition and is not one that I find objectionable. At the same time, however, her assumptions about the United States and how its agency relies on a set of values leads her argument into dangerous territory.[44] Moreover, an engagement with the conception of political and especially state agency suggested above can provide some critical distance from Elshtain's argument, distance that allows a critical reading not just of her work but of more broadly accepted justifications for the war on terror.

Recall that Morgenthau's conception of state agency, at least as I have developed it here, rests on an Aristotelian framework in which agents pursue ends moderated by the need for prudence and in the context of a political community. Morgenthau also agrees with Aristotle that action cannot be divided into means and ends, but that the idea of a human telos pursued through political action implies that all acts constitute the agent. It is the ongoing engagement in the political sphere—not a set of policies that tend towards a distant endpoint—that constructs the political agent. As I have argued above, this Aristotelian insight can be deployed in Morgenthau's understanding of how the political leader and diplomat engage in foreign policy.

To return to Elshtain, Morgenthau would agree that there are certain values that constitute the United States. In his *The Purpose of American Politics*, Morgenthau focuses on the interrelationship of equality and freedom as those values that distinguish the United States from other political agents. But those values are not things that stand in need of defence in the way that Elshtain construes them. Rather, they inform the ongoing practices of American foreign policy, giving meaning to its policies but not determining them. More importantly, as Morgenthau develops in that same book, those concepts do not exist as values without any relation to the historical progression of the political community. The experience of slavery in the United States was for Morgenthau, and remains today, a central issue that cannot be ignored—as was seen in the racially driven political conflicts that arose in the wake of Hurricane Katrina in New Orleans. As Elshtain articulates a politics of American values that celebrate these virtues, her account fails to take into account how those values remain works in progress, always susceptible to the political.

How would Morgenthau's notion of political agency lead to a different set of recommendations? While we cannot know how he would respond to the attacks of September 11 as an individual scholar, it would not be surprising if Morgenthau agreed that a retaliatory strike on Afghanistan was justified. Based on the idea of political agency proposed here, it is unlikely that such a response would be framed in terms of defending American values. Morgenthau was an astute enough social and political critic of American politics to avoid a politics based on values. But, as a theorist of prudent political agency, Morgenthau would not hesitate to act. A Morgenthau-inspired reaction to the attacks of September 11 would certainly include military force, and would undoubtedly seek the capture and perhaps even death to those who organized the attacks. But construing those attacks as part of a 'war on terror' to defend American values does not seem to correspond to Morgenthau's vision of politics.

One further way in which Morgenthau's theory of agency provides some critical distance from the dominant discourses in the war on terror concerns the means being used to prosecute the war. Elshtain's arguments focused primarily on the justification of the overall war, what one might call the jus ad bellum standards. Others, such as Michael Ignatieff,[45] have argued that the war on terror might justify means that would be disallowed otherwise. One might call these claims a version of the supreme emergency argument in which the justness of a cause and the extreme danger of a situation justify manifestly immoral means.[46] In the light of Morgenthau's statement above, that actions cannot be divided into means and ends, but must be seen as part of a whole that motivates and constitutes an agent's politics, justifying unjust actions in pursuit of a justified end cannot be allowed. For all actions undertaken by an agent, especially an agent pursuing foreign policy in a system of states, demand evaluation according to the criterion of prudence. They also should arise from, and take into account, the interests and aims of other agents in the system, not only for benevolent reasons, but for prudential reasons, that is in the future the agent may itself be subject to similar treatment (or its citizens will, in the case of a state).

My reading of Morgenthau suggests that assuming the state is a settled agent pursuing clearly defined and morally justified ends is misleading. In fact, I have proposed a reading of Morgenthau that corresponds more to certain constructivist strands in IR theory. As noted at the outset of the chapter, Morgenthau goes beyond much of the constructivist framework by pushing agency into a normative sphere as well. Not only, then, does Morgenthau reveal a state that is constructed by the international community of which it is a part, he also presents a state agent that is shaped by and pursues normative goals in a world of anarchy. In other words, I have created a Morgenthau more attuned to critical theory than the realism with which he is so often associated.[47]

1.5. **Conclusion**

These reflections on Morgenthau and the potential response to theorists such as Elshtain should not be seen as the last word on how Morgenthau would respond to the war on terror. Rather, the point of this chapter has been to draw out of Morgenthau's work a conception of political agency, including state agency, that is more contingent and historically sensitive than that proffered by the defenders of the war on terror.

Morgenthau's work is rich enough that it can be utilized for a wide range of alternative political ideas. Such a strategy reflects the wide range and sophistication of his insights. I have tried to highlight here how he draws from Aristotle an alternative conception of agency that informed his theory of international politics. If my reading of Morgenthau and Aristotle together suggests some alternative conceptions of both theory and practice, it will have served its purpose.

⬜ NOTES

1. Hans J. Morgenthau, *Political Theory and International Affairs: Hans J. Morgenthau on Aristotle's The Politics*, edited by Anthony F. Lang, Jr. (Westport, CT: Praeger, 2005).

2. See Annette Freyberg-Inan, *What Moves Man: The Realist Theory of International Relations and its Judgment of Human Nature* (Albany: SUNY Press, 2004) for a critical analysis of these assumptions.

3. See Alexander Wendt, 'The Agent-Structure Problem in International Relations Theory', *International Organization*, 41 (1987), 335–70 and Alexander Wendt, *Social Theory of International Politics* (Cambridge: Cambridge University Press, 1999).

4. See Anthony F. Lang, Jr. with John Williams, 'Between International Politics and International Ethics', in Anthony F. Lang, Jr. and John Williams (eds.), *Hannah Arendt and International Relations: Reading Between the Lines* (New York: Palgrave Macmillian, 2005), 221–32 for an attempt to link agency with responsibility through the work of Hannah Arendt.

5. Kenneth Waltz, *Theory of International Politics* (Boston, MA: Addison-Wesley, 1979).

6. Wendt, *Social Theory of International Politics*, 139–92. Constructivism is a wide ranging term, covering a diverse set of theorists. Wendt has become a leading figure of American constructivist theory largely because he accepts the positivist goal of explanation driven social science. Other constructivists look to the work of Nicholas Onuf, whose work is more attentive to legal and moral philosophy; see Nicholas Onuf, *World of Our Making: Rule and Rules in Social Theory and International Relations* (Columbia, SC: University of South Carolina Press, 1989).

7. See James Crawford (ed.), *The International Law Commission's Articles on State Responsibility: Introduction, Text and Commentary* (Cambridge: Cambridge University Press, 2001) and Nina H. B. Jogensen, *The Responsibility of States for International Crimes* (Oxford: Oxford University Press, 2000).

8. See Malgosia Fitzmaurice and Dan Sarooshi (eds.), *Issues of State Responsibility before International Judicial Institutions* (Oxford: Hart, 2004).

9. Aristotle, *The Nichomachean Ethics*, Book I, Ch. 7, 1098a15 in *The Basic Works of Aristotle*, edited by Richard McKeon (New York: Random House, 1941), 943. For a sophisticated updating of Aristotelian moral theory see George W. Harris, *Agent-Centered Morality: An Aristotelian Alternative to Kantian Internalism* (Berkeley, CA: University of California Press, 1999).

10. Hans J. Morgenthau, 'Another "Great Debate": The National Interest of the U.S.', *American Political Science Review*, 46: 4 (1952), 983.

11. Hans J. Morgenthau, *Politics Among Nations: The Struggle for Power and Peace* (New York: Alfred Knopf, 1948), 267–9. All references throughout this chapter will be to this, the first edition, unless otherwise noted.

12. Greg Russell, *Hans Morgenthau and the Ethics of American Statecraft* (Baton Rouge, LA: Louisiana State University Press, 1990) and Joel Rosenthal, *Righteous Realists: Political Realism, Responsible Power and American Culture in the Nuclear Age* (Baton Rouge, LA: Louisiana State University Press, 1991).

13. Christoph Frei, *Hans J. Morgenthau: An Intellectual Biography* (Baton Rouge, LA: Louisiana State University Press, 2001), 107.

14. Frei, *Hans J. Morgenthau: An Intellectual Biography*, 170. In the first edition of *Politics Among Nations*, Morgenthau also links Nietzsche with Hitler and Mussolini as harbingers of an ethos devoted only to the will of power; *Politics Among Nations*, 170.

15. M. Benjamin Mollov, *Power and Transcendence: Hans J. Morgenthau and the Jewish Experience* (Lanham, MD: Lexington, 2002).

16. A. J. H. Murray, 'The Moral Politics of Hans Morgenthau', *The Review of Politics*, 58: 1 (1996), 81–108.

17. Frei, *Hans J. Morgenthau: An Intellectual Biography*, 113

18. 'Notes on Lectures', Winter Quarter 1947. Hans J. Morgenthau Papers, Box 76, Library of Congress, Washington, DC.

19. 'Philosophy of International Relations', 1949. Hans J. Morgenthau Papers, Box 81, Library of Congress, Washington, DC; quote on persistence of Aristotle from p. 17.

20. Personal email contact from Professor Kenneth Thompson, University of Virginia, 8 March 2004.

21. See letter of Robert J. Myers to Mr. Victor Schmalzer, W. W. Norton, 1 June 1983, in the archives of the Carnegie Council on Ethics and International Affairs, New York City.

22. Morgenthau, *Political Theory and International Affairs*.

23. Hans J. Morgenthau, *Scientific Man and Power Politics* (Chicago, IL: University of Chicago Press, 1946), 220.

24. I would also suggest that Morgenthau's views on agency were influenced by Hannah Arendt, with whom he had a close personal relationship. He lists Arendt's book, *The Human Condition*, as one of the ten most influential books he had ever read and cites her *Origins of Totalitarianism* in a few locations as well. Making this case would require a detailed treatment. For one comparison of the two thinkers, see Douglas Klusmyer, 'Hannah Arendt's Critical Realism: Power, Justice and Responsibility', in Lang and Williams (eds.), *Hannah Arendt and International Relations*, 113–79.

25. The other, more well-known, instance of this project is *Scientific Man vs. Power Politics* (Chicago, IL: University of Chicago Press, 1946) which focuses on the failures of emerging positivist social science to grasp the realities of politics.

26. Hans J. Morgenthau, 'The Evil of Politics and the Ethics of Evil', *Ethics*, 56: 1 (1945), 1.

27. 'The Evil of Politics and the Ethics of Evil', 11.

28. Ibid. 18.

29. Hans J. Morgenthau, 'Thought and Action in Politics', *Social Research*, 51 (1984), 152; reprinted from *Social Research*, 38: 4 (1971), 617–24.

30. *Politics Among Nations*, 186.

31. For an overview of virtue ethics, see Daniel Statman (ed.), *Virtue Ethics: A Critical Reader* (Washington, DC: Georgetown University Press, 1997).

32. *Political Theory and International Affairs*, 59.

33. Hans J. Morgenthau, *The Purpose of American Politics* (New York: Alfred A. Knopf, 1960), 222–31.

34. See *Politics Among Nations*, 419–45.

35. Ibid. 105.

36. See, for example, Patrick T. Jackson, et al., 'Forum on the State as a Person', *Review of International Studies*, 30: 2 (2004), 255–316.

37. For one approach that does address the status of state responsibility, see Toni Erskine (ed.), *Can Institutions Have Responsibilities?* (New York: Palgrave, 2003).

38. See, for example, George Kennan's classic statement, *American Diplomacy, 1900–1950* (Chicago, IL: University of Chicago Press, 1951).

39. See Michael Williams, *The Realist Tradition and the Limits of International Relations* (Cambridge: Cambridge University Press, 2005), 197–203 and John Hulsman and Anatol Lieven, 'The Ethics of Realism', *The National Interest*, 80 (2005), 37–43.

40. Williams, *The Realist Tradition and the Limits of International Relations*, 185–92.

41. Morgenthau, 'The Evil of Politics and the Ethics of Evil', 9.

42. Jean Bethke Elshtain, *Just War Against Terror: The Burden of American Power in a Violent World* (New York: Basic Books, 2003).

43. Elshtain, *Just War Against Terror*, 23.

44. For another critical account of Elshtain's book, one with which I have much sympathy but which draws upon a different set of assumptions, see Nicholas Rengger, 'Just War Against Terror? Jean Elshtain's Burden and American Power', *International Affairs*, 80: 1 (2004), 107–16.

45. Michael Ignatieff, *The Lesser Evil: Political Ethics in an Age of Terror* (Edinburgh: Edinburgh University Press, 2004).

46. See Brian Orend, 'Is There a Supreme Emergency Exception?' in Mark Evans (ed.), *Just War Theory: A Reappraisal* (Edinburgh: Edinburgh University Press, 2005), 134–56 for a critical analysis of this argument.

47. See my use of Morgenthau and Arendt to construct a theory of state agency that corresponds to the account here, although not drawing as explicitly on Aristotle, in *Agency and Ethics: The Politics of Military Intervention* (Albany, NY: SUNY Press, 2002), 1–30.

2 'The Twilight of International Morality'? Hans J. Morgenthau and Carl Schmitt on the end of the *Jus Publicum Europaeum*

Chris Brown

The relationship between Carl Schmitt and Hans J. Morgenthau was fraught with all kinds of tensions.[1] Both were, at least in the 1920s, conservative legal theorists who were critical of liberal accounts of politics and the law. Schmitt was approximately 20 years Morgenthau's senior, and initially the latter appears to have regarded him as a potential mentor, sending him a copy of his doctoral thesis which offered a friendly critique of Schmitt's very influential *Concept of the Political* (1st edn. 1927). Schmitt's initial response was also friendly, but a meeting between the two was disastrous, with Morgenthau convinced that he had been snubbed by Schmitt.[2] What was worse, Morgenthau believed that Schmitt had plagiarized him in the second edition of the *Concept* (1932), adopting elements of his critique without acknowledgement—in fact, Schmitt rarely acknowledged any contemporary source, and not many non-contemporary sources, so there is no reason to think that there was anything unusual in this treatment, although Morgenthau could be forgiven for not ignoring it on that account. The coming to power of the Nazis in 1933 ended any possibility of a further meeting of minds. Having previously been associated with anti-Nazi, but very right-wing, military circles, Schmitt became, for a while at least, a Nazi Party member and an important regime intellectual. Morgenthau, as a Jew, was obliged to flee the country, and after unsatisfactory sojourns in Switzerland, France, and Spain, ended up in the United States. After the war, Schmitt refused to accept the legitimacy of the process of de-Nazification and moved into a kind of internal exile; Morgenthau, on the other hand, became enormously influential as a public intellectual at the University of Chicago, a colleague of Leo Strauss, a friend of Hannah Arendt, and the leading figure in the 'realist' school of thought on IR. In various titbits of intellectual autobiography, Morgenthau always referred to Schmitt with great hostility; Schmitt, on the other hand, does not, as far as I know, refer to Morgenthau with any frequency after the war.

In spite of this distance, in the 1940s both scholars addressed what was effectively the same issue in IR theory, namely the collapse of the old European international order, and its replacement by a world in which any principles of order were difficult to discern—although it should be said that to characterize this issue as one for 'international relations theory' is to jump the gun somewhat. Schmitt certainly did not see himself as contributing to any such discourse, and neither, one suspects, did Morgenthau at that stage of his career. In any event, the fact that they use quite similar terms to describe this collapse and the new world that followed from it raises questions of influence, and, since Schmitt was clearly the senior figure in the 1940s and unlikely to be aware of Morgenthau's writings on IR, this resolves itself into the question as to whether Morgenthau's work drew on that of the elder scholar. Schmittians are open to this interpretation, which, unsurprisingly, is resisted by Morgenthau's intellectual heirs who share the latter's distaste for the former. In fact, I would suggest, we do not need to raise this question in the first place because both Schmitt and Morgenthau were drawing on a substantial body of literature on the European states system and statecraft, and much of what is common in their separate accounts is a product of this heritage. What we have here is not so much a case of two scholars independently coming to the same conclusions, but of two scholars reflecting on the same body of material and coming to conclusions which are interestingly similar, but also, at times, interestingly different. It is because of these similarities and differences that a 'compare and contrast' exercise here is highly worthwhile.

In order to carry out this exercise, I will examine two texts, Schmitt's *The Nomos of the Earth* and an essay by Morgenthau entitled 'The Twilight of International Morality'.[3] Schmitt's work was originally published in 1950 (although the English translation is of the 2nd edn. 1974) and appears to have been written in substance during the Second World War. It is certainly the fullest account of Schmitt's international thought available in English, and, as far as I know, the extensive amount of untranslated German texts do not modify substantially the position Schmitt takes therein. Morgenthau's essay was drawn from his text *Politics Among Nations*.[4] The status of this work is much contested amongst Morgenthau scholars; it is often seen as a rather crude oversimplified version of his ideas, certainly by comparison with more philosophically demanding works such as *Scientific Man versus Power Politics*, but Morgenthau himself referred to the work as a distillation of his thought, and seems to have regarded it as his greatest achievement.[5] By relying on the *Ethics* paper I hope to dodge this issue, on the assumption that he would have ensured that this essay in one of the most prestigious journals in American intellectual life, edited from his new home base in Chicago, would accurately reflect his thinking, with no oversimplification or concessions to a student readership. In any event, what were the issues involved here? Since it is a larger text, I will present Schmitt's account first.

2.1. **Carl Schmitt and the *Jus Publicum Europaeum***

In *The Nomos of the Earth*, Schmitt offers an account of the rise of the modern European territorial state, and the spatial differentiation upon which that institution is based, that runs contrary to a great deal of the conventional wisdom of the early twenty-first century, although, as noted above, much of what he has to say would have been a commonplace a century earlier. Whereas a number of modern writers have noted with disapproval the emergence of a clear distinction between intra- and extra-European international politics and with it notions of 'difference' that have, arguably, underpinned European racism and imperialism, Schmitt regards the emergence of this distinction as a basic achievement of Renaissance humanism.[6] Equally, the Catholic natural lawyers of the Salamanca School, usually admired nowadays for their defence of human equality and decent treatment for the 'Indians' of the Americas, are regarded by Schmitt as reactionaries trying to sustain an outmoded, theological conception of world order. Schmitt's reasoning here is largely based on his critique of the notion of the Just War, which he regards as an essentially theological notion which actually worked to legitimize total war. Just War theorists may have attempted to limit the role of violence in human affairs, and the Catholic church in the Middle Ages certainly did try to use its influence to ban certain weapons and enforce truces, but these measures were always subverted by the basic logic of the Just War. The latter, Schmitt argues, by inviting the judgment that one side in a conflict is 'just' involved identifying the other as 'unjust', with the concomitant that the unjust must be defeated whatever the cost, even if this involved using banned weapons or taking a conflict to extremes.[7]

This line of argument parallels many contemporary critiques of Just War thinking from left and right.[8] However, while most such critics rest their case on a kind of generalized beneficence which is difficult to relate to a coherent world view, Schmitt most decidedly does defend an alternative conception of world order. This alternative framework emerges from the development of the sovereign, territorial state in Europe, which involved a spatial reordering of the Continent that undermined the jurisdiction of the Catholic Church and the Empire and in so doing sidelined notions such as the Just War, notions which drew what strength they had from their association with the universal principles those institutions represented. The political order is no longer explicitly committed to the preservation of God's Order in the world and the prevention of the reign of the Antichrist, but instead is based on Reason of State.[9] The European princes create amongst themselves a *Jus Publicum Europaeum* (JPE), a secular legal order under which they recognize each other's rights and interests, *within Europe* (the proviso here is crucial). Beyond the line, in the extra-European world, Europeans engage in large-scale appropriations of land, respecting neither the rights of the locals nor each other's rights, but within Europe a different modus vivendi is possible.

The spatial dimension of this new disposition is central for Schmitt. The very idea of *Nomos* (drawn from the Greek term usually translated as 'convention' or, very loosely, 'law' and generally set in opposition to *Physis* or 'nature') is employed by Schmitt to convey the idea of a set of principles of world order which necessarily have a spatial dimension, and our current woes, he argues, stem from the lack of such a *Nomos*. This spatial dimension is central for Schmitt—but it is not clear to me that it is actually as critical for this particular argument as he, and Schmitt scholars more generally, would argue.[10] Certainly, Morgenthau gets across much the same point without the employment of the term *Nomos* or the same stress on the spatial; perhaps this illustrates his lack of philosophical sophistication, but perhaps not.

In any event, in the extra-European world appalling atrocities occur which, at least in principle, would not happen in Europe.[11] As between European rulers within Europe, war became 'bracketed'—rationalized and humanized. Rather than a divine punishment, war became an act of state. Whereas in the Medieval order the enemy must necessarily be seen as unjust (the alternative being that one was, oneself, unjust—clearly an intolerable prospect), the new humanitarian approach to war involved the possibility of the recognition of the other as *justi hostes*, an enemy but a legitimate enemy, not someone who deserves to be annihilated, someone in whom one can recognize oneself, always a good basis for a degree of restraint. This for Schmitt is the great achievement of the age, and the ultimate justification for—glory of, even—the sovereign state.

[An] international legal order, based on the liquidation of civil war and on the bracketing of war (in that it transformed war into a duel between European states), actually had legitimated a realm of relative reason. The equality of sovereigns made them equally legal partners in war, and prevented military methods of annihilation.[12]

The new thinking about war also opened up the possibility of neutrality as a legal status; since war was no longer justified in accordance with a theological judgment based on notions of good and evil, it became possible for third parties to stand aside if their interests were not engaged. Equally, the ordinary subjects of belligerent rulers need not feel obliged to become emotionally engaged in the fray; war becomes a matter for sovereigns and their servants, civil and military—the kind of wider involvement that might be appropriate to a war between good and evil becomes strictly optional. Thus, during the Seven Years War between Britain and France—more accurately, of course, between George II and Louis XV—the English novelist Laurence Sterne describes in *A Sentimental Journey* his absent-minded attempt to take the regular packet-boat between Dover and Calais, the war having slipped his mind. Fortunately he was able to attach himself to the entourage of a French nobleman returning to Paris after a trip to London, so all was well. Even during the Napoleonic Wars, where national emotions were certainly engaged, there was a regular cross-channel service under a flag of truce, and British scientists attended conferences in France under safe conducts, and vice versa.

Thus was established what Schmitt clearly regarded as a kind of golden age in European international politics, a golden age that would be sabotaged in the twentieth century by the United States, with the reluctant, ambiguous, assistance of the United Kingdom—two maritime powers whose commitment to the JPE was highly qualified in the case of the UK, non-existent in the case of the US. Before examining this end, it might be worth asking whether this 'golden age' has any basis in historical fact? This is a very big question but the simple answer is 'perhaps'—but only for a brief period from the early mid-eighteenth century to its end. For a while war was 'bracketed' but critically for Schmitt's story (and perhaps Morgenthau's) this took place some time *after* the establishment of the sovereign state as the key European actor.

2.2. The ending of the *Jus Publicum Europaeum*

A superficial reading of Schmitt might take the concept of the JPE to be synonymous with the notion of international law (*Völkerrecht*), but for Schmitt the two notions are completely different, indeed opposed to one another. International law is, from his point of view, a quintessentially *American* project, and this for two interconnected reasons, both of which distinguish the notion from the Public Law of Europe. First, international law lacks the spatial aspect which is central to the JPE; it purports to offer a universal account of international order, blurring the crucial distinction between the European and the non-European world. But second, and more important, international law is, for Schmitt, a progressive, liberal project which is subject to the same critique that he delivers against liberalism in general, namely that it undermines the political and acts as a cover for special interests. This point requires some elaboration.

Schmitt's account of politics is developed in opposition to liberalism. For Schmitt, liberalism purports to undermine the key feature of politics, the distinction between friend and enemy.[13] Liberalism, he argues, seeks to moralize and legalize politics, reducing the political process to a set of authoritative rules, attempting, as it were, to take the politics out of politics. This is a doomed enterprise—in any political constitution what is crucial is the ability to decide upon the 'exception', the point at which the rules no longer apply—but it is also a pernicious enterprise because it involves covering particular political interests with a cloak of morality, pretending that a political decision emerging out of the friend–enemy distinction is actually the product of a moral judgment that cannot be opposed without falling into moral turpitude. From Schmitt's perspective there is nothing necessarily unjust about an enemy; indeed, the new humanitarian approach to war described above involved the possibility of the recognition of the other as *justi hostes*, an enemy but a legitimate enemy, not someone who deserves to be annihilated—it is only on this basis that war can be 'bracketed'. Liberalism, by moralizing the political, makes the same kind of category error that led to the development of Medieval Just War thinking, with all the horrors this allegedly entailed.

It is easy to see how this position feeds into a reading of progressivist international law; indeed, this position gels with, at least part of, the classic realist critique of the latter—on which see, for example, E. H. Carr's critique of utopian moralizing as a strategy employed by the 'haves' against the 'have-nots'.[14] It is equally easy to see how Schmitt associates this notion of international law with the USA—but it is worth noting that for Schmitt, unlike Carr and other realists, the liberal internationalism of Woodrow Wilson is not central to this critique, or rather *is* central, but only as a continuation of early American policies. The key date for Schmitt is not 1919, but 1823, the proclamation of the Monroe Doctrine which symbolizes the emergence of a new kind of imperial rule. The Monroe Doctrine purports to warn-off European powers from attempting to take new territories in the Americas, but actually involves an assertion of American power over the rest of the Western hemisphere.[15] This is a new kind of Empire, a hegemony under which the US dominates usually without actually formally ruling; the US often intervenes in the affairs of the lesser American powers, and sometimes does so militarily, but always in the name of progressive values and in the putative interests of the locals—this is a form of rule that is both more effective than traditional empire because it does not involve the usual administrative costs, but also more hypocritical, because it denies its own nature, pretending to exercise power only in the interests of others. The US is revealed by the Monroe Doctrine to be an anomalous power— neither 'European' in the spatial sense conveyed by the notion of the JPE but equally not non-European. It is this anomalous status (partly shared by the other English-speaking sea-power) which, once US power becomes actual rather than latent and the form of rule embedded in the Monroe Doctrine becomes potentially universal, destroys the old order, in a way that a purely outside power (Bolshevik Russia, for example) could not, although the Bolsheviks could, perhaps, physically destroy the old Europe.

The League of Nations Covenant (which specifically underwrites the Monroe Doctrine) represents the extension of US hegemony from the Americas to, potentially, the world. The US did not join the League, but American economic power underwrote the peace settlement, and, eventually, in the Second World War, US military power was brought to bear to bring down the JPE and replace it with 'international law', and liberal internationalism. On Schmitt's account, the two World Wars were fought to bring this about—and the barbarism of modern warfare is to be explained by the undermining of the limits established in the old European order. In effect, the notion of a Just War has been reborn albeit without much of its theological underpinnings. The humanized warfare of the JPE with its recognition of the notion of a 'just enemy' is replaced by the older notion that the enemy is evil and to be destroyed—in fact, is no longer an 'enemy' within Schmitt's particular usage of the term but a 'foe' who can, and should, be annihilated.[16] The Allied strategic objective of 'unconditional surrender' in the Second World War (insisted upon by Roosevelt over Churchill's misgivings) represents this perspective, as does the tactics of blockade in the first War and area bombing in the second.

From Schmitt's perspective, the German stance in the Second World War is essentially defensive, a war fought to preserve the old European Order, but also essentially futile because that order was destroyed in 1914–18. The latter point explains, perhaps, why Schmitt was not entirely persona grata with the Nazis in these years, a point that is sometimes made in his favour by modern writers who wish to acquit him of Nazism, or at least gloss over his record during the Nazi years—but it is well worth stressing that this was how Schmitt saw the war, as a futile exercise, rather than, for example, as the product of a criminal act of aggression by Germany in 1939, waged with inhuman methods in the East and generally accompanied by atrocities. The notion that the Second World War was essentially defensive on the part of Germany is as difficult to take now as it was then for many of the countries that were forcibly incorporated into the German realm. Perhaps the best we can say for this point of view is that, at the time, many of those who collaborated with the Nazis in Western and Northern Europe (and this was a much larger group of people than it became fashionable to acknowledge after 1945) did tell themselves that they were defending European values against both the Bolshevik menace and, crucially, the nascent 'Anglosphere'.

2.3. **The twilight of international morality**

Turning to Morgenthau's writings, one experiences a strange dislocation. Morgenthau is, very obviously, telling the same story, but, equally clearly, he is telling a very different story. Think *Rashomon*. Admittedly, there are some immediate differences. He does not employ the technical terminology that is central for Schmitt; there is no reference to JPE—a relatively minor point—but, rather more important, neither the notion of *Nomos* nor the term itself features in his account. The spatial dimension of the old European order—the clear distinction between the JPE and the rules that exist elsewhere in the world—which is so central for Schmitt is made little of by Morgenthau. It is clear that Morgenthau is actually writing about the old European order, but the distinction between this order and the order that Europeans created elsewhere in the world is not part of his story. Partly, no doubt, this is because his account of the transition from the Medieval to the Modern does not involve the theological dimension that is present in Schmitt's work; as noted above, for the latter, the Medieval political order was designed to prevent the rule of the Antichrist, and it was only after this project lost its immediate significance that the system of sovereign states could emerge. This is a line of argument that means nothing to Morgenthau, who resisted the notion of giving a theological twist to his work—it is noteworthy that, according to Frei, he was reluctant to acknowledge that there was any close resemblance between his position and that of Reinhold Niebuhr, a Protestant theologian whose position was more congenial to Morgenthau than Schmitt's rather strange Catholicism.

Still, in spite of these important differences, the core story he tells is clearly the same story that Schmitt tells, but with several twists. Common to both versions of the story is the idea that the Medieval notion of a Just War actually undermined the business of placing limits on the exercise of force, and that such limits could only emerge once war was conceptualized as a duel between sovereigns, fought by the armies of the belligerent states—only then could the distinction between combatant and non-combatant emerge. Equally, both Schmitt and Morgenthau agree that these limits on the exercise of force have to a large extent disappeared in the twentieth century. They offer, however, very different interpretations of this core story. There are, I think, three key moments with respect to these different interpretations, given here in ascending order of importance.

First, for Morgenthau, but perhaps not for Schmitt, the limitations imposed on force in the old European order developed over time and became more and more effective. Gradually, Morgenthau argues, the basic principle of respect for human life is elaborated, and comes to reflect

[a] moral conscience which feels ill at ease in the presence of violence or, at least, certain kinds of it on the international scene. The existence of such a conscience is attested to, on the one hand, by the attempts at bringing the practice of states into harmony with ethical principles through international agreements and, on the other hand, by the universal justifications of, and excuses for, alleged violations of these agreements in ethical terms.[17]

Schmitt, one can be sure, would have rejected the contents of both these 'hands'. The basis for restraint and the bracketing of war was, from his angle, the recognition of the other as a legitimate enemy, and not adherence to some kind of universal code, most especially not a code that could be found in Hague or Geneva Protocols, much less such quintessentially 'American' treaties as the Kellog-Briand Pact of 1928, which purported to outlaw war. Such legal devices do not represent moral progress but rather the degeneration of the JPE; his notion of war as a duel, something that can be bracketed as between *justis hostes*, is specifically based on the principle that the use of force does *not* have to be justified, not to any external authority nor, for that matter, to oneself. This is an essential feature of the 'humanized war' that Schmitt endorses as an alternative to the horrors of Just Wars. Although he does not put the matter in this way, he is effectively offering to us a devil's bargain; accept that violence is simply a part of human existence—forget the attempt to require that violence be justified— and in exchange you will have a world where violence will actually be more controlled and less dangerous to human well-being than it otherwise would be.[18]

To put the matter differently, in the old European order, war was a tool of foreign policy, a political instrument, but, says Morgenthau, this is no longer acceptable:

[It] is especially in the refusal to consider seriously the possibility of preventive war, regardless of its expediency from the point of view of the national interest, that the ethical condemnation of war as such has manifested itself in recent times in the Western world. When war comes, it must come as a natural catastrophe or as the evil deed of another nation, not as a foreseen and planned culmination of one's own foreign policy.[19]

The different attitudes of Morgenthau and Schmitt to this shift are revealing: for Schmitt, this changing conception of war is disastrous because it represents a reversion to the notion that the other, instead of being a legitimate enemy, is again a 'foe' to be annihilated; this undermines the bracketing of war as a duel between princes and leads to unrestrained total war. For Morgenthau, on the other hand, this new conception of war represents genuine moral progress, but is profoundly dangerous nonetheless because those states, people, and statesmen who adhere to this non-political conception of war as a catastrophe to be avoided if at all possible have to deal with people who do not, both people who still regard war as a usable political instrument, and, more dangerously, with people who accept no limits, political or otherwise, on the exercise of force; as Neville Chamberlain illustrated in his dealings with Hitler, this places them at a very considerable disadvantage.[20]

There are, Morgenthau argues—and Schmitt would agree, I think—more people today who do not accept limits on force than there were a generation or two ago. For example, Bismarck and Hitler both faced the problem of potential German encirclement: Bismarck accepted the terms of the problem, that is, the existence of France and Russia as neighbours to the new *Reich*, and tried to solve it by diplomacy—Hitler, on the other hand, accepted no restraints, and tried to eliminate both France and Russia.[21] Schmitt, of course, would not agree with this particular analysis, but he would have agreed that the limitations on force were breaking down in the twentieth century. On his account this comes about because of the breakdown of the JPE under American/universalist pressure. How does Morgenthau explain the shift? Here the differences between the two scholars become really interesting.

Morgenthau presents two reasons for the dissolution of moral limitations on international politics: 'the substitution of democratic for aristocratic responsibility in foreign affairs and the substitution of nationalistic standards of action for universal ones'.[22] Schmitt would clearly take issue with the latter—but, first, what of the former? How is the 'substitution of democratic for aristocratic responsibility' to be understood?

Morgenthau's argument here is quite complex. On the one hand, he is making rather an English School point about the culture of international society—and, interestingly, he uses the term 'international society' in a very Bull/Wight/Watson way throughout this article (and the relevant section of *Politics Among Nations*). The diplomats who staffed the Chancelleries of Europe had a lot in common, usually more with each other than with their employers, and these employers were not necessarily fellow-nationals. Morgenthau tells a nice story of Bismarck leaving his post as Prussian Ambassador in St. Petersburg to return to Berlin, conventionally expressing to the Czar his regrets at leaving, and, in response, being offered a post in the Russian diplomatic service—an offer that Bismarck politely declined, but did not regard as either ludicrous or inappropriate. Standards of international morality were partly preserved as a by-product of codes of gentlemanly behaviour—certain things were simply 'not done'.

This argument would not be too difficult to cast in Schmittian terms, but Morgenthau has another point to make about the nature of moral responsibility. The key shift is the arrival of officials who are 'legally and morally responsible for their official acts, not to a monarch, that is a specific individual, but to a collectivity, that is a parliamentary majority, or the people as a whole'.[23] More,

[Government] by clearly identifiable men, who can be held personally accountable for their acts, is therefore the precondition for the existence of an effective system of international ethics. Where responsibility for government is widely distributed among a great number of individuals with different conceptions as to what is morally required in international affairs, or with no such conception at all, international morality as an effective system of restraints upon international policy becomes impossible.[24]

Here Schmitt's version and Morgenthau's version of the common story can be seen to be pulling apart, but then coming together again. Schmitt would reject the very idea of an effective system of international ethics as something either possible or desirable and so this whole line of argument would have been mistaken from his point of view. But he would certainly recognize the contrast being drawn between the apolitical faceless bureaucrat and the Prince or the Prince's agent; the latter could be genuinely 'political' in Schmitt's sense—basing his/her behaviour on the friend–enemy distinction—in a way that a purely constitutional figure could not be.

The big difference between the two scholars, however, comes over the issue of pluralism, which is at the heart of Morgenthau's second reason for the collapse of the old order. For Morgenthau, as noted in the above quotation, the emergence of a number of 'different conceptions as to what is morally required in international affairs' undermines the limits on force that have grown up over the years even when these different conceptions are held by members of the same polity (although to have no such conception at all is, of course, worse). For Schmitt this is really neither here nor there—not simply because the important limits on force are not based on a moral conception at all, but also because pluralism is, in general, a positive virtue rather than a defect of the system.

The central point here is that Morgenthau's account of the functioning international society that was disappearing in the mid-twentieth century contains a very strong cosmopolitan, universalist, even supranational component—counter-intuitive though this may be with respect to a figure who is rightly regarded as the archetypical realist. In fact, his description of this component in the final pages of 'The Twilight of International Morality' will be immediately familiar to English School theorists of international society—the extended quote he presents from Gibbon on the nations of Europe forming 'one great republic', with the same system of arts and laws and manners is regularly used by the English School.[25] Somewhat off the point, it is worth noting that the correspondence between Morgenthau's views and those of the English School is not actually surprising given that—to generalize a point made in the introduction to this chapter—both he and they draw heavily upon the European diplomatic tradition. The English School is only 'English' in the same way that the Frankfurt School is 'Frankfurt', that is because its prime movers were located there, not because its ideas are particularly national—it is worth making this point partly to reinforce the sense that both Morgenthau and Schmitt were building on past writings for the core elements of the common story they tell, but also to undermine the idea that there is a clear distinction to be made between the English School and so-called 'American' realism.

In any event, to return to the main line of the argument, for Morgenthau this universal conception of international society has now broken down, and in its place three competing universalisms have emerged—the Nazi bid for universality has just been defeated, but in the late 1940s the contest between the communist and democratic versions of universal values is very much under way. In these circumstances, moral limitations on the use of force are difficult to sustain; there are competing international moralities, which, for Morgenthau, is much the same as saying there is no international morality. The cosmopolitan and moral element of this diagnosis is, for Schmitt, beside the point, but, suitably transformed, the notion of competing universalisms can be worked into his analysis. One feature of The Nomos *of the Earth* not discussed so far is Schmitt's notion of the *Grossraum*, a political unit that is neither a large state nor quite an Empire, but rather a kind of extended hegemony with an empire at its centre. This notion is drawn from antiquity, but can be reworked quite easily to fit the notion of competing universalisms in the modern world. US hegemony over Latin America, signalled by the Monroe Doctrine, is the key modern example of a *Grossraum* offered by Schmitt, and on his account this political order has obvious universalist tendencies—indeed, according to Schmitt, the US *Grossraum* has been transformed from its territorial base in the Americas into the universal order envisaged in the League of Nations, a global order dominated by the United States. It is not too difficult to see how the Nazi and Soviet Realms could be seen as harbouring similar kinds of ambitions to be universal orders. In any event, and again Schmitt's argument parallels that of Morgenthau, as between *Grossräume* the kind of accommodation that made possible the JPE is simply not possible because these are not the kind of political orders that are capable of admitting the existence of equals or *justi hostes*, legitimate enemies.[26]

Once again, we see the same story told in different ways. To return to the beginning of this discussion, for Schmitt the spatial ordering of the world is of central importance—this is where the essentially untranslatable term *Nomos* comes in. The JPE constitutes such a *Nomos* but has been destroyed and there is no new *Nomos*. Morgenthau by way of contrast sees (essentially) the same phenomena in (essentially) normative terms—it is the civilization that constituted European international society that has been destroyed, not a spatial ordering *as such*, and it is the failure to agree on a new basis for civilization rather than the absence of a new *Nomos* of the earth that brings about the twilight of international morality.

2.4. **Under an empty sky**

Both texts under consideration here are elegies; they look back with a degree of nostalgia to a better world. Morgenthau's instinctual approach to politics seems to have been deeply conservative, and he sees much to mourn about in the passing of the old order, and little to hope for from the coming of the new. His repeated and invariably favourable references to Bismarck as the representative statesman of the old order—tough, ruthless, but recognizing a moral code nonetheless—are best understood in this light. An added attraction of the old Chancellor may also have been that he represented a Germany with which the conservative Morgenthau could identify, as opposed to the Germany ruled by the ruffians who had expelled him from what he had thought of as his home on the basis of his race. Equally elegiac is Schmitt, who had, for a while at least, identified with these ruffians, but whose particular brand of conservatism was centred on the past, the old European order rather than the new, anti-Semitic populism of the Nazis.

   Both writers believed that this world was gone for good. Both saw the contest of their day as being between two constellations of forces ('The West' and 'Soviet Communism') neither of which was remotely interested in, or indeed capable of, recreating the old order. Both were deeply depressed by this perception. Schmitt's sense of alienation from the post-war world is well known, but Morgenthau's pessimism is, perhaps, worth documenting. The final paragraphs of 'The Twilight of International Morality' (which also appear in *Politics Among Nations*) set out a picture of a struggle with

[a] ferocity and intensity not known to other ages. . . . [Thus], carrying their idols before them, the nationalistic masses of our time meet in the international arena, each group convinced that it executes the mandate of history, that it does for

humanity what it seems to do for itself, and that it fulfils a sacred mission ordained by providence, however defined.

Little do they know that they meet under an empty sky from which the gods have departed.[27]

Schmitt might, I think, have agreed with the sentiment if not the phraseology; the world of the JPE is gone and gone for good. Much to his regret the old European world has been undermined by the new universalism. The successive attempts by Wilhelm II and Hitler to carve out for Germany an imperial identity (a *Grossraum*) as the dominant power in the Eurasian landmass have been defeated by the universalist principles represented, albeit in very different ways, by the Anglo-Saxons and the Bolsheviks. *The Nomos of the Earth* has an elegiac tone which, from Schmitt's perspective is understandable, though, as noted below, it is less clear why this position would be endorsed by any twenty-first century thinker with progressivist tendencies.

Still, while Schmitt remained true to this pessimism, Morgenthau's later career and writings counteract this sentiment and suggest a qualified optimism. Although he was never a Cold Warrior in the full sense of the term, he seems, reasonably enough one might think, to have seen the cause of the US and the West as clearly morally superior to that of the Soviet Union; his education of the American people and political class in the realities of statecraft was designed to help them to defend themselves against a cruel and cynical enemy. At the same time, the American people seem to have educated him into an appreciation of the imperfect virtues of a liberal democratic state. The essays collected in *Truth and Power* and written over the decade of the 1960s paint a self-portrait of a scholar who, while certainly critical of the excesses of American power and especially of US involvement in Vietnam, nonetheless developed an admiration and affection for American political culture and the American people.[28] The very fact of his engagement in such anti-Vietnam activities as the teach-ins of the 1960s indicates a commitment to American life and American democracy which is at odds with the pessimism of the above quotation. This commitment is to be contrasted with Carl Schmitt's attitude towards the Federal Republic of Germany, which he always kept at an arm's length, refusing to engage with its politics, or to recognize its status as the most successful polity that Germany has ever managed to produce. For Schmitt, the post-1945 world held no redeeming features, and the elegiac pessimism of *The* Nomos *of the Earth* stayed with him for the rest of his long life—he died in 1985, at the age of 96.

In this context, the posthumous reputations of the two scholars are of some interest. After years of neglect, if not actual obloquy, Schmitt has become an iconic writer not simply, as one might have expected, for thinkers of the right, but also for the post-Marxist, post-modern left. His *Concept of the Political* is widely seen as a compelling assault on contemporary liberalism; the autonomy of the political and the notion of the 'friend–enemy' distinction is seen as a necessary corrective to the liberal reduction of politics to morals.[29] The terminology of much of *The* Nomos *of the Earth* is gnomic enough to appeal to many post-positivist international political theorists, and Schmitt is beginning to be seen as a major theorist of IR—for example, the September 2004 ECPR Pan-European International Relations Conference at the Hague ran a Section on 'The International Thought of Carl Schmitt' which attracted twenty-seven papers running over eight sessions.[30] In spite of Schmitt's appalling political record in the 1930s and subsequently, this revival of interest in his work ought to be welcomed; in any event, it is, perhaps, worth noting that giving one's allegiance to Stalin in the 1930s has never attracted the kind of opprobrium associated with a dalliance in the other political direction. Perhaps it should, and there can be no excuses for Schmitt's fellow-travelling with the Nazis, but for all that, he is a genuinely original thinker whose geopolitical take on the JPE is certainly well worthy of attention, even if the uncritical praise it sometimes receives is unwarranted.

It is fair to say that the upward trajectory of Hans Morgenthau's posthumous reputation has not been as steep. Within the literature of IR theory, he is now more highly regarded than he was at the time of his death in 1980, but partly for reasons not directly connected to the merits of his own work, but rather connected to the use of that work as a stick to beat other scholars. As realism in IR theory became associated with rational choice theory, largely as an unintended by-product of the recasting of the discourse by Kenneth Waltz, so critics of this turn began to look to the past and a 'classical realism' of which Morgenthau was a prime exemplar; the process of reassessment began as long ago as 1984 in the post-structuralist work of Richard Ashley, and has continued via more extended explorations of an Augustinian realism that can be contrasted with Waltzian 'neo-realism'.[31]

For all that this process will certainly continue—as this volume testifies—there are natural limits to the extent to which Morgenthau's reputation can rise. The simple truth is that he was not a philosophically deep writer; there is more meat in Schmitt's account of the JPE than there is in Morgenthau's account of the twilight of international morality. At the same time, it is right and proper that Morgenthau's work should receive attention because there is more to life than philosophical depth. At its best, his writing displays qualities of common sense and practical wisdom that are conspicuously absent from works such as *The* Nomos *of the Earth*. His account of the old European order is much more accessible than Schmitt's; perhaps for precisely that reason it is less fashionable, but accessibility should be recognized for the virtue it is. In terms of content and general relevance for the twenty-first century, Morgenthau has at least as much to say as Schmitt, and perhaps more, but what is actually rather more important is that he offers us an account of what it is to be a socially concerned theorist in a democratic state; 'speaking truth to power' is something conspicuously absent from Schmitt's life, but exemplified by Morgenthau's.

☐ NOTES

1. This account draws in particular on Christoph Frei, *Hans J. Morgenthau: An Intellectual Biography* (Baton Rouge, LA: Louisiana State University Press, 2001); William C. Scheuerman, *Carl Schmitt: The End of Law* (Lanham, MD: Rowman & Littlefield, 1999) Ch. 9; and Michael C. Williams, *The Realist Tradition and the Limits of International Relations* (Cambridge: Cambridge University Press, 2005).
2. When Morgenthau arrived to see Schmitt, someone more important was present, and Schmitt more or less ignored the young scholar; Schmitt presents here a familiar figure, the man who while talking to you at a party is constantly looking over your shoulder to see if there is anyone more interesting in sight.
3. Carl Schmitt, *The* Nomos *of the Earth in the International Law of the* Jus Publicum Europaeum, translated and with an Introduction by G. L. Ulmen (New York: Telos Press, Ltd., 2003). Hans J. Morgenthau 'The Twilight of International Morality', *Ethics*, 58: 2 (1948), 79–99.
4. Hans J. Morgenthau, *Politics Among Nations: The Struggle For Power and Peace*, 1st edn. (New York: Knopf, 1948).
5. *Scientific Man versus Power Politics* (Chicago, IL: University of Chicago Press, 1947).
6. See, for example, T. Todorov, *The Conquest of America* (New York: Harper Torchbooks, 1987) for an account of the inability of either the conquistadors or their critics to develop the notion of 'different but equal'. For another example, see the

account of the different rules that apply within Europe and in the rest of the world in Edward Keene, *Beyond the Anarchical Society* (Cambridge: Cambridge University Press, 2002). Both Keene and Todorov regret the distinctions that Schmitt regards as central and desirable.

7. The argument here is set out in Part II Chapters 1 and 2 of Schmitt, *The Nomos of the Earth*.

8. See, for example, Ken Booth, 'Ten Flaws of Just Wars', in Booth (ed.), The Kosovo Tragedy, a Special Issue of *The International Journal of Human Rights*, 4 (2000), 315–24.

9. There is a line of thought in Schmitt interpretation that sees him as essentially a theological writer who places the issue of God's order in the world at the centre of all his thought; a central concept here is that of the *katechon*, the being referred to in a (contested) interpretation of 2 Thessalonians, 2: 1-8 as having the role of staving off the Apocalypse and the coming of the Antichrist. Although in the original Greek text *ho katechon* seems to refer to a person, Schmitt interprets the term more widely; in this context, it should be noted that, to Schmitt's way of thinking, although the modern state system does not understand itself as *ho katechon*, it operates as such by preventing the world unity that is a necessary precondition for the Apocalypse. I am grateful to Will Hooker for this point.

10. Gary Ulmen's Introduction to the English Translation of *The Nomos of the Earth* is the best source for mainline Schmitt interpretation on this, and, indeed, most other issues.

11. The 'Amboyna Massacre' of 1623, the murder of English and Japanese traders by their Dutch rivals is perhaps the most famous illustration of this point. A graphic account is given in Giles Milton's best-seller *Nathaniel's Nutmeg* (London: Hodder and Stoughton, 1999).

12. Schmitt, *The Nomos of the Earth*, 142.

13. Key texts available in English here are *The Concept of the Political*, trans. George Schwab (Chicago, IL: University of Chicago Press, 1996) and *The Crisis of Parliamentary Democracy*, trans. Ellen Kennedy (Cambridge, MA: MIT Press, 1985).

14. E. H. Carr, *The Twenty Years Crisis*, ed. Michael Cox (London: Palgrave, 2001).

15. It is, perhaps, worth making the point that most modern historians would be sceptical of this interpretation, pointing out that for most of the nineteenth century the Monroe Doctrine was underwritten by British naval power.

16. Whether there is actually a distinction between 'enemy' and 'foe' is contested amongst Schmittians; although Schmitt himself does not explicitly employ the distinction it seems to me to be implicit in his approach—the notion of *justi hostes* makes little sense without some such distinction. I am grateful to Douglas Bulloch for comments on this point.

17. Morgenthau, 'Twilight', 84.

18. For a similar recent argument, see Edward Luttwak, 'Give War a Chance', *Foreign Affairs*, 78 (1999), 36–45.

19. Morgenthau, 'Twilight', 85.

20. There is an interesting contemporary parallel here: both Robert Kagan and Robert Cooper argue (albeit in rather different ways) that the Continental (West) Europeans have been so successful at eliminating force amongst themselves that they assume there is no place for force in the modern world—but there are serpents outside rather than inside this paradise, and they may have to get used to the idea that there are two sets of moral rules that apply, one to intra-European/Western relations the other to dealings with much of the rest of the world. Kagan, *Of Paradise and Power* (London: Atlantic Books, 2004), Robert Cooper, *The Breaking of Nations* (London: Atlantic Books, 2003).
21. Morgenthau, 'Twilight', 81.
22. Ibid. 88
23. Ibid. 91.
24. Morgenthau, 'Twilight', 93. I hope to consider further Morgenthau's critique of liberal-democratic foreign policy in a later paper. A recent series of workshops on the responsibilities of institutions can be seen as an attempt to disprove his contention. See, e.g., Toni Erskine (ed.), *Can Institutions Have Responsibilities? Collective Moral Agency and International Relations* (Basingstoke: Palgrave Macmillan, 2003).
25. Morgenthau, 'Twilight', 98.
26. *Nomos* is a more complicated notion than this summary conveys; a very good commentary is provided by Gary Ulmen in his Introduction to *The* Nomos *of the Earth*, 22ff.
27. Morgenthau, 'Twilight', 99.
28. Morgenthau, *Truth and Power: Essays of a Decade 1960–70* (London: Pall Mall Press, 1970).
29. The writings of Chantal Mouffe are central here: see, e.g., *The Return of the Political* (London: Verso, 1993) and Mouffe (ed.), *The Challenge of Carl Schmitt* (London: Verso, 1999). It is interesting that in Britain the Schmitt revival has been led by an explicitly left-wing publishing house (Verso is the modern name for what used to be New Left Books, associated with what still is the *New Left Review*). The same house published Gopal Balakrishnan's *The Enemy: An Intellectual Portrait of Carl Schmitt* (London: Verso, 2002).
30. The first part of this paper draws on my 'From Humanised War to Humanitarian Intervention: Carl Schmitt's Critique of the Just War Tradition' which was presented at The Hague. See: http://www.sgir.org/conference2004/ for the full programme of Section 11 'The International Thought of Carl Schmitt' and many of the papers in PDF. format.
31. Kenneth Waltz, *Theory of International Politics* (Reading, MA: Addison-Wesley, 1979); Richard Ashley, 'The Poverty of Neorealism', *International Organisation*, 38 (1984); 225–86; Joel Rosenthal, *Righteous Realists* (Baton Rouge, LA: University of Louisiana Press, 1991); Alasdair Murray, *Reconstructing Realism* (Edinburgh: University of Keele Press, 1996); Richard Ned Lebow, *The Tragic Vision of Politics* (Cambridge: Cambridge University Press, 2003); Michael C. Williams, *The Realist Tradition*.

3 Carl Schmitt and Hans Morgenthau: Realism and beyond

William E. Scheuerman[1]

We now know that the young Hans Morgenthau was involved in an intense 'hidden dialogue' with Carl Schmitt, twentieth-century Germany's most significant right-wing authoritarian political thinker.[2] In his earliest Weimar-era writings, Morgenthau responded to Schmitt's influential reflections on the 'concept of the political': Morgenthau's assertion that Schmitt plagiarized core arguments from his 1929 dissertation is fundamentally accurate. As Morgenthau noted, his dissertation was partly intended as a critical response to a 1927 essay by Schmitt in which the right-wing theorist had defined 'the political' as constituting a fundamentally distinct and independent sphere of activity, existing alongside alternative modes of human activity. Morality concerns the problem of good and bad, aesthetics is occupied with the distinction between beautiful and ugly, economics is preoccupied with profitability and unprofitability, whereas only politics concerns the contrast between what Schmitt famously described as 'friend and foe'.[3] The young Morgenthau astutely diagnosed the conceptual Achilles' heel of this initial definition of politics: Schmitt's exposition misleadingly implied that political activity was limited to a pre-given set of objects or concerns, thereby obscuring the possibility that *any* conceivable sphere of activity could take on 'political' qualities. In its stead, Morgenthau proposed that politics be described as 'a characteristic, quality, or coloration which any substance can take on . . . '.[4] The distinctive attribute of political activity was captured best by focusing on 'the degree of intensity' of the conflict at hand. Although drawing their substantive concerns from any of a host of (moral, aesthetic, and economic) arenas of human activity, identifiably political concerns were those in which a high 'degree of intensity' of conflict had surfaced.[5] Although admitting the difficulty of determining at what specific juncture a particular conflict had become 'intense' and thus genuinely political, Morgenthau's 1929 dissertation insisted that his alternative 'model of intensity' offered a superior way of capturing the distinctive traits of political life. Schmitt seemed to agree. As Morgenthau noted in a 1978 autobiographical essay for the journal *Society*, Schmitt not only wrote him a complimentary letter praising his conceptual innovations, but also 'changed the second [1932] edition of the *Concept of the Political* in the light of the new propositions of my thesis without lifting the veil of anonymity from their author'.[6] In fact, Schmitt's 1932 study tends to drop misleading imagery of politics as a distinct or separate sphere, instead following Morgenthau's conceptualization of politics as concerning conflicts characterized by intense enmity.[7]

Morgenthau's 1978 comments remain surprising. Why would a German-Jewish refugee who went on to become the leading light of post-war realist IR theory proudly proclaim that he had significantly influenced Schmitt, whom Morgenthau himself described, not unfairly, as having aspired to become the 'Streicher of the legal profession' in 1930s Germany?[8] Why not let the sleeping dogs lie, especially in light of Schmitt's poor treatment of the young Morgenthau, as bitterly recounted in his reflections, as well as Schmitt's enthusiastic embrace of Nazism? To be sure, Morgenthau *did* wait many decades before bringing this intellectual connection to an English-speaking audience probably unfamiliar anyhow with Schmitt and his nefarious quest to become the 'crown jurist' of National Socialism.[9]

Let me suggest one explanation for Morgenthau's concession: Morgenthau reminded his audience that he influenced Schmitt's reflections on the 'concept of the political' because it represents the tip of the iceberg in terms of the deep intellectual ties between the two authors. Although I leave it to others to speculate on Morgenthau's psychological motives, an element of 'bad conscience' characterizes his 1978 comments. Just as Schmitt borrowed significantly from Morgenthau's ideas about the nature of politics without bothering to acknowledge his intellectual debts to the young Jewish doctoral student, Morgenthau was inspired by Schmitt's *substantive views* about international relations without openly conceding how much he owed to Schmitt. In fact, some of Morgenthau's most provocative observations about American foreign policy build directly on Schmitt's reflections. In developing his famous critique of American liberalism, Morgenthau clearly builds on a number of Schmitt's criticisms. Unfortunately, his arguments also reproduce Schmitt's blind spots (I). As a number of commentators have noted, Morgenthau's post-war writings are tension-ridden. While insisting on the necessity of establishing a world-state alone fully capable of minimizing the destructive potential of contemporary warfare, Morgenthau's realist intellectual instincts forced him to decry even relatively modest attempts at global governance. With growing theoretical and intellectual acumen, Morgenthau tackled the horrible prospect of nuclear war. Yet deeply rooted intellectual presuppositions prevented him from undertaking the necessary theoretical and political revisions to realism. Consequently, his attempts to influence the study of international relations as well as US policymakers always remained no less tension-ridden. Morgenthau's hidden dialogue with Schmitt can help us understand the origins of these tensions (II).

Thus far, IR scholars—in contrast to some political theorists—have shown limited interest in Morgenthau's intellectual ties to Schmitt. What could arcane theoretical disputes about the 'concept of the political' possibly have to do with the empirical realities of world politics? As I hope to show in this essay, the substantive overlap between the two authors is extensive. A proper understanding of that overlap is indispensable if we are to make sense of Morgenthau's idiosyncratic brand of realism.

3.1. Schmitt and Morgenthau on the pathologies of American power

Morgenthau's 1929 dissertation, *The International Judicial System: Its Essence and Its Limits*, offers a clear response to Schmitt's ideas about the 'concept of the political'. But it also refers to key arguments of one of Schmitt's most important early books on international relations, the 1926 *Key Questions of the League of Nations* [*Die Kernfrage des Voelkerbundes*], where Schmitt offered an initial formulation of his far-reaching critique not only of twentieth-century liberal visions of international law, but also the United States and the predominant role, Schmitt argued, it played in the destruction of superior pre-liberal models of international politics.[10]

Morgenthau was clearly familiar with Schmitt's core arguments about both international politics and the special role played by the United States on the global scene. Some evidence suggests that he followed the development of Schmitt's ideas about international law well into the post-war era.[11] At the very least, a number of striking parallels can be found between Schmitt's criticisms of US foreign policy and Morgenthau's.

3.1.1. THE WESTPHALIAN STATE SYSTEM AS HISTORICAL NOSTALGIA

Schmitt offers a deeply nostalgic vision of the early Westphalian system and traditional early modern European model of international law, according to which the moralistic and legalistic liberalism of the United States— as represented most clearly by the figure of Woodrow Wilson—played a decisive role in the destruction of a fundamentally pacific European-dominated state system. After the religious wars, Schmitt claims, the European continental powers successfully defused explosive political tensions by 'de-theologizing' and neutralizing international relations.[12] As clearly articulated in the political and legal theory of Thomas Hobbes, legality and morality were strictly separated. Traditional religiously inspired notions of Just War were jettisoned for a formalistic conception of warfare, according to which every state possesses an equal chance to wage war as it deems appropriate. A crucial implication of Hobbes' critique of traditional natural law and his famous postulate that only the sovereign state offers an adequate framework for a shared definition of justice is that

[i]n contrast to religious, civil, and factional wars, wars between states cannot be measured with the yardstick of truth and justice. War between states is neither just nor unjust; it is an affair of state and as such does not have to be just . . . What is therefore essential to international law, which governs relations between states, is law that does not distinguish between just and unjust, a nondiscriminatory concept of war.[13]

In this account, the only (formal) prerequisites of the right to wage war consisted of minimal features of sovereignty (e.g. a centralized monopoly on legitimate coercion) which all modern states potentially possess. Because of the resulting 'neutralization' of international strife, warfare lost the horrible traits it had acquired during the 1500s and 1600s, when Protestant and Catholics competed to see who could most brutally slaughter their religious opponents. 'Only by means of the full elimination of the question of the *justa causa* [just cause]...did the taming of European war succeed.'[14] To be sure, the non-European world functioned as a bloody site where European powers were permitted to vent their rivalries; Schmitt concedes that non-Europeans rarely benefited from the civilizational achievements of post-1648 European international law.[15] Yet at least *in* Europe, a 'neutral' conception of the right to wage war put to rest the self-destructive dynamic of moralistic civil war and internecine religious conflict. In contrast to the brutalities of the preceding religious wars, warfare on the European continent subsequently took the form of a highly ritualized duel, conducted according to strict mores and norms of behaviour, between equal (sovereign state) partners. In the ritualized wars of early modern Europe where states could no longer plausibly make universally binding claims to the religious or moral superiority of their cause, both combatants and non-combatants were spared the worst horrors of political violence. The spectre of more-or-less permanent civil war, in which self-righteous crusaders insisted on the universal validity of their moral ideas before unleashing unmitigated horrors against their enemies, was abandoned in favour of relatively civilized wars between equal sovereign states.

The early modern system rested on two pillars, however, both of which have crumbled in the twentieth century: the balance of powers, which in turn only functioned effectively because of a far-reaching consensus concerning basic ideals and values shared by all European states. When the state system embraced non-European powers as equals and thereby tolerated heterogeneous elements, this original cultural and ideological consensus collapsed. In Schmitt's argument, any effective system of supranational legal coordination must rest on a substantial dose of homogeneity, which he saw—at least before 1933—as potentially taking many different forms.[16] In the literal sense of the term, a fair and effective system of *international* law remains impossible because no such homogeneity can be found on the world scene. Amid the profound moral, political, and ethnic antagonisms of our deeply divided globe, any system of 'international' law in reality necessarily rests on the specific political vocabulary and legal ideals of a particular set of power interests.

Morgenthau offers a remarkably similar nostalgic portrayal of the trajectory of modern international law. For both writers, the history of modern international politics is essentially a *Verfallsgeschichte* [story of decay], in which a fundamentally sound early modern European-dominated system is destroyed by a far more explosive (liberal) twentieth-century model no longer based on the balance of powers and a shared European cultural background. Although Morgenthau tends to translate Schmitt's German theoretical terminology (e.g. the 'political') into language more acceptable to English-speaking readers ('power politics'), he not only endorses the broad outlines of Schmitt's account, but also reproduces many of its specific claims as well.[17] Morgenthau's readers will encounter similar comments about Hobbes, the positive role of the balance of power and European moral consensus in the traditional state system, relations between the European and non-European worlds, and the profound limitations of international law and 'world public opinion' in the contemporary era.[18] Even Morgenthau's famous quest to show that realism is by no means immoral or amoral in its fundamental orientation mirrors Schmitt's use of Hobbes: the security of the sovereign state is a fundamental presupposition of moral experience, and to the extent that the pursuit of the 'national interest' is indispensable to security, its pursuit makes an indispensable contribution to the realization of moral life.[19]

Unfortunately, Morgenthau probably reproduces the weaknesses of Schmitt's original rendition of the argument as well. Despite their shared enthusiasm for Hobbes, both authors have a hard time both defending Hobbes and simultaneously making sense of the fact that the English thinker was such a significant influence on the legal positivism so abhorred by both of them. Both conveniently overlook historical evidence suggesting that their nostalgia for a 'golden age' of pre-liberal international relations is misplaced. Between 1648 and 1914, terrible violence not only characterized relations between European and non-European states, but oftentimes relations between and among European states as well.[20] Both risk simplifying the complex nature of the nexus between morality and legality that emerged in European legal thought and, to some extent, within European legal reality in the early modern period. Legality was not 'cleansed' of morality, as the argument sometimes misleadingly suggests. Instead a new and more nuanced—but indisputably *normative*—understanding of the relationship between morality and legality emerged which allowed for the possibility of avoiding crude *conflations* of traditional morality and legality. Indeed, that new understanding—whose outlines emerged most clearly during the European Enlightenment—clearly partook of 'universalistic' moral and political ideals. As Juergen Habermas has repeatedly pointed out in arguing against Schmitt, universalistic normative ideals not only provide powerful conceptual ammunition against a crude moralization of legality, but they are probably indispensable if we are to defend a plausible distinction between law and morals in the first place.[21] For Schmitt, however, modern universalism is the *source* of the brutalities of twentieth-century world affairs rather than a foundation for precisely that delineation of morals from law that he considers essential to the greatest achievements of the European state system. To be sure, Morgenthau is more appreciative of the role universalistic normative ideals played in humanizing the pre-1914 European state system.[22] Yet like Schmitt, he ultimately is reluctant to concede that such ideals can play, under the guise of modern liberal notions of international law, a fundamentally positive role. In accordance with Schmitt, Morgenthau repeatedly depicts the twentieth-century international legal offspring of Enlightenment universalism—most prominently: the League of Nations and United Nations—in a negative light.

3.1.2. AMERICAN LIBERALISM AND THE ORIGINS OF TOTAL WAR

Of course, Schmitt and Morgenthau are by no means the only analysts of modern international politics to offer a nostalgic gloss on the pre-twentieth-century European state system. Nor are they the only writers who trace decisive breaks to the traditional order to Wilsonian liberalism. However, many features of Morgenthau's account arguably build directly on the idiosyncrasies of Schmitt's. Both authors attribute many of the brutalities of twentieth-century global politics to the increased power of the United States. Of course, in Morgenthau's account, in striking contrast to Schmitt's, Nazi Germany plays a key role in the demolition of the traditional balance of power; Morgenthau dates the demolition of the traditional state system to 1933.[23] However, his polemical discussions of the pathologies of US foreign policy often mirror Schmitt's tendency to emphasize the central role played by the United States in undermining an otherwise sound European-dominated system.

The universalistic aspirations of American liberalism engender a remoralization of international relations that paves the way for the ills of total

war. Although neither Schmitt nor Morgenthau neglects the technological sources of total war, both underline the importance of the revival
of the traditionalistic garb of 'just war', now dressed in the fashionable
form of American liberalism and the messianic Wilsonian fantasy of a
war 'to end all wars'. American liberalism generates a self-righteous brand
of pseudo-humanitarianism blind to the terrible dangers of state violence
waged under the banner of a (fictional) singular humanity. Waged in the
name of humanity, 'liberal wars, far from fulfilling the liberal hopes [to
end war], even brought about the very evils which they were supposed
to destroy. Far from being the "last wars", they were only the forerun-
ners and pioneers of wars more destructive and extensive than pre-liberal
ones.'[24] Those who oppose the American-dominated liberal international
system constitute pariahs and criminals deserving of harsh punishment.[25]
Blurring any meaningful distinction between legality and morality, those
who dare to oppose the American-dominated vision of an international
legal community are demonized and accordingly subjected to terrible brutalities. Warfare reverts to the horrors of the pre-Westphalian era, when
foreign foes were more than mere duelling partners: they were deemed
morally inferior and potentially subhuman in character. Even worse: modern technology heightens the destructive capacity of modern warfare and
makes unprecedented acts of violence relatively commonplace. The apex
of liberal self-righteousness is the view that liberal wars no longer even
deserve to be described as 'wars'. Although their technological prowess
permits liberal states to kill innocent civilians in any corner of the globe,
they purportedly undertake 'police action' (or, in more recent parlance,
humanitarian intervention) for the sake of enforcing international law,
whereas only outcast (non-liberal) states who dare to challenge liberal
hegemony continue to engage in the barbarism of war. The exclusionary
character of liberal universalism is thereby taken to its logical conclusion:
liberal international law requires what Schmitt describes as a *discriminatory
concept of war*.[26] In stark contrast to the Hobbesian traits of the early
Westphalian system, sovereign states no longer possess equal or 'neutral'
rights to wage war. As Morgenthau observes, liberals criticize autocratic
and totalitarian wars, yet 'on the other hand, [when] the use of arms is
intended to bring the blessings of liberalism to peoples not yet enjoying
them or to protect them against despotic aggression, the just end may
justify means otherwise condemned'.[27]

This vision of liberal international law rests on a false universalism because self-interested liberal great powers (e.g. the USA and UK) skillfully exploit it in order to pursue their specific power interests. Liberal international law is not, in fact, representative of a mythical 'world public opinion': it reflects specifically Anglo-American political and economic ideals. Following Schmitt, Morgenthau believes that one can still detect an instinctual sense for 'the political' (or, in Morgenthau's terminology, sound pursuit of 'power politics' and the 'national interest') behind the moralistic and legalistic rhetoric of American foreign policy.[28] American global influence rests, Schmitt similarly argues, on an uncritical acceptance by the world community of a set of inherently imperialistic liberal categories that dutifully reflect US (and sometimes Anglo-American) political and economic interests.[29]

To be sure, Morgenthau modifies core elements of this story. Most significantly, his writings offer a vastly more subtle appreciation of the political culture and intellectual traditions of his adopted country: like so many of the German-Jewish refugee intellectuals who made their homes in the United States, Morgenthau soon came to embrace, though by no means uncritically, many features of the US political tradition.[30] In this spirit, he struggled to identify indigenous voices who might be interpreted as having anticipated some of his own theoretical and political proclivities: Morgenthau delighted in holding up the examples of Alexander Hamilton and Abraham Lincoln as exemplars of authentically political thinkers. Yet Morgenthau's harsh assessment of contemporary American foreign policy means that he typically is forced to locate these more attractive elements of the American political tradition in the distant past. He complements his Schmitt-inspired nostalgia for the early modern European system with a nostalgic portrayal of the early years of the American republic and yet another *Verfallsgeschichte*.[31] *In the Defense of the National Interest* argues that the earliest years of US foreign policy alone endorsed the verities of realist doctrine, whereas decadent 'ideological' and 'utopian' modes of foreign policy superceded this brief foundational shining moment of realist intellectual hegemony.[32]

Morgenthau's critical account of the Schmittian bugbear of liberal universalism is also more plausible than the original version. Rejecting Schmitt's open-ended broadsides against universalism (or, in Schmitt's own polemical terminology, 'normativism'), Morgenthau offers a more convincing analysis of how modern political ideologies absorbed the universalistic pretensions of the European past while simultaneously disfiguring their worthwhile elements. Noble moral and cultural ideals claming universal validity are replaced by disturbingly parochial political visions (e.g. an American version of liberalism derived from special conditions of nineteenth-century US political development) that inherit the claim to universal validity found in traditional moral ideals and aspirations. The immediate result is secularized 'political religions' claiming universal validity but insensitive to their own time- and place-based limitations. The rise of political religions not only contributes to the destruction of the shared moral and cultural consensus of European society, but it also proves inconsistent with the complicated operations of elite-dominated diplomacy and balance of power politics. Reminiscent of Schmitt, Morgenthau envisions the post-1945 era as a 'global civil war' pitting two political religions claiming universal validity (American liberalism and Soviet communism) in a life-or-death struggle. Given the rigid dynamics of a bipolar world, the most attractive features of the traditional state system undergo dramatic decay: the 'two superpowers and their allies and satellites face each other like two fighters in a short and narrow lane'.[33] Here as well, Morgenthau shares Schmitt's anxieties about the decline of European civilization, while simultaneously amending them: whereas Schmitt clearly sees American and Soviet domination of Europe as an unmitigated disaster, Morgenthau tends to emphasize the cultural and political commonalities of European and American civilization. In this manner, the United States is reinterpreted, *pace* Schmitt, as a *defender* of an embattled European civilization.[34]

For both authors, the history of American foreign policy rests on a reckless dialectic of 'interventionism and isolationism'; both argue that these seemingly disparate features of American foreign policy really represent two sides of the same coin.[35] They also offer a number of shared observations about the specific operations of American power. For example, Schmitt considers the *non-intervention treaty* to be one of the most creative US innovations in modern international law. The non-intervention treaties pursued by the United States in Latin and South America are *in fact* intervention treaties since the United States maintains the right to intervene if certain vaguely defined conditions—'public order', 'the protection of life, liberty, and property', etc.—are not violated.

In the case of all of these nonintervention agreements it is important to note that due to the indeterminacy of their concepts the hegemonic power decides at its discretion and thereby places the political existence of the controlled state in its own hands.[36]

The de facto military and political prowess of the United States means that in most cases it unilaterally determines the meaning of the vague legal clauses at hand. Morgenthau not only refers expressly to Schmitt's analysis of the non-intervention treaty,[37] but he similarly underscores its significance as an instrument of US power. Not the main body of the general norms of the non-intervention treaty, but rather its declaration of a series of exceptions to the rules of non-intervention allows us best to understand the real state of affairs between the great powers and lesser states. Like Schmitt, Morgenthau asserts the 'impossibility of developing a coherent [legal] doctrine of nonintervention'.[38] Power politics, not the legal niceties of treaty makers, ultimately determines the dynamics of intervention and non-intervention. Great powers in pursuit of their national interests will also be forced to undermine the express spirit of non-intervention treaties.

3.1.3. BACK TO THE MONROE DOCTRINE?

Despite his nostalgia for the Westphalian state system, Schmitt early on grasped that its days were numbered. Anticipating contemporary debates about globalization, Schmitt quickly reached the conclusion that the nation state was no longer sufficiently attuned to the regulatory and military challenges of contemporary political life.[39] But if ambitious liberal models of international law were unacceptable, what alternative political forms presented themselves as plausible alternatives? Schmitt's answer to this question, which he formulated between the 1930s and 1950s, was clear enough: *regionalization*. Regionally based political and economic blocs, dominated by a single hegemonic power (in Schmitt's terminology from the Nazi period, a *Reich*), was both the best way to avoid the pathologies of universalistic liberal international law and ensure effective state action. During the Nazi period, Schmitt's preference for regional political and economic blocs meshed neatly with Nazi imperialism: Schmitt enthusiastically sketched out the conceptual foundations for a Nazi-dominated European 'greater region' [*Grossraum*] as an alternative to the twin universalistic sisters of Anglo-American liberalism and Soviet communism.

The most provocative facet of this argument is Schmitt's attempt to employ a selective reading of US political experience as a justification for a German-dominated European 'greater region'. According to Schmitt, it was the *Americans* who in fact uncovered the organizational and normative virtues of regionalization; Wilsonian liberalism, it turns out, represents an abandonment of earlier more sound US ideas about international politics. Even Schmitt's early Weimar-era writings exhibit a fascination with the manner in which the Monroe Doctrine functioned as an instrument of US domination in Latin and South America. During the nineteenth century, Schmitt argues, the Monroe Doctrine possessed an authentically 'political' character, based on its acknowledgement of the life-or-death existential threat posed to the fledgling American Republic by European monarchies. In stark contrast to the League of Nations and other ambitious liberal visions of supranational legal order, the Monroe Doctrine helped assure a necessary dose of homogeneity within the Americas: it allowed the United States to intervene in order to guarantee that a particular (liberal democratic) vision of political and social order would be established by all American states.[40] In a revealing 1932 essay, Schmitt can barely restrain his enthusiasm for the 'astonishing political achievement' of the Monroe Doctrine: the Monroe Doctrine is of 'world-historical significance', a true manifestation of a 'real and great imperialism'.[41] The Americans have taught the rest of the world that the essence of effective power is the manipulation of elastic legal clauses (e.g. the exception clauses of non-intervention treaties) for the sake of swallowing up small- and medium-sized states whose sovereignty is unlikely to survive the rapid economic, technological, and military transformations of the present era. In conjunction with its manipulation of the legal instruments of the nonintervention treaty, the Americans have brilliantly employed the Monroe Doctrine to unveil the future face of international relations: the globe is destined to be carved up into a small group of 'huge complexes', encompassing entire continents or more, in which a single political entity exercises de facto sovereignty over its neighbours.[42] The United States' de facto domination of the Americas represents the future of international politics everywhere. Schmitt enviously observes in 1932 that 'as a German' examining the US usage of the Monroe Doctrine 'I can only have the feeling of being a beggar in rags talking about the riches and valuables of strangers.'[43]

In 1939, Schmitt directly appealed to the Monroe Doctrine in order to suggest how Germany might successfully join the ranks of the world's great powers. Schmitt argued that the Nazis would have to develop their own version of the Monroe Doctrine in order to establish a European 'huge complex' destined to swallow up small- and medium-size European states by subjecting them to de facto Nazi control. In a clever polemical move, Schmitt claimed that Nazi Germany could learn from the foreign policy of the United States in order to offer a viable alternative to Wilsonian liberalism: American liberalism could be fought with its own impressive arsenal of weapons. Of course, the Nazis would have to discard the 'decadent' liberal democratic ideals with which the Americans had always packaged the Monroe Doctrine. According to Schmitt, not until the conclusion of the nineteenth century did the Americans recklessly subordinate the sensible core ideas of the Monroe Doctrine to the dangerous missionary impulses of universalistic liberalism. An identifiably Nazi 'greater region' would do well to embrace the Monroe Doctrine's original geopolitical ideas, which presciently anticipated the twentieth-century trends towards regionalization by insisting that 'alien' powers had no legitimate political role in the Americas. Just as the United States in the nineteenth century had monopolized the task of warding off 'alien' (e.g. European powers), so too did it now fall to Nazi Germany to 'protect' Europe from 'alien' (American liberalism and Soviet communism) political threats.[44]

For self-evident reasons, Morgenthau was always hesitant to acknowledge his dependence on Schmitt's interpretation of the Monroe Doctrine. Of course, he never endorsed Schmitt's cynical appeal to the Monroe Doctrine as a justification for Nazi imperialism, and when he expressly refers to Nazi ideas of a 'greater region', he does so with obvious disdain.[45] Nonetheless, Morgenthau's discussion of the Monroe Doctrine bears Schmitt's mark. Notwithstanding his nostalgia for the Westphalian system, Morgenthau, like Schmitt, early on presciently acknowledged the 'obsolescence of the nation state' while also rejecting ambitious liberal models of international law.[46] For him as well, the Monroe Doctrine suggested the possibility of a possible alternative.

In his 1929 dissertation, Morgenthau offers a detailed discussion of the Monroe Doctrine in which he acknowleges Schmitt's view of its centrality to US foreign policy, but similarly underscores its authentically 'political' traits. As Schmitt had similarly argued, the Monroe Doctrine is a 'political act' in the truest sense of the term and thus an expression of its fundamental 'life interests'.[47] This argument reappears in many of Morgenthau's subsequent writings on US foreign policy, which repeatedly present the Monroe Doctrine as a paradigmatic exemplar of genuine power politics. Morgenthau seems no less preoccupied with the significance of the Monroe Doctrine than Schmitt. For both authors, the genuinely political character of the Monroe Doctrine makes it one of the rare highpoints in the otherwise unfortunate history of American foreign policy, which too often has succumbed to naive and ultimately irresponsible legalistic and moralistic impulses. In this spirit, *In Defense of the National Interest* begins with what amounts to a eulogy for the Monroe Doctrine: Morgenthau commences his depressing *Verfallsgeschichte* by praising the farsightedness of early US political leaders, and the Monroe Doctrine serves him as a symbol of what once was right about American foreign policy: '[t]he Monroe Doctrine and the policies implementing it express that permanent national interest of the United States in the Western Hemisphere.'[48] Echoing Schmitt, Morgenthau occasionally suggests that attempts at the end of the nineteenth century to extend the scope of the Monroe Doctrine beyond the Americas represented an abandonment of its original function as a sound instrument of *hemispheric* power politics; since McKinley, attempts to apply it have been polluted by inappropriately ambitious universalistic models of political organization.[49] Finally, Morgenthau draws the same tight link between the US employment of non-intervention treaties and the Monroe Doctrine, essentially accepting Schmitt's view that they represent two sides of the same coin of US regional domination in the Americas.[50]

Even more striking is the manner in which Morgenthau again reproduces the blind spots of Schmitt's arguments. Neither author seems particularly concerned with the high price paid by Latin and South American peoples for US regional hegemony; on the contrary, both consider the Monroe Doctrine a fundamentally positive political achievement. Schmitt's celebration of what both authors describe as 'imperialism' is hardly surprising given his basic normative commitments. However, Morgenthau's avowed commitment to basic liberal democratic political ideals meshes less well with his embrace of US hegemony in the Americas.[51] In addition, the argument suffers from a number of historical oversights. The dominant power in South America until the end of the nineteenth century was probably the UK, not the USA. In contrast to the Schmitt–Morgenthau interpretation, American foreign policy in the nineteenth century hardly resisted *all* European intervention, and the United States was not always the dominant power in some sort of American 'greater region'. The scope of the Monroe Doctrine was indeed extended beyond its original geopolitical boundaries at the end of the nineteenth century, but the driving forces in that expansion were very different from those described by Schmitt and Morgenthau. As reinterpreted by Theodore Roosevelt and defenders of US expansionism in the Far East, the Monroe Doctrine was given a Social Darwinian and racist gloss, as captured concisely by Senator Albert J. Beveridge, who piously declared in 1900 that 'God has made us adepts in government that we may administer government among savage and senile peoples.'[52] The move to transform the Monroe Doctrine into an instrument of global domination in fact rested on missionary impulses in US political consciousness, but *pace* Schmitt and Morgenthau as well, it is misleading to attribute those impulses to moralistic liberalism or liberal legal 'normativism'.

A decisive difference separates Morgenthau's discussion of the Monroe Doctrine from Schmitt's, however. Whereas Schmitt argues that the Monroe Doctrine offers a constructive game plan for establishing new modes of regionally based imperialism, Morgenthau is openly sceptical of proposals for revitalizing the Monroe Doctrine as the core of US foreign policy. According to Morgenthau's post-war writings, this is precisely what isolationists and neoisolationists want: they naively believe that the United States can remove itself from non-American affairs while comfortably maintaining its hegemony in Latin and South America. For Morgenthau, such proposals fail to tackle the novel political challenges of the mid-twentieth century. They ignore the profound threats posed to the United States by extra-American powers, and naively continue to consider the hemispheric isolation of the United States a source of security. They also ignore the fact that the Monroe Doctrine always required a rough balance of power in Europe which prevented any single European power from gaining too much power and thereby potentially threatening US hegemony in the Americas. If such a balance of power were to be preserved after 1945, he repeatedly argues, the United States would have to be actively involved on the European theatre of the Cold War—in order to prevent Soviet domination of Europe and ultimately a Soviet threat to US domination of the Americas.[53]

As Morgenthau quickly recognized after 1945, the advent of high-speed air warfare[54] and atomic weapons rendered any easy return to the Monroe Doctrine as the key feature of US foreign policy anachronistic. The Monroe Doctrine remained a model of sound realist foreign policy thinking, but no object of blind veneration.

3.2. **Schmitt and Morgenthau versus the world state**

Morgenthau's post-war writings pursue the dual goal of reshaping the study of IR and influencing US foreign policy. Unfortunately, a striking tension plagues his intellectual and political project. After 1945, Morgenthau emphasized the obsolescence of the nation state as well as the necessity of a world state in order to guarantee lasting peace. As Morgenthau stated with characteristic bluntness, 'there is no shirking the conclusion that international peace cannot be permanent without a world state'.[55] Yet he stubbornly continued to underscore the utopian character of most attempts to create ambitious models of supranational governance: *Politics Among Nations* notes 'that international peace through the transformation of the present society of sovereign nations into a world state is unattainable under the moral, social, and political conditions' of our times.[56] Morgenthau's most influential post-war work then proceeds to pillory both the League of Nations and United Nations. Ours is, indeed, a tragic situation: the dominant moral traditions of the West condemn the brutality of war; war can only be effectively avoided by a world state; aspirations for a world state remain unrealizable and, indeed, potentially dangerous if allowed to join ideological forces with moralistic and legalistic liberalism.

By the late 1950s, Morgenthau presciently grasped that the real possibility of thermonuclear destruction implied a qualitative and not simply quantitative shift in the character of modern warfare. The risky quest for power among nation states might now rapidly culminate in a war that would decimate the human species. The means of warfare might easily undermine the ends (the 'national interest') since atomic warfare would not only destroy the modern state system but humankind itself. 'Because they render meaningful military victory impossible, nuclear weapons fundamentally alter the traditional relationship between force and for-eign policy.'[57] If atomic weapons were left under the control of individual nation states, 'their increase and improvement increase the danger. Thus, it becomes the task of all governments to make themselves superfluous as the guardians of their respective territorial frontiers by transferring their nuclear weapons to an agency whose powers are commensurate with the worldwide destructive potentialities of these weapons.'[58] The only solution, Morgenthau posited, was ultimately the establishment of a fundamentally novel global order in which control over weapons of mass destruction would be taken out of the hands of individual nation states.

As Campbell Craig has observed, Morgenthau was able 'to glimpse—not to design, to glimpse—a *new*, that is, unforeseen political process whereby a condition of anarchy evolves in a new Leviathan; a world state that comes into being merely because of the *prospect* of a nuclear war of all against all'.[59] Morgenthau only *glimpsed* the necessity of a novel global order, however, because it went against the grain of so many of the basic tenets of his thinking. Most important, it clashed fundamentally with the realist assumption of the fundamentally 'anarchic character of the international environment'.[60] Nonetheless, a striking shift characterizes his writings in the 1960s and early 1970s. Although remaining steadfast in his view that the establishment of a world government remained remote, he now often emphasized the *moral imperative* of its establishment at least as much as the pathologies of the dominant attempts to move in this direction (e.g. the United Nations). In Craig's view, Morgenthau reluctantly began to concede that 'the prospect of thermonuclear war had caused the utopian and realistic approaches' in IR to merge.[61]

Unfortunately, Morgenthau never succeeded in undertaking the neces-sary theoretical synthesis. In his late writings, aphoristic existential anxi-eties about the fate of humankind exist uneasily alongside his familiar bat-tery of criticisms of universalism and liberal international law.[62] His policy advice to US foreign policymakers oscillates uneasily between nostalgic appeals to salvage old-fashioned elite-dominated diplomacy and increas-ingly ambitious proposals for supranational governance. Morgenthau's debts to Schmitt play a significant role in his unsuccessful attempt to over-come the basic tensions of his thinking. It would be mistaken to attribute Morgenthau's embrace of the necessity of the world state and simultaneous emphasis on its impracticality exclusively to his 'tragic vision of politics'.[63]

Morgenthau was never able to think creatively enough about the possibility of a novel global order because he carried too much Schmittian intellectual baggage.

To be sure, Morgenthau himself was partly aware of the underlying tensions in his theory. He consequently struggles to describe paths by which we might move closer to a world state and avoid the horrors of contemporary warfare, while also resisting the false temptations of Wilsonian liberalism. In this vein, he repeatedly underscores the virtues of traditional diplomacy: 'If the world state is unattainable in our world, yet indispensable for the survival of that world, it is necessary to create the conditions under which it will not be impossible.... This method of establishing the preconditions for permanent peace we call peace through accommodation. Its instrument is diplomacy.'[64]

Morgenthau then offers his famous 'plea for the restoration of diplomacy to the eminence of its high days in old Europe, when its coolness of head and its clarity of sight prevailed over a public opinion not yet made unruly by mass ideologies...'.[65] Revealingly, this nostalgic vision of diplomacy builds directly on his Schmitt-inspired account of the 'golden age' of the early modern European-dominated international system. What the contemporary world urgently needs, Morgenthau asserts, is a revival of elite-dominated diplomacy and, to the extent still possible, traditional balance of power thinking. These constitutive features of the Westphalian system, it seems, provide the best immediate protection against the spectre of nuclear war.

As many commentators have noted, however, Morgenthau's recourse to traditional diplomacy seems at best naive and at worst misguided. Having established the far-reaching *structural* roots of its decline, Morgenthau is able to offer little more than a desperate plea for its re-establishment without really explaining how traditional diplomacy might thrive in a political environment fundamentally hostile to its operations. Characteristically, Morgenthau also downplays the least appealing implications of his nostalgia. As James Speer has pointedly observed, a return to traditional diplomacy would necessitate 'the repeal of the nineteenth and twentieth centuries, which have witnessed the rise of popular sovereignty and ideology'.[66] In fact, when describing the pathologies of contemporary foreign policymaking, Morgenthau underscores the eminently democratic 'vices' of publicity and majority decision making.[67] He also worries about excessive legislative controls on US foreign policymaking in the United States—a surprising concern given the awesome expansion of executive prerogative during the twentieth century.[68] Despite his best efforts, Morgenthau never really succeeds in explaining how a revival of traditional diplomacy might be synthesized with modern democracy. In Schmitt's nostalgic account of the Westphalian system, its anti-democratic elements generate no theoretical tension since Schmitt is hostile to modern notions of popular sovereignty anyhow. For Morgenthau, however, dependence on this nostalgia produces profound theoretical difficulties since he rejects Schmitt's authoritarian political preferences. One immediate result of this tension are the increasingly shrill criticisms Morgenthau levels at *individual* US policymakers: at times he seems to believe that it is simply the (democratically based) *intellectual and professional mediocrity* of American leaders that constitutes a central source of the pathologies of US foreign policy. No wonder that Morgenthau repeatedly cites Tocqueville's conservative arguments about the tensions between modern democracy and foreign policymaking.[69] If only the United States could recapture the farsighted wisdom of the pre-democratic statesmen of early modern Europe!

A second argumentative strategy points to Morgenthau's Weimar background as well. Although he rejects potentially reckless attempts, including Schmitt's, to rely on the Monroe Doctrine as an immediate guide for reconstructing the international system, Morgenthau similarly exhibits some sympathy for political and economic regionalization, under the auspices of a regional great power and resting on some form of homogeneity. In Schmittian terms: supranational organization can only work when (*a*) it rests on a far-reaching set of shared values and commitments and (*b*) acknowledges the dominant position of one state or group of states. *In Defense of the National Interest* thus argues that Americans should drop their hostility to the traditional notion of a 'sphere of influence': 'it is indeed obvious... from the political history of the human race that the balance of power and concomitant spheres of influence are of the very essence of international politics.'[70] A division of the globe by means of a 'negotiated settlement' into distinct spheres of influence, each dominated by one of the superpowers, offers the best possibility for peace and stability between the 'free world' and its Russian rival.[71] Even Morgenthau's most creative proposals for reordering the global system are haunted by the ghosts of Weimar. The ambitious *Purpose of American Politics*—where Morgenthau hints clearly at the possibility of merging realist and 'utopian' views of IR—advocates a supranational 'free-world association', under US leadership, whose main achievement would be to take the first step towards breaking the increasingly explosive chain between statehood and the monopoly on violence by placing the control of nuclear weapons under supranational control. Only by such a 'free association of [liberal democratic] states' would America 'share its purpose with its associates'.[72] Significantly, this free-world association would be 'more intimate' than traditional alliances or ad hoc alignments, and it would rest on a modicum of ideological homogeneity since it would consist of like-minded states sharing the American commitment to 'equality in freedom'.[73] Only then might the United States successfully 'use its predominant power on behalf of a purpose that would be not only its own but also one in which the non-Communist world could recognize its distinct character and in whose achievement it could experience a common destiny'.[74] In contradistinction to doomed universalistic models of supranational organization, this prospect is more than a vague dream because 'the interests that tie the United States to its European allies are more profound, more comprehensive, and more stable than the interests upon which alliances have traditionally been based . . . [T]hese interests enclose the national identities of all its members within a common civilization threatened by an alien and oppressive social system.'[75]

Morgenthau always conceded that even the most ambitious regionalist models of supranational organization were at best steppingstones to a world state that alone could ensure lasting peace. Thus, his regionalist theoretical tendencies ultimately leave the riddle of his post-war theory unsolved: in the face of nuclear extinction, we desperately require a world state, yet such a state remains at best a distant possibility.

Unfortunately, Morgenthau builds on another facet of Schmitt's thinking that ultimately prevents him from moving beyond this dead end. Morgenthau does not simply consider a world state *unrealistic* given present conditions. Like Schmitt, he also tends to consider it *unattractive* to the extent that it would unduly violate the 'autonomy of the political'. Morgenthau is generally less blunt than Schmitt in advancing this second fundamentally *normative* argument against ambitious modes of supranational organization. Nonetheless, it remains a crucial source of the underlying tensions of his brand of realism, as well as a central reason why he seems so hesitant to reconsider its core tenets despite his acknowledgement of the fundamental novelty of the nuclear era.

In the 1932 version of *The Concept of the Political*, rewritten with Morgenthau's conceptual innovations in mind, Schmitt writes:

> A world in which the possibility of war is utterly eliminated, a completely pacified globe, would be a world without the distinction of friend and enemy and hence a world without politics. It is conceivable that such a world might contain many interesting antitheses and contrasts, competitions and intrigues of every kind, but there would not be a meaningful antithesis whereby men could be required to sacrifice life, authorized to shed blood, and kill other human beings.... The phenomenon of the political can be understood only in the context of the ever present possibility of the friend-and-enemy grouping....[76]

'[R]ejecting the illusory security of a status quo of comfort and ease', while 'holding in low esteem a world of mere entertainment and the mere capacity to be interesting', Schmitt attacks ambitious liberal democratic proposals for supranational rule.[77] A world without 'intense' conflicts, characterized by the *possibility* of killing the 'enemy', would devalue and potentially trivialize human existence. It also rebels against human nature: Schmitt directly links his 'concept of political' to a pessimistic version of philosophical anthropology.

Morgenthau shares Schmitt's concern with defending the 'autonomy of the political', and similarly delights in attacking liberalism for 'depreciating' the centrality of the struggle for power to human existence. To the extent that he also links his interpretation of the concept of the political to the fundaments of human nature, any attempt to rid the universe of 'the political' similarly must seem not only unrealistic but also undesirable.[78] By necessity, ambitious models of transnational government potentially represent an assault on human nature because they would rid human experience of those conflicts that are most intense and thus authentically political in nature. To be sure, Morgenthau stresses that the struggle for power can manifest itself in many arenas of human activity. Presumably, even a world state would provide opportunities for such struggles. Yet he also suggests that *interstate* conflicts—characterized by what Schmitt dubbed the 'real possibility of killing' the enemy—represent the most authentic expression of 'the political'. Within the terms of Morgenthau's own 'model of intensity', the attempt to eliminate interstate violence by means of ambitious transnational governance necessarily undermines the rightful place in human existence of political conflict. Not surprisingly, Morgenthau, like Schmitt, repeatedly criticizes novel experiments with global political decision making—most important: the League of Nations and United Nations—as misguided and characteristically liberal attempts to supplant 'the political' with inappropriate forms of legalism and moralism. Such experiments constitute a denial of the pluralistic character of human experience since they subject a legitimate and necessary form of human action to the laws of competing modes of action.

Unfortunately, the resulting theoretical paradox for Morgenthau is obvious enough: the world state is an existential necessity, but the last century's most impressive quests to achieve a new transnational order are ultimately anti-political and thus intrinsically flawed. No wonder Morgenthau struggles unsuccessfully to show how we might move from interstate anarchy to the world state we purportedly need so desperately.

Interestingly, Morgenthau is dismissive of proposals for pacific *federations* or *confederations* of states. This is, of course, crucial because many if not most modern cosmopolitan theorists—including Immanuel Kant—have advocated something alone these lines rather than a centralized world state.[79] This hostility is motored by the assumption—probably borrowed from Schmitt—that international law typically proves at best of limited value and more often counterproductive when resting on heterogeneous political, cultural, and ideological elements.[80] Morgenthau never really takes such proposals seriously for a second reason as well: they conflict with his ideas about sovereignty. At times clearly echoing Schmitt's interpretation of sovereignty as the capacity to act effectively during a crisis or emergency,[81] Morgenthau writes that in a democracy, the exercise of sovereignty 'lies dormant in normal times, barely visible through the network of constitutional arrangements and legal rules'. Democratic systems 'purposefully obscured the problem of sovereignty and glossed over the need for a definition location of the sovereign power' with legalistic and constitutional niceties masking the real nature of power.[82] 'Yet in times of crisis and war that ultimately responsibility asserts itself', when 'a man or a group of men'—Morgenthau's examples for his primarily American audience are Lincoln, Wilson, and the two Roosevelts—exercise supreme and fundamentally undivided power. Sovereignty cannot, in fact, 'be vested in the people as a whole, who, of course, as such cannot act'.[83] If states are to act 'in times of crisis', undivided and supreme sovereignty must be placed in the hands of some individual or group of individuals. Because *indivisibility* and *supremacy* are constitutive features of sovereignty, and every effective state requires sovereignty, proposals for supranational government that fall short of a centralized world state are intrinsically incoherent:

> We have heard it said time and again that we must 'surrender part of our sovereignty' to an international organization for the sake of world peace, that we must 'share' our sovereignty with such an organization, that the latter would have a certain 'limited sovereignty' while we would keep the substance of it.... We shall endeavor to show that the conception of a divisible sovereignty is contrary to logic and politically unfeasible...[84]

Not only is divisible—or in present-day parlance, 'differentiated'—sovereignty inconsistent with the very nature of the state, but any supranational political and legal institutions committed to realizing confused ideas about sovereignty are destined to founder in the face of war or dire crisis. For Morgenthau, the League of Nations' failure to act in the face of Japanese and German aggression always represented paradigmatic examples of such failures.[85]

Morgenthau's definition of sovereignty, like its Schmittian inspiration, suffers from a misleadingly one-sided focus on the emergency or crisis; its *personalistic* emphasis on the necessity of decision making by 'one man or group of men', along with its dismissal of the notion of *popular sovereignty*, inadvertently reproduces Schmitt's anti-democratic views. Here as well, we encounter Morgenthau's deeply rooted nostalgia for early modern Europe: his conception of sovereignty builds upon ideas about *state* sovereignty that emerged in European Absolutism. Morgenthau probably fails to appreciate how ideas of *popular* sovereignty break with such traditional notions of state sovereignty.[86] Not surprisingly, he misses how the American Republic reshaped traditional ideas of sovereignty, interpreting the US founding in overly traditional terms and misleadingly suggesting that all the Philadelphia Convention 'did was to replace one constitution, one sovereignty, one state with another one, best resting upon the same pre-existing community'.[87] In this interpretation, the United States takes the form of a fundamentally conventional (European-style) nation state resting on a far-reaching set of shared values and cultural commitments.[88]

Speer has countered Morgenthau's definition of sovereignty by responding that:

[i]f sovereignty means supremacy, supremacy as to what? If it means supremacy as to all things, then sovereignty logically is present only in the totalitarian state. If it means less than all things, then sovereignty logically is present where there is supremacy as to only some things. And if this is true, then one government can be supreme as to some things while another government is supreme as to some other things.[89]

For this reason, Morgenthau's hostility to alternative forms of relatively decentralized supranational organization rests on sand: 'It is the essence of the federal principle that different things are done by different governments...each government acting within its own sphere of authority upon the same individual human beings.'[90] Thus, effective state action is by no means inconsistent with any of a host of complex forms of complex or differentiated sovereignty potentially realizable at the transnational level. *Pace* Morgenthau (and Schmitt), various proposals for federal or cofederal supranational government might very well prove consistent with sovereignty.

If the *only* conceivable form of transnational rule, in the final instance, is a centralized world state outfitted with indivisible and supreme sovereign power, no wonder that Morgenthau ultimately remained so worried about its potential dangers. Most cosmopolitan theorists might easily endorse his concern that a world state can only be achieved by illegitimate force and consequently might entail nothing more than 'a totalitarian monster resting on feet of clay' forced to 'maintain complete discipline and loyalty'.[91]

To Morgenthau's enormous credit, his refreshing awareness of the illusions of great power political pretences often made him suitably critical of the pathologies of American foreign policy.[92] He also came to see that human well-being in the nuclear era required a fundamental break with traditional forms of international organization. Unfortunately, deeply rooted intellectual proclivities—many of which emerged in his complex 'hidden dialogue' with Carl Schmitt—prevented Morgenthau from seriously considering possible alternatives to a centralized world state.

3.3. **Conclusion**

A number of Morgenthau's most influential ideas about US foreign policy emerged in the context of a 'hidden dialogue' with Carl Schmitt. Those ideas played a crucial role in Morgenthau's ultimately unsuccessful attempt to synthesize realism with what he typically dismissed as 'utopianism' in IR. But are there any contemporary lessons we might draw from this story?

Once again, we are witnessing a revival of ambitious and arguably utopian models of transnational political and legal order.[93] And once again, we also see a resurgence of realist theory that delights in poking holes in the ideas of 'legalistic' cosmopolitanism.[94] To Morgenthau's credit, he understood that we would need to move beyond this theoretical divide and consider the possibility of fruitfully merging cosmopolitan and realist ideas about IR. His own failure to do so also underscores the profound difficulties inherent in the attempt to do so. In particular, it is unlikely that any normatively desirable cosmopolitan vision will be able to borrow much if anything from the political thought of Carl Schmitt; Morgenthau's own failures stem at least in part from his unwieldy Schmittian intellectual baggage. Nonetheless, Morgenthau's intellectual challenge needs to be taken seriously. For those of us, like Morgenthau, willing to acknowledge the potential misuse of universalistic political rhetoric as a fig leaf for great power imperialism, while also recognizing the necessity of fundamentally reordering the international system in order to guarantee human survival, a cosmopolitanism able to integrate the best insights of realism remains a desirable intellectual aspiration.

☐ NOTES

1. I am grateful to all the participants at the conference on 'Reconsidering Realism: The Legacy of Hans Morgenthau in International Relations', University of Wales, 9–11 October, but especially to Michael Williams for words of encouragement, and Chris Brown, Ned Lebow, Michael Cox, and Michael Smith for astute criticisms of my argument.

2. The term 'hidden dialogue' comes from Heinrich Meier, *Carl Schmitt and Leo Strauss: The Hidden Dialogue* (Chicago, IL: University of Chicago, 1985). This essay builds on Chapter Nine of my *Carl Schmitt: The End of Law* (Lanham, MD: Rowman & Littlefield, 1999), 225–52 ['Another Hidden Dialogue—Carl Schmitt and Hans Morgenthau'], where I offer a detailed discussion of Morgenthau's dialogue with

Schmitt about 'the concept of the political'. There is now a small cottage industry on the nexus between Schmitt and Morgenthau. See Christoph Frei, *Hans J. Morgenthau: An Intellectual Biography* (Baton Rouge, LA: Louisiana State University Press, 2001), 118–19, 123–32; Jan Willem Honig, 'Totalitarianism and Realism: Hans Morgenthau's German Years', in Benjamin Frankel (ed.), *Roots of Realism* (London: Frank Cass, 1996), 283–313; Martti Koskenniemi, *The Gentle Civilizer of Nations: The Rise and Fall of International Law 1870–1960* (Cambridge: Cambridge University Press, 2001), 413–509; Hans-Karl Pichler, 'The Godfathers of "Truth": Max Weber and Carl Schmitt in Morgenthau's Theory of Power Politics', *Review of International Studies*, 24 (1997), 185–200; Michael C. Williams, 'Why Ideas Matter in International Relations: Hans Morgenthau, Classical Realism, and the Moral Construction of Power Politics', *International Organization*, 58 (2004), 633–65.

3. Carl Schmitt, 'Der Begriff des Politischen', *Archiv fuer Sozialwissenschaft und Sozialpolitik*, 58 (1927), 1–33.

4. Hans J. Morgenthau, *Die internationale Rechtspflege, ihr Wesen und ihre Grenzen* (Leipzig: Universitaetsverlag von Noske, 1929), 67.

5. Morgenthau, *Die internationale Rechtspflege*, 69.

6. Hans J. Morgenthau, 'An Intellectual Autobiography', *Society*, 15 (1978), 67–8.

7. Schmitt, *The Concept of the Political*, trans. George Schwab (New Brunswick, NJ: Rutgers University Press, [1932] 1976). For a detailed discussion, see Scheuerman, *Carl Schmitt*, 224–42.

8. Morgenthau, 'An Intellectual Autobiography', 68.

9. Morgenthau also clearly possessed a significant dose of intellectual integrity. Perhaps he simply thought it best to call a spade a spade and let others sort out the complexities of his intellectual relationship to Schmitt.

10. Carl Schmitt, *Die Kernfrage des Voelkerbundes* (Berlin: Duemmlers, 1926). Schmitt discusses the United States' role in global affairs at many junctures. For an overview, see Scheuerman, *Carl Schmitt*, 141–74. For the specific references to Schmitt's 1926 book in Morgenthau's dissertation, see Morgenthau, *Die internationale Rechtspflege* 3, 88, 116. Schmitt's impact on Morgenthau—here and elsewhere—is undoubtedly greater than these meager citations suggest, however. In fact, Morgenthau is terribly ungenerous when crediting other authors. Although his dissertation is clearly meant as a response to Schmitt's 'concept of the political' (and he even admits as much in subsequent years), for example, he never bothers to cite Schmitt's 1927 article! In a similar fashion, his postwar writings rarely mention debts to other realist authors (most importantly, E. H. Carr).

11. Because many of Morgenthau's most important works lack traditional academic citations altogether, or at best include only a select bibliography, it is difficult to prove that he was necessarily familiar with many of Schmitt's specific writings on international relations. However, it is telling that Morgenthau refers in 1978 to Schmitt's 'voluminous scholarly production, excelling in originality and brilliance and shedding light, for instance upon the nature of guerrilla warfare and the new aspects of [post World War II] international law' (Morgenthau, 'An Intellectual

Autobiography', 67). The comment about guerrilla warfare is surely a reference to Schmitt's *Theorie des Partisanen. Zwischenbemerkung zum Begriff des Politischen* (Berlin: Duncker & Humblot, 1963); 'the new aspects of international law' likely refers to Schmitt's most important contribution to the study of international relations, *Der Nomos der Erde* (Berlin: Duncker & Humblot, 1950). The latter work builds directly on Schmitt's writings from the 1930s and 1940s. It is also telling that Morgenthau's biographer points out that his reading lists from the late 1920s and early 1930s mention only a few authors represented by several book titles. Carl Schmitt is among them (Frei, *Hans J. Morgenthau*, 108).

12. This nostalgic argument is developed in many texts, but the most cogent statement of it is found in Schmitt's *Der Nomos der Erde.*

13. Carl Schmitt, *The Leviathan in the State Theory of Thomas Hobbes* (Westport, CT: Greenwood, [1936] 1996), 47–8.

14. Schmitt, *Der Nomos der Erde*, 136–7.

15. Schmitt, *Der Nomos der Erde*, 62–5, 101; compare Hans J. Morgenthau, *Politics Among Nations: The Struggle for Power and Peace*, 2nd edn. (Chicago, IL: University of Chicago Press, 1954), 331–4.

16. Schmitt, *Die Kernfrage des Voelkerbundes*, 63–79. After 1933, homogeneity was conceived in ethnic and racial terms.

17. The clearest statement of this nostalgic account is probably found in Morgenthau, *Politics Among Nations.*

18. On Hobbes, see Hans J. Morgenthau, *In Defense of the National Interest* (New York: Knopf, 1951), 34; 'The Problem of the National Interest' [1952], in his *The Decline of Democratic Politics* (Chicago, IL: University of Chicago Press, 1958), 79–112; *Politics Among Nations*, 469; on the balance of power and decline of European moral consensus, see also *Politics Among Nations*, 155–204; *Defense of the National Interest*, 40–68; on the limits of global public opinion, international morality, and international law, see *Politics Among Nations*, 205–310. For a useful discussion of the status of moral arguments in Morgenthau's realism, see A. J. H. Murray, 'The Moral Politics of Hans Morgenthau', *Review of Politics*, 58 (1996), 81–108. Also, Robert Jervis, 'Hans Morgenthau, Realism, and the Scientific Study of International Politics', *Social Research*, 61 (1994), 867–9.

19. Morgenthau, *Defense of the National Interest*, 33–9.

20. I realize that the conventional military historiography shares this nostalgia for the period after 1648. Yet one should remain sceptical of it. For example, in the Seven Years War (1756–63), Prussia lost 180,000 soldiers and one-ninth of the country's entire population; Frederick conceded that his subjects 'had nothing left except the miserable rags which covered their nakedness' (cited in M. S. Anderson, *War and Society in Europe of the Old Regime, 1689–1789* [Guernsey: Sutton, 1988], 180). Armies still spread terrible illnesses: in 1771, soldiers returning from battles with Turks on the south Russian steppe spread a plague that killed 60,000 in Moscow, 14,000 in Kiev, and 10,000 in the Ukraine (Anderson, *War and Society in Europe,*

180). I criticize Schmitt's nostalgic interpretation of early modern international law—as well as his oftentimes crude anti-Americanism—in 'International Law as Historical Myth', *Constellations*, 11 (2004), 537–50.

21. For the theoretical argument, see Juergen Habermas, *Die Einbeziehung des Anderen* (Frankfurt: Suhrkamp), 226–36. Also, Habermas, *Der Gespaltene Westen* (Frankfurt: Suhrkamp, 2004), 187–93.

22. Morgenthau, *Politics Among Nations*, 205–48.

23. Morgenthau, *Politics Among Nations*, 200. Schmitt, in contrast, interprets the Nazis as trying to build on the best elements of the traditional international system while warding off its real foe—the United States. Despite this significant difference, Morgenthau's argumentation often follows Schmitt's.

24. Hans J. Morgenthau, *Scientific Man vs. Power Politics* (Chicago, IL: University of Chicago Press, 1946), 67.

25. See Morgenthau's sceptical comments about the liberal idea that 'police actions' must be undertaken against 'criminal aggressors' in the international arena (*In Defense of the National Interest*, 94–5). See also Morgenthau, 'The Nuremberg Trial', in *The Decline of Democratic Politics*, 377–9.

26. This concept is already hinted at in Schmitt's Weimar writings, but it is formulated most bluntly in his *Die Wendung zum diskriminierenden Kriegsbegriff* (Munich: Duncker & Humblot, 1938).

27. Morgenthau, *Scientific Man vs. Power Politics*, 51. On total war as well as the revival of just war thinking, see *Politics Among Nations*, 217–20, 230–4, 343–62.

28. This is a common theme in Morgenthau's reflections on US foreign policy. See, for example, *Defense of the National Interest*, 4–7.

29. Schmitt, 'Voelkerrechtliche Formen des modernen Imperialismus' [1932], in *Positionen und Begriffe im Kampf mit Weimar-Genf-Versailles* (Hamburg: Hanseatische Verlagsanstalt, 1940), 179.

30. This is perhaps most clear in Hans J. Morgenthau, *The Purpose of American Politics* (New York: Knopf, 1960). On this issue, Morgenthau is reminiscent of (his friend) Hannah Arendt, who similarly combines a critical account of present-day US politics with a nostalgic portrayal of its foundations (see her *On Revolution* [New York: Penguin, 1963]).

31. As we will see, even this feature of his thinking mirrors Schmitt, who also argued—though in a much less developed manner than Morgenthau—that Wilsonian liberalism represented a betrayal of superior 'political' notions of international relations influential in the nineteenth century.

32. Morgenthau, *Defense of the National Interest*, 3–39.

33. Morgenthau, *Defense of the National Interest*, 50; *Politics Among Nations*, 205–48, 311–40.

34. Morgenthau, *Purpose of American Politics*, 177–81.

35. Morgenthau, *Defense of the National Interest*, 91–138; Schmitt, *Nomos der Erde*, 270–85.

90 WILLIAM E. SCHEUERMAN

36. Schmitt, 'Das Rheinland als Objekt internationaler Politik' [1925], in *Positionen und Begriffe im Kampf mit Weimar-Genf-Versailles*, 29. For a discussion, see Scheuerman, *Carl Schmitt*, 142–52.

37. Morgenthau, *Die internationale Rechtspflege*, 116; Morgenthau, 'Understanding American Foreign Policy' [1959], in his *The Impasse of American Foreign Policy* (Chicago, IL: University of Chicago Press, 1962), 6–7.

38. Hans J. Morgenthau, *A New Foreign Policy for the United States* (New York: Praeger, 1969), 117. See also *Politics Among Nations*, 295–6.

39. This rather prescient feature of Schmitt's thinking has been neglected in the English-language secondary literature. For an exception, see Jan-Werner Mueller, *A Dangerous Mind: Carl Schmitt in Postwar European Thought* (New Haven, CT: Yale University Press, 2003).

40. Schmitt, *Die Kernfrage des Voelkerbundes*, 72–3.

41. Schmitt, 'Voelkerrechtliche Formen des modernen Imperialismus', 169, 178.

42. Schmitt, *Die Kernfrage des Voelkerbundes*, 11; 'Voelkerrechtliche Probleme im Rheingebiet' [1928], in his *Positionen und Begriffe*, 107.

43. Schmitt, *Positionen und Begriffe*, 179.

44. Schmitt, *Voelkerrechtliche Grossraumordnung mit Interventionsgebot fuer raumfremde Maechte* (Berlin: Deutscher Rechtsverlag, 1939).

45. Morgenthau, 'The National Socialist Doctrine of World Organization' [1941], in *The Decline of Democratic Politics*, 241–6.

46. Morgenthau, 'An Intellectual Autobiography', vii.

47. Morgenthau, *Die internationale Rechtspflege*, 107–9.

48. Morgenthau, *In Defense of the National Interest*, 5.

49. In his discussion of the Monroe Doctrine, Morgenthau notes that 'moralism' has plagued our extra-hemispheric expansion 'since McKinley', *In Defense of the National Interest*, 6.

50. Morgenthau, 'Understanding American Foreign Policy', in *The Impasse of American Foreign Policy*, 6–7.

51. Schmitt, 'Voelkerrechtliche Formen des modernen Imperialismus'; Morgenthau, *Politics Among Nations*, 53.

52. Cited in Morgenthau, *Politics Among Nations*, 44. For a useful critical discussion of many of the misleading ideas about the Monroe Doctrine posited by Schmitt (and, unfortunately, Morgenthau as well), see Lothar Gruchmann, *Nationalsozialistische Grossraumordnung. Die Konstruktion einer deutschen 'Monroe-Doktrin'* (Stuttgart: Deutsche Verlagsanstalt, 1962).

53. See, for example, Morgenthau, *Defense of the National Interest*, 28–33, 128–38; Morgenthau, *Purpose of American Politics*, 110–11, 117–27, 182–3.

54. Morgenthau, *Defense of the National Interest*, 53–7, where he follows Schmitt in underscoring the manner in which air warfare 'compresses space and time'.

55. Morgenthau, *Politics Among Nations*, 481.

56. Ibid. 505.

57. Jervis, 'Hans Morgenthau', 862.

58. Morgenthau, *Purpose of American Politics*, 308. See also Morgenthau, 'The Four Paradoxes of Nuclear Strategy', *American Political Science Review*, 58 (1964), 23–35; and Morgenthau, *Science: Servant or Master?* (New York: New American Library, 1972). His reading of Karl Jaspers' *The Future of Mankind* probably helped stimulate his reflections on the novel implications of atomic warfare (Morgenthau, 'Review of Jaspers, The Future of Mankind', *Saturday Review*, 18 February 1961, 18–19.

59. Campbell Craig, *Glimmer of a New Leviathan: Total War in the Realism of Niebuhr, Morgenthau, and Waltz* (New York: Columbia University Press, 2003), xvii. See also James Speer, 'Hans Morgenthau and the World State', *World Politics*, 20 (1968), 207–27.

60. Richard Ned Lebow, *The Tragic Vision of Politics: Ethics, Interests and Orders* (Cambridge: Cambridge University Press, 2003), 14.

61. Craig, *Glimmer of a New Leviathan*, 109.

62. See especially Morgenthau, *Science: Servant or Master?*

63. See Lebow, *Tragic Vision of Politics*. Lebow downplays the impact of Schmitt on Morgenthau. On the Weberian background to Morgenthau, see Michael Joseph Smith, *Realist Thought from Weber to Kissinger* (Baton Rouge, LA: Louisiana State University Press, 1986). Weber, of course, shared a similar sense of tragedy.

64. Morgenthau, *Politics Among Nations*, 505.

65. Speer, 'Hans Morgenthau and the World State', 215.

66. Ibid. 222.

67. Morgenthau, *Politics Among Nations*, 519–26.

68. Morgenthau, *Purpose of American Politics*, 274–92, 311–41. This theme is even more pronounced in *Defense of the National Interest*. On the US executive and foreign policy, see Louis Fisher, *Presidential War Power* (Lawrence, KS: University of Kansas Press, 1995).

69. Morgenthau, *Politics Among Nations*, 134–5.

70. Morgenthau, *Defense of the National Interest*, 154–5.

71. Ibid. 139–58.

72. Morgenthau, *Purpose of American Politics*, 309.

73. Ibid. 308–9.

74. Ibid. 178.

75. Morgenthau, *Purpose of American Politics*, 181. In fairness to Morgenthau, some of his regionalist considerations—most important: his fascinating discussion of early moves towards European integration—hardly fit the Schmittian mode (see Morgenthau, *Politics Among Nations*, 496–500; for a discussion, see Lebow, *Tragic Vision of Politics*, 244–6).

76. Schmitt, *Concept of the Political*, 35.

77. Meier, *Carl Schmitt and Leo Strauss*, 41. Meier sees overlap between Schmitt and Strauss on this point.

78. See, for example, Morgenthau, *Politics Among Nations*, 25–34. Here, as at so many other junctures, his theory is both prescriptive and descriptive. Politics possesses an unchanging essence, namely the fact that conflicts can take an 'intense' coloration.

Yet political actors also are normatively obliged to understand 'the political' and abide by its laws.

79. See Mathias-Lutz Bachmann and Jim Bohman (eds.), *Perpetual Peace: Essays on Kant's Cosmopolitan Ideal* (Cambridge, MA: MIT Press, 1997).

80. Where federations have worked successfully, Morgenthau argues, they rest on a 'pre-existing community' based on extensive shared ties (*Politics Among Nations*, 483–4). Like many contemporary Euro-sceptics, Morgenthau is sceptical that novel supranational legal and political institutions can play a decisive role in initiating and cementing such common ties. As in the case of Schmitt, this insistence on the importance of homogeneity is a convenient argument because it often takes a conceptually imprecise form. It is, however, clearly directed against formalistic and proceduralistic models of legal coordination and decision-making.

81. Schmitt defines sovereignty as 'he who decides on the exception', *Political Theology: Four Chapters on the Concept of Sovereignty*, translated by George Schwab, (Cambridge, MA: MIT Press, 1985 [1922]), 5. Note also the personalistic overtones of Schmitt's definition, which Morgenthau reproduces.

82. Morgenthau, *Politics Among Nations*, 305.

83. Ibid. 306.

84. Ibid. 303.

85. Ibid. 441.

86. On confused ideas about sovereignty in recent political thought, and especially the problematic tendency to conflate ideas of state and popular sovereignty, see especially Ingeborg Maus, *Zur Auflaerung der Demokratietheorie* (Frankfurt: Suhrkamp, 1992).

87. Morgenthau, *Politics Among Nations*, 485. For an alternative view, see Arendt, *On Revolution*.

88. A more complex view appears, however, in his later writings (see *Purpose of American Politics*).

89. Speer, 'Hans Morgenthau and the World State', 226.

90. Ibid.

91. Morgenthau, *Politics Among Nations*, 482.

92. Lebow, *Tragic Vision of Politics*, 310–59.

93. For example, see David Held, *Democracy and the Global Order: From the Modern State to Cosmopolitan Governance* (Stanford, CA: Stanford University Press, 1995).

94. Danilo Zolo, *Cosmopolis: Prospects for World Community* (Cambridge: Polity Press, 1997).

4 The image of law in *Politics Among Nations*

Oliver Jütersonke[1]

Interest in 'classical' variants of the realist school in IR theory has recently gone beyond realism's typical functions of acting as a surrogate for qualifying standard arguments and providing a convenient point of departure from which to launch one's own diverging theory or approach. By and large, this renewed substantive appeal stems from a dissatisfaction with the way mainstream schools of thought in IR (broadly categorized into neorealist, constructivist, and liberal-institutionalist approaches) fail to pay enough attention to the production of foreign policy, from the sense that rational choice approaches are unable to adequately explain cooperation, and from an overall feeling that in the face of a single superpower waging a 'war on terror', IR theory requires a return to ethics and insights from the humanities. All this is coupled with a growing acknowledgement of interpretive approaches to the study of texts, which often leads to an acute frustration with the way 'classical' authors continue to be appropriated for a particular 'tradition', with little appreciation for the gaping chasm between standard renditions and a more nuanced, contextual reading of works that are considered as part of the canon.[2]

Hans Joachim Morgenthau, famous for his textbook *Politics Among Nations*,[3] has been one of those classical scholars receiving particular attention. This in itself is hardly surprising, for as Michael C. Williams has recently reiterated, 'no assessment of the development of IR can overlook the importance of Morgenthau in the intellectual evolution of the field, and his role in placing Realism at the centre of that evolution'.[4] Yet the interpreter's view obviously has a great influence on which aspects of

Morgenthau's thought are deemed important, and on what is consequently ignored, or at least understudied. For while the interests of the predominantly Anglophone IR community, quite firmly grounded in the discipline of Political Science, has entailed a growing acknowledgement of the utility of an accurate reading of the works of scholars such as Morgenthau, there is also a degree of unwillingness to step into the unknown territory of other disciplines from which many of the émigrés emerged in order to do so. As will be shown in this chapter, the fact that Morgenthau came from the field of International Law is of no slight importance for an appreciation of his intellectual roots, and thus also for more complete understanding of his most oft-cited work, *Politics Among Nations*.

An exception to this pattern is the interest in the 'hidden dialogue' between Morgenthau and the legal theorist Carl Schmitt. Schmitt was certainly no negligible player in Morgenthau's development, and important groundwork has already been undertaken to flesh out the relationship.[5] Yet Schmitt was not the only influence on Morgenthau, and a subsidiary argument of this chapter is to point out that the link should not be exaggerated. Indeed, one might almost be inclined to argue that the focus on the hidden dialogue between Morgenthau and Schmitt stems more from a renewed fascination, especially in Political Science, with the 'forbidden' thinker Schmitt and his devastating critique of liberalism,[6] than from a true interest in Morgenthau. Be that as it may, this chapter will show that other key thinkers in the German law tradition, in particular the household names of Hans Kelsen and Hersch Lauterpacht, had an equally prominent place in the picture gallery of Morgenthau's intellectual mentors.

As this chapter will demonstrate, Morgenthau's interactions with Lauterpacht and Kelsen form the basis for what would later become his realist theory of international politics. While in no way attempting to give a comprehensive account, this chapter will nonetheless seek to make good on this claim by outlining a number of key elements of the legal debates Morgenthau engaged. It will do so by going back to his two early publications on the justiciability of disputes (Sections 4.2 and 4.3), which were commented on and reviewed in detail by Lauterpacht. As will be shown, the vision of international law and politics he would retain through to the publication of *Politics Among Nations* was in large part a reaction to the criticism he received from Lauterpacht. Section 4.4 will then focus on Morgenthau's work on the 'reality' of norms, which is written under the obvious influence of Kelsen and the Vienna School. After showing how all of this is reflected in *Politics Among Nations* (Section 4.4), a concluding section will then briefly discuss what lessons can be drawn from the insights gathered for a more comprehensive understanding of Morgenthau and his place within the 'canon' of IR theory.

4.1. **Tension and dispute**[7]

Renewed interest in the writings of Carl Schmitt have brought to the fore his controversial 'concept of the political', famously based on the distinction between friend and foe.[8] Yet Schmitt's concept has been appropriated by Political Science—and IR—in a way that often fails to appreciate the specific context from which the notion of 'the political' derived its relevance in legal thought. More precisely, the concept of the political is intricately related to legal debates on the justiciability of disputes, or rather to what is commonly called the doctrine of non-justiciable disputes. As Hersch Lauterpacht informs us, this doctrine of the inherent limitations of the international judicial process is 'the work of international lawyers anxious to give legal expression to the State's claim to be independent of law'.[9] It is thus the logical consequence of the concept of state sovereignty, which found expression in positivist international law through the right of a state to determine which rules it accepts as binding, and, by implication, which interstate disputes it is willing to submit to international arbitration. Based on 'the alleged fundamental difference' between two categories of disputes, varyingly termed 'legal and non-legal, legal and political, justiciable and non-justiciable, disputes as to rights and disputes arising out of conflicts of interests', the doctrine connotes that there are certain disputes that, owing to the nature of the international system, are outside of the field of judicial settlement understood within the framework of obligatory arbitration.[10]

Morgenthau began his academic career working on precisely this issue. His doctoral dissertation was entitled *The judicial function in the international realm, the nature of its organs and the limits of its application; in particular, the concept of the political in international law*,[11] and dealt with the extent to which states felt obliged to submit their disputes to international arbitration. The starting point for Morgenthau was the clause relating to matters of honour and (national) interest, which represents the classical expression of the attempt by states to give their international obligations a form that allows them 'to avoid unforeseen, unwanted consequences of the obligation without breaking the law, by means of a contractual disregard of the agreement'[12]: if a state cannot ignore its obligations under international law, then it had to be made sure that issues of 'vital' interest were formally acknowledged to lie outside of the law's scope. The content of this clause and the theoretical framework of the concept of the political which it is based upon in order to delineate the area of non-justiciable disputes were to be the subject matter of the work.

Morgenthau begins his analysis by 'proving', as he calls it, that the area of competence of international dispute-settlement bodies—with the criterion of justiciability based objectively on the ability of judges to settle a dispute through a decision in a material sense—has indeed no limitations.[13] This in itself was uncontroversial; far more eyebrow-raising was the second part of Morgenthau's thesis, the main claim of which, as Martti Koskenniemi points out, 'deviated from (and was in part directed against) the type of legal formalism represented by the works of his supervisor [Karl] Strupp'.[14] Morgenthau begins by stating the obvious: although in theory all international disputes could be solved by resort to international judicial settlement bodies, it is by no means the case in practice that all interstate disputes were submitted to international arbitration. Following the thought of another well-known jurist of the time, the Swiss internationalist Otfried Nippold, he asserts that while the common 'vertical' distinction between legal disputes and disputes of interest might hold in theory, it is of no value for a practice-oriented analysis.[15] Instead, he advocates a 'horizontal' distinction that singles out certain disputes from the set of legal disputes and disputes of interest, namely 'political' disputes, defined as those related to the honour and vital interests of the disputing parties. All disputes are obviously related to the interests of the parties involved; of importance is whether the interests are such that international judicial settlement is deemed too risky. The concepts of the legal and the political should not be understood as opposing terms, Morgenthau thus claims, and the antithesis of political questions is non-political questions, and not legal questions, which themselves could be of a political or non-political nature.[16]

In principle and by definition, Morgenthau continues, there is no issue of state action to which the word 'political' could not be applied. Only through an empirical analysis is it possible to assert that in a particular situation, a given issue attained a political character; in a different context, the same issue might not be political in nature. This is because the concept of the political has no substance of its own, but is rather a quality that can adhere to all substances—in other words, the field of political disputes cannot be determined through its subject matter: any dispute can, under certain circumstances, be or become a political one. In order to identify this quality, what is thus required is a more precise conceptualization of the political, reaching beyond the more general concept relating 'political' to the purpose of state action (*Staatszweck*). This essential characteristic of this more nuanced concept of the political is, according to Morgenthau, the degree of intensity with which an object of state action is related to the substantiality, or individuality, of the state itself.[17]

As it had hitherto been formulated, then, the concept of the political was inadequate in its function of objectively categorizing a particular type of juridical question within a given legal system. To alleviate this deficiency, Morgenthau argues, it is necessary to distinguish between 'objective' and 'subjective' limits to judicial settlement, a distinction that, he proposes, could be captured by the concept of 'tensions' (*Spannungen*): a disagreement between states would be called a 'dispute' if it could be expressed in legal terms, whereas the word 'tension' refers to a situation 'involving a discrepancy, asserted by one state against another, between the legal situation on the one hand and the actual power relation on the other'.[18] Due to the static nature of the international legal order, formal dispute settlement bodies could not adequately deal with such tensions, and thus, as Martti Koskenniemi succinctly sums up Morgenthau's argument, the law needed to be changed from a static to a dynamic order by equipping it 'with a (legislative) mechanism that would reflect the underlying political transformations and integrative new values and power relations into itself while at the same time limiting States' unilateral right to resort to war'.[19]

This distinction between objective and subjective limits of judicial settlement did not sit well with Morgenthau's reviewers, who included Paul Guggenheim, Hersch Lauterpacht, and Hans Wehberg.[20] The idea that there were certain political tensions which overruled, or preceded, international law's claim of relevance in dealing with interstate disputes was not what those insisting on the binding force and material scope of the law in the international realm wanted to hear. As Wehberg wrote,

It is unclear how one would want to promote the authority of international law by advocating that tensions among states be taken even more into consideration than has already been the case in practice. Here, the author shows himself as a politician of power, rather than one of law.[21]

True to their discipline of International Law, the likes of Lauterpacht tried to undermine the realism of the view that there were practical limits to justiciability by arguing that it is rather the recalcitrance of leaders that is at fault, and that 'it is the refusal of the state to submit the dispute to judicial settlement, and not the intrinsic nature of the controversy, which makes it political'.[22] Morgenthau, most certainly less attached to the well-being of his chosen trade of International Law than Lauterpacht, had far less inhibition to take the analysis to intellectual plains that were beyond the realm of international law altogether. Wehberg's statement about the author's predisposition as an advocate of the centrality of power turned out to be a most perceptive one indeed.

4.2. **The will to power**

When Morgenthau moved to Geneva in February 1932, and had finally managed to overcome the troublesome hurdle of 'passing' his inaugural lecture,[23] he reacted to the reviews he had received for his dissertation with a small volume in French, *La notion du 'politique' et la théorie des différends internationaux*.[24] A large part of the text is basically a translation of sections of his dissertation. Yet whereas the aim of the dissertation had been to associate the work with the ongoing debate over international judicial settlement, Morgenthau was now out to distance himself from it, asserting that his reflections were of a purely theoretical nature, focused solely on the sociological structure on which international disputes were founded, but drew no consequences for practice with respect to the issue of justiciability:

We believe it necessary to insist on this last point, given that the dominant doctrine has the habit of confusing the empirical and normative points of view, identifying legal disputes with justiciable disputes and political disputes with non-justiciable disputes, and that it is thus tempted to draw, by way of classification only, certain immediate practical consequences.[25]

Obviously Morgenthau believed attack to be the best means of defence: positive international law does not have the necessary tools to fully grasp the concept of the political, he charged. All attempts to do so, including those of Lauterpacht, consequently have to resort to defining the concept of the political in opposition to the notion of legal questions or questions susceptible to a juridical solution.[26]

Morgenthau's attack on Lauterpacht, however, was somewhat misguided. Having read and reviewed Morgenthau's dissertation, Lauterpacht cited the work on numerous occasions between 1930 and 1933.[27] Morgenthau was aware of this, and in *La notion du 'politique'* remarked in the conclusion that Lauterpacht was undoubtedly the one who had devoted the most attention to his theory.[28] Yet what Morgenthau failed to appreciate sufficiently, it seems, was that Lauterpacht was just as opposed to the distinction between legal and political, justiciable and non-justiciable, as he was himself. The difference, rather, lay in the consequences each drew from the recognition of these misleading conceptualizations: whereas Lauterpacht concludes that 'all international disputes are, irrespective of their gravity, disputes of a legal character in the sense that, so long as the rule of law is recognised, they are capable of an answer by the application of legal rules',[29] Morgenthau chose to take the apologetic route of arguing that the substance of the 'political' falls into the domain of social reality.[30]

The term 'apologetic', in the way it is used here, relates to Martti Koskenniemi's landmark study *From Apology to Utopia*.[31] There, Koskenniemi argues that in their constant concern to demonstrate that their subject matter is distinct from politics, international lawyers attempt to show that international law is both concrete and normative. The concreteness of international law refers to its responsiveness to changes in the behaviour, will, and interests of states, and, by consequence, normativity refers to the degree of autonomy that international law has from state behaviour. Without concrete processes, international law would face the charge of being utopian, as it would mean assuming the existence of a natural morality independent of the behaviour, will, and interests of states. Without normative rules, however, international law would be unable to demonstrate its independence from state policy, hence opening up to the charge of being apologist. Thus, from the perspective of the lawyer who attempts to make his or her work appear coherent, 'modern discourse will appear as the constant production of strategies whereby threats to the argument's inner coherence or to its controlling assumptions are removed, or hidden from sight, in order to maintain the system's overall credibility.'[32]

This brings us back to Morgenthau, and his argument in *La notion du 'politique'*. Both Lauterpacht and Morgenthau were opposed to the distinction between legal and political disputes. Lauterpacht still tried to reconcile the demands of normativity and concreteness by positing a wide material scope of the law, thereby downplaying the role that political considerations had on the actual workings of the international legal system. Morgenthau, by contrast, decided to prioritize the analysis of this social reality of the political, and in *La notion du 'politique'* proposed to unravel what he called the concept's philosophical and sociological foundations.[33] Morgenthau was no longer trying to produce a strategy that would uphold a sense of internal coherence and order in international legal discourse. By doing so, he slid into the disciplinary chasm between legal and political theory, into a grey-zone in which, though embedding his argument into the legal language of international dispute settlement, he was no longer addressing his supposed target audience of international lawyers: though responding to Lauterpacht, Morgenthau had made himself the external critic. This disciplinary indeterminateness would remain characteristic of Morgenthau's later work as well, and as we shall see, is also reflected in his seminal book, *Politics Among Nations*.

In 1930, Morgenthau had produced a manuscript that attempted to relate the notion of intensity, with which he had defined the concept of the political, with the primordial lust for power in the human psyche.[34] Now, in *La notion du 'politique'*, this would become his starting point for the refinement of the concept of the political, analysed on the level of the individual. All political action, he asserts, is based on the psychological factor of the will to power (*la volonté de puissance*). This will to power can take on three forms: it can aim at maintaining the acquired power, increasing it, or demonstrating it.[35] As Christoph Frei rightly notes,[36] and Morgenthau would later admit,[37] one finds much the same in Max Weber's essay *Politik als Beruf*.[38] While the first two forms of the will to power are related to objects which themselves, independent of the will in question, have an objective value, the will to demonstrate one's power entails an often 'grotesque' disproportion between its objective value and the intensity of the will to affirm it, Morgenthau continues. In the words of Hamlet:

'Rightly to be great—Is not to stir without great argument—But greatly to find quarrel in a straw—When honour's at the stake.'[39]

Contrary to this view, Morgenthau writes, is the theory expounded by Carl Schmitt, to whose concept of the political he now turns for a discussion, somewhat irrelevant to his argument, spanning 18 pages.[40] Morgenthau seemed to be very aware of the necessity of engaging with Schmitt's conceptualization of the political in order for his work to be deemed academically sound, although this in itself, he also knew, was not reason enough for devoting space to him. The result is a rather rambling (and perhaps ultimately unsuccessful) qualification in which Morgenthau argues that Schmitt's 'doctrine', as he calls it, is a metaphysical one, and is very far from historical and psychological reality. Although not in the least irrelevant to an elaboration of the content of the political sphere, Morgenthau reasons, Schmitt's distinction between friend and foe is of no use to the stated goal of distinguishing the political from other spheres of human action.

Having dismissed Schmitt's conceptualization, Morgenthau proceeds to go back to his own argument and his typology based on the will to power. Now, he claims that the insights that were made in the domain of human life could 'find their verification' in the external relations of states:

All foreign policy is nothing but the will to maintain, increase or demonstrate its power, and these three manifestations of political will denote the fundamental empirical forms of the policy of the status quo, the policy of imperialism, and the policy of prestige.[41]

With this assertion, the scene was set. Throughout his doctoral dissertation, Morgenthau had circumscribed a concept of the political that was compatible with the doctrine of the non-justiciability of disputes in international law, that is one formulated for the actions of sovereign states. He then completely left the field of International Law to indulge in psychological reflections on the nature of human desire, only to then transpose his insights back onto the plain of international dispute settlement. Now armed with the 'will to power' of states, and the triad of maintaining, increasing, or demonstrating that power, Morgenthau heavy-handedly closed the door on any hope of reconciling his views with those in the legal profession. For the static and dynamic elements in international law were now aligned with the goal of maintaining and increasing one's power, respectively. Given the complete lack of any enforcement mechanisms, international law, he charged, was bound by the willingness of states, and this willingness was only present when the distribution of power was such that maintaining one's share was the policy to follow. The moment this 'balance of power' was in jeopardy, international law lacks the necessary rules of peaceful change—hence Morgenthau's distinction between 'disputes' and 'tensions'. According to this logic, there are two levels of conflict, the first covered by mechanisms of international law and correspondingly termed disputes, the second being out of the grasp of 'rational regulation', and representing a lower level of generally latent conflict which only manifests itself indirectly, save for the occasional 'violent explosion'.[42]

4.3. **Norms and sanctions**

When Morgenthau accepted the invitation to come to Geneva, he was in the process of writing his *Habilitationsschrift*, which he now planned to submit there. Although intended to entail a critique of Kelsen, the work—published in 1934 under the title *La réalité des normes*[43] (even before he was granted his *Habilitation*)—is generally compatible with Kelsen's attempt to portray law as a purely normative science. Indeed the similarities between the thought of the two scholars are more striking than the (at times pedantically constructed) points of divergence Morgenthau tries to highlight throughout. Before proceeding with an analysis of Morgenthau's text, it thus makes sense to give an overview of the literature he was trying to latch on to.

Throughout the first decades of the twentieth century, the German (international) legal tradition is characterized by successive attempts to overcome the nineteenth century idealism established by the likes of Hegel and Savigny, which was based on an organic theory of the state that conceived of the state as embodying the unity of the people (*Volk*). In the realm of international law, the question was how to relate such an understanding of the state with a normative order that lies beyond it, but that nonetheless entails a notion of obligation. The particular problem faced by any conceptualization of international law was how to overcome the fact that in the absence of a central authority establishing and enforcing norms, the creators and subjects of international law were identical. Late nineteenth century debates in German-speaking academic circles thus oscillated between the 'objective principle' of Carl von Kaltenborn, according to which the community of states represented a supranational legal community in which states functioned as organs of this legal order, and the Hegelian 'subjective principle' that considered international law to be based on a voluntarism derived from the will of sovereign states.[44] Georg Jellinek, undoubtedly the most prominent legal theoretician of the late nineteenth and early twentieth century, tried to find a synthesis between these two perspectives by positing a two-sided conception of statehood (*Zwei-Seiten-Lehre*): the state exists both in empirical reality (*Sein*) and, through the will of the *Volk*, in the normative 'ought' (*Sollen*). The result of his reflections is his doctrine of self-limitation (*Selbstverpflichtungslehre*), which posits that by equating the binding force of the law with the will of the state, it is possible to conceive of domestic and international law as two separate normative systems that are in a relation of coordination, not subordination, to one another.[45]

Perhaps the most famous reaction to the dominance of Jellinek came from Hans Kelsen and his colleagues of the so-called Vienna School (in particular Joseph L. Kunz and Alfred Verdroß), known in particular for its influential and controversial 'pure theory of law'. Kelsen's critique of the dominant German public law tradition is already found in his early works, which begin with his voluminous *Hauptprobleme*, published in 1911.[46] Under the influence of neo-Kantian philosophy, which posited a strict separation of *Sein* and *Sollen*, Kelsen reacted to Jellinek by arguing that it was methodological syncretism to try and blend legal with moral-political analysis.[47] *Rechtswissenschaft* should be a purely normative discipline based on the notion of imputation (*Zurechnung*): to every (legal) norm is attached a coercive sanction that is the (legal) consequence of non-compliant behaviour. An elaboration of this idea led Kelsen to postulate the identity of state and law (*Identitätsthese*), and the corollary that the dualistic conceptualization of considering international and state law to be separate normative systems was logically unsound. Instead, Kelsen formulated an 'objective' construction in which national and international law were conceived as forming a monistic system based on the principle of delegation: every norm can be ascribed to another norm that is superordinate to it, with the delegated norm deriving its validity from the latter. The result is the hierarchical structure of norms (*Stufenbaulehre*) Kelsen borrowed from his colleague Adolf Julius Merkl, which culminates in the basic norm (*Grundnorm*) that represents a hypothetical 'fiction' embodying the unity of the legal system.[48] And in terms of the monistic conceptualization of state and international law, we are left with the non-legal (i.e. moral-political) choice between two epistemological hypotheses: either one considers state law to be the highest form of law (*der Primat der staatlichen Rechtsordnung*) or one takes international law to override it (*der Primat des Völkerrechts*). In each case, the relationship is one of delegation.

By itself, however, this did not yet entail a reply to those who denied that international law was 'law' because of the lack of enforcing authority. In order to overcome this dilemma, Kelsen needed to show that the international legal order was a coercive one, that is, that international law was 'law' because its norms were still of the structure: if A (sanction-inducing behaviour), then B (sanction). From Kaltenborn, he took the idea that the difference was that the system was decentralized, because enforced by individual states. It was 'primitive' law, as the sanction was still based on the principle of self-help, but it was 'law', nonetheless, with its system of sanctions, understood within the framework of the *Primat des Völkerrechts*, comprised of reprisals (under customary law) and war.[49]

This, with the broadest of brushstrokes, is the setting for Morgenthau's *Habilitationsschrift, La réalité des normes*. Kelsen's 'immense theoretical progress', Morgenthau begins, is his application of Kantian thought to the field of law, but it must be saved from the hollow conceptualizations of neo-Kantianism: for the opposition between *Sein* and *Sollen* is not absolute, but relative: the *Sollen* does have a reality, a *Sein*, even it it does not have 'existence' (*Da-Sein*)[50]—the result is a highly theoretical and at times cumbersome text (written in poor French), which Paul Guggenheim, who evaluated the manuscript, promptly deemed to be 'pretentious', not very original, and filled with obscure passages.[51] In the end, it was actually only due to the fact that Kelsen himself came to Geneva after having lost his chair at the University of Cologne (he read one morning in the newspaper that he had been indefinitely put on leave, '*beurlaubt*'[52]), and commended him for having tackled 'the most difficult problem in normative theory', that Morgenthau finally managed to receive his *Habilitation* at all.

This most difficult problem in normative theory was the issue of the 'reality' of norms. The study of norms, Morgenthau claimed, can be broken down into four fundamental categories: the logical structure of norms, the reality of norms, the content of norms, and the realization of norms. The Vienna School generally deals with the first of these, as it is the only one that it considers truly scientific and normative by nature. The content of norms is the subject matter of traditional 'positivist' jurisprudence, and the realization of norms is sociological by nature, and deals with the relation between norms and that part of reality they are supposed to form— Morgenthau's own concept of tensions is a relation of this sort. The reality of norms, however, had yet to be treated, and was thus to be the focus of the work.

What did Morgenthau mean by the 'reality of norms'? The issue of reality, he tells us, contains three aspects, the first epistemological (the relation between the content of our ideas and the content of empirical being), the second ontological (the nature of being as such), and the third the phenomenological relation between the idea as such and being as such. The reality of norms thus deals not with the idea (I have to walk), but rather with the psychophysical act through which this 'ought' is expressed (I walk, I think about walking, etc.). It is this third aspect that Morgenthau sought to engage with: following Husserl's distinction between real and imaginary definitions,[53] Morgenthau argues that 'reality' in such a pure-phenomenological approach signifies abstract (as opposed to normative) 'validity'. It is this equation of 'reality' with 'validity' that is key to Morgenthau's approach, and also completely in line with the work of Kelsen.[54]

Morgenthau begins with Wilhelm Wundt's definition of a norm as 'a prescription of will that designates, from among the set of possible actions, the one that *should* be chosen';[55] it is the fact that it is derived from human will, a will that wishes to maintain or change a facet of reality, that distinguishes a norm from other types of rules. Paralleling Kant's distinction between autonomous and heteronomous will,[56] Morgenthau asserts that depending on whether or not the will that establishes the norm is identical with the will for which it is destined, one can distinguish between autonomous and heteronomous norms, with legal norms falling into the latter group.[57]

In order to distinguish one category of norms from another (Morgenthau treats three types of norms: morals, mores, and legal norms), it does not suffice to look at the content alone. Rather, it must be remembered that a norm has two constitutive elements: the first is its normative disposition (the expression of a will intending to realize something, either by itself or by another will—in other words, its content), the second its validity. Validity here signifies what Léon Duguit called 'the intensity of the social reaction brought about by its violation':[58] a norm is only valid, is only 'real', if it is backed up by an enforceable sanction. The reality of a norm lies in the abstract ability of a particular will to determine the content of its own or another's will for the realization of what the norm was destined to bring about.

Norms, Morgenthau continues, can thus be categorized according to the type of validity pertaining to them. Norms of morality are autonomous (the author of the norm and the recipient constitute the same will) and their validity is derived from human conscience. Mores and legal norms, on the other hand, are heteronomous. The distinction between the two lies in the fact that for the case of mores, validity is derived, in the realm of social psychology, from the spontaneous and arbitrary reaction by a large or key part of the community, which supports the realization of a certain normative order. The validity of a legal norm, by contrast, is itself based on another system of norms—that is, it is normatively determined. This is Kelsen's conceptualization of a hierarchical structure of norms.

Morgenthau, however, is interested in international law. And whereas in his earlier work the focus was on the absence of a legislative mechanism that is able to cope with the 'tensions' that international dispute settlement bodies had to deal with, the attention is now turned to the nature of sanctions, and to the absence of a centralized enforcement mechanism. Following Kelsen, international law is no different from state law, in that it is an order of constraint, with each rule consisting of an illegal act and a sanction. An international delinquency is only a special case of unlawful action, and if there is a key difference between the international and domestic spheres, then it lies in the fact that international law is a primitive type of law because it is decentralized. The consequence of this is the identity of the holders of validity and the subjects of the international legal order: the normative reality of international law depends almost exclusively and most often directly on the will of the states and their representatives who are at the same time the subjects of international law.[59]

According to Morgenthau, this state of affairs has only one possible logical conclusion, which he lays out in his two-part article on a theory of sanctions in international law, published in 1935.[60] Contrary to the belief of the Anglo-American anti-sanction school, he argues that public opinion is an insufficient tool for the existence of an international legal order. The reality of international law requires a system of effective sanctions, and given its decentralized nature, these sanctions can only be enforced through a balance of power. As Koskenniemi points out, Morgenthau, like Kelsen, describes international conflict as the clash of two effective national systems of sanctions whose relationship can only show their relative power.[61]

4.4. *Politics Among Nations*

Let us now have another look at *Politics Among Nations*. Most readers of this volume will be familiar with the book, which has rightly been called 'the single most important vehicle for establishing the dominance of the realist paradigm within the field [of IR]'.[62] Many will have been taught with it, or have used the book for teaching purposes themselves, and readers may therefore have already noticed the many familiarities of the arguments presented in the preceding sections of this chapter. Indeed, the similarities are stunning.

In exactly the same terms as in 1933, Morgenthau asserts that this strug-gle for power, the manifestation of all politics, can be reduced to three 'basic types': 'A political policy seeks either to keep power, to increase power, or to demonstrate power'; moreover, to these three patterns of politics correspond three foreign policies: the policy of the status quo, the policy of imperialism, and a policy of prestige, respectively.[63] Again, just as in 1933, Morgenthau highlights the ad hoc nature of this typology, warning that '[i]t should be noted that these formulations are of a provisional nature and are subject to further refinement'.[64] Refine them, however, he never did.

States' aspiration for power leads to a constellation called the balance of power, Morgenthau continues. What is more, we should not fall prey to the 'basic misconception' that there is a choice 'between power politics and its necessary outgrowth, the balance of power, on the one hand, and a different, better kind of international relations, on the other'.[65] For power is 'a crude and unreliable method of limiting the aspirations', Morgenthau argues, and although a system based solely on such Machiavellian notions of political expediency would indeed resemble Hobbes' state of nature as a war of all against all, such a scenario would not be part of political reality. This is where the ethical aspect inherent in Morgenthau's thought becomes clear, for he elaborates: 'Actually, however, the very threat of such a world where power reigns not only supreme, but without rival, engenders that revolt against power, which is as universal as the aspiration for power itself'.[66] And the substance of this revolt, though often taking on ideological connotations by those trying to conceal their aims of power, is to be found in the normative orders of ethics, mores, and law—the three types of norms that were the focus of his 1934 book. The argument is the same: every rule of conduct, Morgenthau tells us, entails two elements, the command and the sanction. 'No particular command is peculiar to any type of norm . . . It is the sanction that differentiates these different types of rules of conduct'.[67]

After chapters on international morality and world public opinion, Morgenthau then turns to the subject of international law. As in the cases of morality and public opinion, he begins by warning against the extreme views of exaggerating the importance of international law, on the one hand, and denying its existence, on the other.[68] And contrary to what one might expect from the 'theoretician of power', one soon reads that '[i]t is also worth mentioning, in view of a widespread misconception in this respect, that during the four hundred years of its existence international law has in most instances been scrupulously observed'.[69] Nevertheless, just as in his works of 1934 and 1935, Morgenthau tells us that international law is 'a primitive type of law' because it is almost completely decentralized law with respect to its three basic functions of legislation, adjudication and enforcement.

Yet this is not all. The last part of *Politics Among Nations* discusses the issue of attaining international peace, with one possible remedy being 'judicial settlement and peaceful change'. That chapter is taken straight from his doctorate: an analysis of international conflict needs to distinguish between disputes (i.e. legally formulated conflicts) and tensions (or 'unformulated conflicts of power').[70] Shakespeare's *Hamlet* is again cited, and it is concluded that 'political disputes—disputes which stand in relation to a tension and in which, therefore, the over-all distribution of power between two nations is at stake—cannot be settled by judicial means.'[71]

In sum, Morgenthau debunks international law as simply fulfilling the ideological function for policies of the status quo. 'Law in general', he writes, 'and, especially, international law is primarily a static social force.'[72] And whereas in the domestic context the presence of legislative, judicial, and enforcement mechanisms enables law to influence the distribution of power, in the international sphere it is dependent on a stable equilibrium to exist at all. Nevertheless, Morgenthau concludes, the creation of such mechanisms remains the only way to attain a lasting peace, and this, he speculates, lies in the establishment of a world state, although current conditions make this creation 'unattainable'. He nonetheless remains optimistic on this point: 'If the world state is unattainable in our world, yet indispensable for the survival of that world, it is necessary to create the conditions under which it will not be impossible from the outset to establish a world state.'[73] The foundations for such a position clearly lie in the cosmopolitan project of Kelsen and the Vienna School, based on the monistic notion of a hierarchically structured, unified system of law in which state law is only a part. Only then do you come to the conclusion that the current system is primitive, and that the teleological 'ideal' is the *civitas maxima*, or world state.

At the time of writing *Politics Among Nations*, Morgenthau appeared reluctant to make the extent of his indebtedness to Kelsen explicit; later in life, he would go on to dedicate his anthology, *Truth and Power*, to him in 1970.[74] Indeed, the main thrust of the criticism which would finally lead to the demise in influence of the Vienna School was precisely that their 'stateless' theoretical construction of international law was unrealistic. Hedley Bull, for instance, would later write: 'The idea of international law as a coercive order based on a system of sanctions which is decentralized is a fiction which, when applied to reality, strains against the facts.'[75] And John H. Herz, another disciple of Kelsen in his pre-emigration life, would go on to label Kelsen's international legal framework 'the most sophisticated natural law theory' of IR.[76] In any event, Morgenthau confines any reference to Kelsen in *Politics Among Nations* to the list of further readings, and chooses to end the book with an appeal to diplomacy rather than law—here again, we witness Morgenthau's discursive grey zone in which he uses the building blocks of international legal theory, but makes himself the external critic. The underlying logic, however, is unmistakably Kelsenite.

4.5. **Conclusion**

This chapter has shown that much of the substance of *Politics Among Nations*, in particular the image of law it propagates, is a result of Morgenthau's reactions to Lauterpacht's review of his work and of his own engagement with the work of Kelsen. Of course, Morgenthau was now writing for a different audience, and under different circumstances, and he certainly shared with many of his fellow émigrés the disillusionment with liberalism after the traumas of Versailles and Weimar. Nevertheless, there is a high degree of continuity in Morgenthau's thought. What lessons should we learn from this?

The first and most obvious point to be made is that it is misleading to interpret Morgenthau by establishing a break in his oeuvre, and hence assuming there to have been a 'European' Morgenthau engaged in legal theory and then an 'American' Morgenthau disillusioned with liberal internationalism and preaching the virtues of power politics.[77] As this chapter has shown, the continuity in his writings is startling. As a corollary, it seems that the authors he subsequently does not cite are just as important as those he did. To be sure, the 'hidden dialogue' with Carl Schmitt is an important step towards a more comprehensive understanding of Morgenthau's thought, but it is only the tip of the iceberg. The likes of Kelsen, Lauterpacht, Nippold, Guggenheim, and Wehberg are there as well, and form the backdrop to Morgenthau's stage, the supporting actors required for the leading role to flourish and evolve.

The second, and perhaps more important, point concerns our reading of *Politics Among Nations* itself. Contrary to common conceptions, it is misleading to consider the work a book on what today would be called IR theory, constituted in the vein of political science. It is a work on the practical limitations to the use of law in the international realm, written at a time when peaceful change seemed an increasingly futile endeavour, and the bipolar stalemate that was to become the Cold War an ominous reality. Students of international law had to be aware of this reality, and textbooks were drawn up attempting to describe the contemporary international scene. One thinks of Friedmann's *Introduction to World Politics*, Schwarzenberger's *Power Politics*, or Niemeyer's *Law Without Force*.[78] These are works written by international lawyers, not political scientists, and were never intended to be anything other than a commentary on—and not a theory of—international politics. In this regard, it is useful to cite Morgenthau's review of the first edition of Schwarzenberger's *Power Politics*, in, tellingly, the *American Journal of International Law*:

Whoever published a volume ten years ago on the general problems of international affairs, the forces determining them, and their possible solutions, could not fail to indicate in the title the importance of international law or the League of Nations for his subject matter. Dr. Schwarzenberger himself, together with Professor Keeton, dealt with this subject as late as 1939 under the title *Making International Law Work*. His more recent 'Introduction to the Study of International Relations and Post-War Planning,' however, he simply calls *Power Politics*. Yet the new title indicates a change of emphasis rather than a new approach.[79]

'A change of emphasis rather than a new approach': neither Schwarzenberger nor Morgenthau intended to frame a *theory* of political power à la Charles E. Merriam, for instance.[80] It is often forgotten that the famous chapter entitled 'A Realist Theory of International Politics', in which Morgenthau outlines his 'Six Principles of Political Realism' that would become the starting point for the bulk of subsequent writing on the subject,[81] was only added in the second edition. In 1948, it seems unlikely that Morgenthau had contemplated drawing up anything resembling a 'theory' of international politics.

The horrors of the National-Socialist regime, a Second World War, and the prospect of an uncertain future were omnipresent in the minds and writings of the many scholars who suddenly populated American universities and think-tanks. Morgenthau was certainly no exception. He was one among many academics from the social sciences and law who had to make do with positions that were not in their own field, and that entailed an often significant compromise with respect to their personal research agendas and interests. The result, when reading their work, is the sense that with each line the authors were battling with the inherent tension between their intellectual heritage and the requirements and style of their new academic milieu. In that respect, Morgenthau is a success story. Had he not been as adept at grappling with the sea change in his career, we would not be studying him today.

Yet Morgenthau's firm position in the canon of the realist school should not blind us into thinking that he is now a 'truly American thinker', and that we can treat him without comprehensive reference to his European past. And perhaps more importantly, recognizing the origins and nature of *Politics Among Nations* can also help us appreciate the important shift that took place in the history of the field of IR, namely a conscious shift away from studying international relations from the perspective of International Law to a focus on the methods and research questions of Political Science. The result of this shift is that we are also inclined to write a somewhat imbalanced disciplinary history of IR—a grave error given that many of the field's main 'founding fathers' were not political scientists. Let us not forget that when Morgenthau came to Chicago to replace Quincy Wright in 1943, international law was still the substance of the majority of courses he had to teach. Contextualizing Morgenthau's work requires an interdisciplinary approach that takes due account of his move from International Law to International Relations. Only then will we be able to understand the thought of the man and his place in the history of both disciplines.

NOTES

1. The author would like to thank Peter Haggenmacher, Martti Koskenniemi, Keith Krause, Richard Ned Lebow, and Michael C. Williams for their comments and support.
2. Worth mentioning here are Richard Ned Lebow, *The Tragic Vision of Power Politics: Ethics, Interests and Orders* (Cambridge: Cambridge University Press, 2003); and Michael C. Williams, *The Realist Tradition and the Limits of International Relations* (Cambridge: Cambridge University Press, 2005).
3. Hans J. Morgenthau, *Politics Among Nations. The Struggle for Power and Peace* (New York: Knopf, 1948). The first edition was reprinted eight times before a second, revised and enlarged edition came out in 1954 (reprinted six times), a third in 1960 (reprinted eight times), a fourth in 1967 (reprinted three times), and a fifth in 1973. Kenneth W. Thompson then posthumously published a sixth edition in 1985, a brief edition in 1992, and now a seventh edition in 2005.
4. Williams, *The Realist Tradition*, 82.
5. See Hans-Karl Pichler, 'The Godfathers of "Truth": Max Weber and Carl Schmitt in Morgenthau's Theory of Power Politics', *Review of International Studies*, 24: 2 (1998), 185–200; William E. Scheuerman, *Carl Schmitt: The End of Law* (Lanham, MD:

Rowman & Littlefield, 1999); Martti Koskenniemi, 'Carl Schmitt, Hans Morgenthau, and the Image of Law in International Relations', in Michael Byers (ed.), *The Role of Law in International Politics. Essays in International Relations and International Law* (Oxford: Oxford University Press, 2000), 17–34; and Koskenniemi, *The Gentle Civilizer of Nations. The Rise and Fall of International Law 1870–1960* (Cambridge: Cambridge University Press, 2002); Michael C. Williams, 'Why Ideas Matter in International Relations: Hans Morgenthau, Classical Realism, and the Moral Construction of Power Politics', *International Organization*, 58: 4 (2004), 633–65; and Williams, *The Realist Tradition*.

6. From amongst the literature in English, see for instance John P. McCormick, *Carl Schmitt's Critique of Liberalism: Against Politics as Technology* (Cambridge: Cambridge University Press, 1997); Gopal Balakrishnan, *The Enemy: An Intellectual Portrait of Carl Schmitt* (London: Verso, 2000); and Anthony Carty, 'Carl Schmitt's Critique of Liberal International Legal Order Between 1933 and 1945', *Leiden Journal of International Law*, 14: 1 (2001), 25–76.

7. This and the following section are based on a more detailed account found in Oliver Jütersonke, 'Hans J. Morgenthau on the Limits of Justiciability in International Law', *Journal of the History of International Law*, 8: 2 (2006), 181–211.

8. Carl Schmitt, 'Der Begriff des Politischen', *Archiv für Sozialwissenschaft und Sozialpolitik*, 58: 1 (1927), 1–33; published under the same title in book form in the series, 'Wissenschaftliche Abhandlungen und Reden zur Philosophie, Politik und Geistesgeschichte', Heft 10 (München/Leipzig: Duncker & Humblot, 1932); a slightly altered edition then came out in 1933, published in Hamburg by the Hanseatische Verlagsanstalt; the version of 1932 was then reprinted three decades later: *Der Begriff des Politischen. Text von 1932 mit einem Vorwort und drei Corollarien* (Berlin: Duncker & Humblot, 1963). The 1932 version has also been translated into English: *The Concept of the Political*, translated and with an introduction by George Schwab, foreward by Tracy B. Strong (Chicago, IL: The University of Chicago Press, 1996).

9. Hersch Lauterpacht, *The Function of Law in the International Community* (Oxford: Clarendon Press, 1933), 6.

10. Lauterpacht, *The Function of Law*, 3–4; *idem*, 'The Doctrine of Non-Justiciable Disputes in International Law', *Economica*, 24 (1928), 277–317, especially 277.

11. Morgenthau, *Die internationale Rechtspflege, das Wesen ihrer Organe und die Grenzen ihrer Anwendung; insbesondere der Begriff des Politischen im Völkerrecht* (Leipzig: Noske, 1929).

12. Morgenthau, *Die internationale Rechtspflege*, 4. (This, and all subsequent translations from French and German, are the author's own.)

13. Morgenthau, *Die internationale Rechtspflege*, 42.

14. Koskenniemi, *The Gentle Civilizer*, 445.

15. Otfried Nippold, *Die Fortbildung des Verfahrens in völkerrechtlichen Streitigkeiten* (Leipzig: Duncker & Humblot, 1907), 181 and 186. Nippold argues that talk of the legal limits to judicial settlement is of no value, as they are not related to the nature

of the process of arbitration itself, nor to the nature of modern state disputes: if there are limits to justiciability, these would be found in the realm of practical politics, and are hence outside the scope of international law altogether.

16. Morgenthau, *Die internationale Rechtspflege*, 58, 62.

17. Morgenthau, *Die internationale Rechtspflege*, 65–9. At this point (67), Morgenthau again quotes Nippold's *Fortbildung des Verfahrens in völkerrechtlichen Streitigkeiten*, (143), who writes that 'A legal dispute can turn into a political, and a political dispute into a legal one.' Nippold then proceeds to cite James Goldschmidt, 'Ein Reglement für internationale Schiedsgerichte', *Zeitschrift für das Privat- und Öffentliche Recht der Gegenwart*, 2 (1875), 714–49, who urges that one must not forget 'that the major international conflicts seldom exist in their full intensity from the outset, that originally meagre sprouts can grow into serious threats to the peace'. As there has been much talk of late about Morgenthau's claim that Schmitt 'stole' his notion of intensity (see for instance the contributions by Brown and Scheuermann in this volume), it is worth pointing out that, in any event, the idea was not of Morgenthau's making in the first place.

18. Morgenthau, *Die internationale Rechtspflege*, 78.

19. Koskenniemi, 'Carl Schmitt, Hans Morgenthau, and the Image of Law in International Relations', 20.

20. Paul Guggenheim, review article, in *Juristische Wochenschrift*, 58: 51/52 (1929), 3469–70; Hersch Lauterpacht's book review was published in the *British Year Book of International Law*, 12 (1931), 229–30; Hans Wehberg, in *Die Friedens-Warte*, 30: 1 (1930), 30–1.

21. Wehberg, in *Die Friedens-Warte*, 31.

22. Lauterpacht, *The Function of Law*, 164.

23. Morgenthau held his probationary inaugural lecture in French, in April 1932, only to be told to give it again in German a few days later, as his poor French prevented the faculty from gauging his capacity. After the second attempt, he was given permission to teach provisionally, and only on certain subjects, due to insufficient 'pedagogic' skills. His lecture can be found in the archives: Morgenthau, 'Der Kampf der deutschen Staatslehre um die Wirklichkeit des Staates' (The Struggle of German Theory of the State over the Reality of the State), Geneva, 1932, found in Morgenthau's literary estate, Library of Congress, Washington, DC, Container 110; hereafter cited as 'HJM-Container 110'. After appealing twice, he was finally allowed to give a third inaugural lecture in 1935. Though successful, Morgenthau was already on his way to Madrid when the decision came through. See Frei, *Hans J. Morgenthau*, 44–5.

24. Morgenthau, *La notion du 'politique' et la théorie des différends internationaux* (Paris: Sirey, 1933).

25. Morgenthau, *La notion du 'politique'*, 5.

26. Ibid. 38.

27. See in particular Lauterpacht's 'The Absence of an International Legislature and the Compulsory Jurisdiction of International Tribunals', *British Year Book of International Law*, 11 (1930), 134–57; his Hague lectures, 'La théorie des différends non

justiciable en droit international', *Receuil des Cours de l'Académie du droit interna-tional public* (RCADI), 34 (1930/IV), 493–654; and finally *The Function of Law*.

28. Morgenthau, *La notion du 'politique'*, 89.

29. Lauterpacht, *The Function of Law*, 158.

30. For a short comparison of Lauterpacht and Morgenthau on this issue, see Martti Koskenniemi, 'Hersch Lauterpacht (1897–1960)', in J. Beatson and R. Zimmermann (eds.), *Jurists Uprooted: German-Speaking Emigré Lawyers in 20th Century Britain* (Oxford: Oxford University Press, 2004), 601–61, especially 620–1.

31. Martti Koskenniemi, *From Apology to Utopia: The Structure of International Legal Argument*, 2nd edn. (Cambridge: Cambridge University Press, 2005); first published in Helsinki, Lakimiesliiton kustannus, 1989.

32. Koskenniemi, *From Apology to Utopia*, 158.

33. Morgenthau, *La notion du 'politique'*, 42.

34. Morgenthau, 'Über die Herkunft des Politischen aus dem Wesen des Menschen' (On the derivation of the political from human nature), HJM-Container 151.

35. Morgenthau, *La notion du 'politique'*, 43.

36. Frei, *Hans J. Morgenthau*, 130.

37. In a letter to Max Bodilson, 3 May 1976. HJM-Container 6; see also Frei, *Hans J. Morgenthau*, 130.

38. Max Weber, 'The Profession and Vocation of Politics' [1919], in Weber, *Political Writings* (Cambridge: Cambridge University Press, 1994), 309–69, especially 311. Frei, *Hans J. Morgenthau*, 130, goes further, arguing that almost identical formu-lations can be found in the works of Friedrich Nietzsche, with the work of whom Morgenthau was familiar.

39. Morgenthau, *La notion du 'politique'*, 43–4. Shakespeare's quote is from *Hamlet*, Act 4, Scene 4, of the Second Quarto manuscript of 1604–5.

40. The section—Morgenthau, *La notion du 'politique'*, 44–61—closely follows a Ger-man manuscript from the year 1932, entitled 'Einige logische Bemerkungen zu Carl Schmitt's Begriff des Politischen' (A Few Logical Remarks on Carl Schmitt's Concept of the Political), HJM-Container 110.

41. Morgenthau, *La notion du 'politique'*, 61.

42. Ibid. 78.

43. Morgenthau, *La réalité des normes, en particulier des normes du droit international: Fondements d'une théorie des normes* (Paris: Félix Alcan, 1934).

44. See Jochen von Bernstorff, *Der Glaube an das universale Recht: Zur Völkerrechtstheo-rie Hans Kelsens und seiner Schüler* (Baden-Baden: Nomos, 2001), 13–37.

45. See Jens Kersten, *Georg Jellinek und die klassische Staatslehre* (Tübingen: Mohr Siebeck, 2000), 420. For a concise overview of the German international law tradi-tion see Koskenniemi, *The Gentle Civilizer*, 179–265; also Michael Stolleis, *Geschichte des öffentlichen Rechts in Deutschland, Vol. 2: Staatsrechtslehre und Verwaltungswis-senschaft 1800–1914* (München: Beck, 1992).

46. Hans Kelsen, *Hauptprobleme der Staatsrechtslehre, entwickelt aus der Lehre vom Rechtssatze* [1911], 2nd edn. (Tübingen: Mohr, 1923).

47. Kelsen, *Das Problem der Souveränität und die Theorie des Völkerrechts. Beitrag zu einer reinen Rechtslehre* [1920], 2nd edn. (Tübingen: Mohr, 1928), 2.

48. On Merkl's role in the formulation of Kelsen's '*Stufenbau*' see Martin Borowski, 'Die Lehre vom Stufenbau des Rechts nach Adolf Julius Merkl', in Stanley L. Paulson and Michael Stolleis (eds.), *Hans Kelsen: Staatsrechtslehrer und Rechtstheoretiker des 20. Jahrhunderts* (Tübingen: Mohr Siebeck, 2005), 122–59.

49. See Kelsen, *Unrecht und Unrechtsfolge im Völkerrecht* (Vienna and Berlin: Julius Springer, 1932); 'Théorie générale du droit international public', *Recueil des Cours de l'Académie de Droit International* (RCADI), 42 (1932/IV), 117–352; and in particular Bernstorff, *Der Glaube an das universale Recht*, 69–95.

50. Morgenthau, *La réalité des normes*, 1–9.

51. Cf. Frei, *Hans J. Morgenthau*, 46.

52. Rudolf Aladár Métall, *Hans Kelsen: Leben und Werk* (Wien: Franz Deuticke, 1969), 60.

53. See Edmund Husserl, *Logische Untersuchungen; 1. Band: Prolegomena zur reinen Logik* (Husserliana XVIII) (The Hague: Nijhoff, 1975, 1984), 241.

54. Indeed, Morgenthau only cited Husserl, but not Kelsen, who already in his *Hauptprobleme*, and then more explicitly in *Der soziologische und der juristische Staatsbegriff* [1920], 2nd edn. (Tübingen: Mohr, 1928), made use of Husserl in precisely this way. Morgenthau tries to distinguish himself from Kelsen by denying that there is a third, ideal reality of the ought that is outside the realm of the psychological-physical; Morgenthau, *La réalité des normes*, 11.

55. Wilhelm Wundt, *Ethik: Eine Untersuchung der Tatsachen und Gesetze des sittlichen Lebens*, 3rd edn. (Stuttgart: Ferdinand Enke, 1903), vol. 1, 167 (emphasis in the original); cited by Morgenthau, *La réalité des normes*, 22.

56. Immanuel Kant, 'Grundlegung zur Metaphysik der Sitten' [1785], in Kant, *Werke* (Berlin: Akademieausgabe, 1911), vol. IV, 385–463, at 440–1.

57. Morgenthau, *La réalité des normes*, 23. Taking 'will' and 'norm' to be synonymous is not without its problems, but is an issue too complex to be elaborated upon here. By now, however, it should come as little surprise to the reader that the identity of the two terms is again found in Kelsen's *Der soziologische und der juristische Staatsbegriff*, 193.

58. Léon Duguit, *Traité de droit constitutionnel*, 2nd edn. (Paris: E. de Boccard, 1921), vol. 1, 26; Morgenthau, *La réalité des normes*, 25.

59. Morgenthau, *La réalité des normes*, 242.

60. Hans J. Morgenthau, 'Théorie des sanctions internationales', *Revue de droit international et de législation comparée*, 36: 3/4 (1935), 474–503 and 809–36.

61. Koskenniemi, *The Gentle Civilizer*, 458.

62. John A. Vasquez, *The Power of Power Politics: From Classical Realism to Neotraditionalism* (Cambridge: Cambridge University Press, 1998), 36.

63. Morgenthau, *Politics Among Nations*, 21–2.

64. Morgenthau, *Politics Among Nations*, 22; see also Frei, *Hans J. Morgenthau*, 131–2.

65. Morgenthau, *Politics Among Nations*, 125.

66. Ibid. 169.
67. Ibid. 170.
68. Ibid. 209.
69. Ibid. 211.
70. Interestingly, Morgenthau's conceptualization of conflicts as disputes and tensions was adopted by Charles de Visscher in his *Théories et Réalités en Droit International Public* (Paris: A. Pedone, 1953); translated into English by P. E. Corbett as *Theory and Reality in Public International Law* (Princeton, NJ: Princeton University Press, 1957).
71. Morgenthau, *Politics Among Nations*, 346.
72. Ibid. 64.
73. Ibid. 539.
74. Morgenthau, *Truth and Power: Essays of a Decade, 1960–1970* (New York: Prager, 1970).
75. Hedley Bull, *The Anarchical Society: A Study of Order in World Politics*, 2nd edn. (Basingstoke: Macmillan, 1995), 127.
76. John H. Herz, 'The Pure Theory of Law Revisited: Kelsen's Doctrine in the Nuclear Age', in Salo Engel (ed.), *Law, State and International Legal Order: Essays in Honour of Hans Kelsen* (Knoxville: University of Tennessee Press, 1964), 107–18, at 108; also cited in Bernstorff, *Der Glaube an das universale Recht*, 100.
77. See, for example, the otherwise very commendable work by Joel H. Rosenthal, *Righteous Realists: Political Realism, Responsible Power, and American Culture in the Nuclear Age* (Baton Rouge, LA: Louisiana State University Press, 1991). Even Martti Koskenniemi gives this impression by talking of Morgenthau's 1940 article 'Positivism, Functionalism, and International Law', *American Journal of International Law*, 34: 2 (1940), 260–84, as being Morgenthau's 'legal swan song'; Koskenniemi, *The Gentle Civilizer*, 459.
78. Wolfgang G. Friedmann, *An Introduction to World Politics* (London: MacMillan: 1951); Georg Schwarzenberger, *Power Politics: An Introduction to the Study of International Relations and Post-War Planning* (London: Jonathan Cape, 1941); Gerhart Niemeyer, *Law Without Force: The Function of Politics in International Law* (Princeton, NJ: Princeton University Press, 1941).
79. Morgenthau, in the *American Journal of International Law*, 36: 2 (1942), 351.
80. Charles E. Merriam, *Political Power: Its Composition and Incidence* (New York: Wittlesey House, 1934).
81. Morgenthau, *Politics Among Nations*, 2nd edn. (New York: Knopf, 1954), 3–13. The six principles of political realism claim that politics is governed by objective laws having their roots in human nature (1st principle). Realism's key concept is that of interest defined in terms of power (2nd), which is considered an objective category of universal validity (3rd). Realism is aware of the moral significance of political action (4th), but 'refuses to identify the moral aspirations of a particular nation with the moral laws that govern the universe' (5th)—in short, it represents 'a distinctive intellectual and moral attitude to matters political' (6th).

5 Realism, tragedy, and the anti-Pelagian imagination in international political thought

Nicholas Rengger[1]

For much of the 1990s, realism in IR scholarship was possessed of a kind of intellectual split personality. The dominant forms of realism in the academy, essentially versions of the structural or neorealism associated with Kenneth Waltz, were—as many of their rivals were—dominated by a methodological stance that one of those rivals, Robert Keohane, quite accurately charactareized as 'rationalist'[2]—an offshoot of liberal progressivism in the academy, even if the conclusions in the context of neorealism were certainly not that. At the same time, however, the work of an earlier generation of realists was becoming increasingly studied and—for many at least—reinterpreted,[3] and though its conclusions were not dissimilar to the neorealists, its assumptions, and general philosophical orientation was greatly at odds with theirs.

Of course, it is a commonplace that all realist accounts of politics depict the political realm as a realm of 'recurrence and repetition'[4] where the dichotomies between human moral self-image and the necessities of successful political action are unavoidably confronted to the detriment of the former or the collapse of the latter. Yet between the neorealists of the 1980s and 1990s and their earlier ancestors, there is a clear and, I want to suggest, profound difference of view: and the word that is often used to refer to this difference of view, by many realists, in many different contexts, is tragedy. Indeed, it might be too strong a point to say that even among those who owe a good deal to the methods and assumptions of structural realism the 'tragic' emphasis of so-called 'classical realism' has made an important comeback. Its importance and hold over realist thought can be indicated perhaps by the observation that two recent, and very different, restatements of the realist tradition by senior and very influential scholars both use the term in their titles—Ned Lebow's *The Tragic Vision of Politics* and John Mearsheimer's *The Tragedy of Great Power Politics*.[5]

Of course, the sense of the world as *essentially* tragic is not unique to realism; many other thinkers from a wide variety of assumptions and in a wide variety of historical periods have shared it—including some who have been deeply influential on realism such as Thucydides,[6] but also many who have not, for example Jacob Hamann.[7] Nonetheless, in the twentieth—and now twenty-first—century and at least in connection with politics, it is the realist version of this argument that has been most important.

Indeed, it might be said that in the opening decade of the twenty-first century the sense that *international* politics, at least, is such a realm of 'recurrence and repetition' is stronger than it has been for some time and for obvious reasons. Conflict and war seem to be everywhere in the ascendant; the optimistic assumptions of the early 1990s have been shown up as facile and deluded; Hobbes famous twins 'Force and Fraud' seem once more to be in the driving seat of international affairs. And this, many realists will chorus, is what we have always told you. Only by accepting the necessity of this tragic reality do we have any hope of really being able to deal with it.

Where realists of all persuasions have largely been able to agree, however, is that the liberal, idealist, utopian (and many other) critics of their position have systematically failed to come up with any argument that could seriously dent the realist emphasis on power as the major determinant of international politics and therefore they have felt able to dismiss the growing progressive chorus of the 1990s as just so many wiseacres. One realist, Randall Schweller, asked to comment on a major work by a prominent (and obviously progressive) critical theorist—Andrew Linklater—expressed this point of view for all to see in the title he gave to his paper: 'Fantasy Theory'.[8]

The assumption that seems to underlie realist arguments on this point, however, is that there is a clear choice between a 'realistic' understanding of international politics with all of its—perhaps—tragic connotations and the alternative, progressivist accounts. In this chapter, I want to suggest that there is perhaps an alternative to both. I shall not delineate it in any detail, but rather merely suggest how we might characterize it and view it in comparison with its realist and progressivist opponents.

The chapter is thus divided into four sections. First, I need to say something about the idea of tragedy within realism in general. Second, I shall elaborate a little on what I take to be the most profound version of the tragic realist case in classical realism, Hans Morgenthau's *Scientific Man versus Power Politics*. Third, I shall offer a reading of an engagement with that case from a thinker, Michael Oakeshott, who admired it and, with some important exceptions, agreed with it but who also points in the different direction I mentioned above; and fourth and finally, I shall offer some thoughts about the perspective and why it is preferable even to the tragic realism with which it shares a good deal. As a whole, I hope that the chapter suggests that realism and the various forms of progressivism do not exhaust the possibilities for thinking about politics in general, and international politics in particular, though I freely concede that the proof of the pudding must, so to say, await another occasion.

5.1. **Realisms: Tragic and untragic**

To begin with, we need to clear up what might, on the face of it, appear an obvious problem. Unlike those who dominated earlier discussions of politics, domestic or international, most *contemporary* realists accept very little of what often (indeed usually) has gone with a tragic view of politics— the view, that is to say, that tragedy is a feature of the human condition as such, or at least of the human condition as it pertains to politics as such. For such contemporary realists, at least in the academy, while they seem to consider the world as a dark and haunting place, the academy itself seems to be seen as a place of light and learning where the reasons that make the world the place it is do not obtain.

The most celebrated version of realism in this mode is, of course, Kenneth Waltz's much (and justly) praised *Theory of International Politics*[9] and the reason for his optimism about the academy is, of course, the reason for his pessimism about the world. For the fault, dear Brutus, lies not in ourselves but in our stars, or rather in our structures. It is the *structure* of the international system that causes states (and, thus the individuals who act for states) to act in the manner that they do—unless they do so, their states will simply cease to exist. In his famous phrase, the international system—the world of world politics—is a self-help system.

Waltz does not, of course, deny that actors in international politics can and do act from all kinds of motives, benign and well intentioned as well as malign and vicious; his point is merely that the contexts that create the characteristic behaviour of states in the international system are in a certain sense neither of the above, they are simply shaped by the structure of the system they inhabit—an anarchical system, that is to say—and in such a system, typified by the lack of an overall superior, they *must* act as they do or face annihilation. This was the conclusion Waltz had of course reached in his earlier book, *Man, The State and War* and had expressed in his memorable language of three 'images' of IR, the personal, the state based and the anarchical. Knowing this, however, those of us fortunate enough to reflect upon international politics from a distance can learn a good deal about it and—at least sometimes—aid those who practise the *craft* of international politics to work the system a little better, more efficiently, and with less risk of failure or collapse. As he puts it, in the conclusion to that earlier book, 'reason can work only within the framework that is suggested by viewing the first and second images in the perspective of the third'.[10]

Waltz himself does not use the term 'tragic' to describe this situation, though others who share a good deal with him do. But partly the reason for the absence of tragedy from Waltz's lexicon—at least in *Theory of International Politics*—has to do with the general approach to theory—and especially to method—that that work adopts and the much more assertive methodological scientism that political science as a whole has adopted from the mid-1960s onwards. 'Tragedy' smacks—obviously—of 'value' and thus has no place in a 'value free' social science. Is it only from the perspective of Perfidious Albion that the claim that the pure unfettered light of reason can work in the academy but never in politics, looks slightly odd?

More worryingly still for such realists, however, an awful lot is being carried by the claim that the 'structure' of the system is what makes the difference. In his book, Waltz illustrates the difference between systemic theories (his) and reductionist theories (everyone else's) by pointing to the difference between the two statements 'He is a troublemaker' and 'he makes trouble'. His argument is simply that 'the second statement does not follow from the first one if the attributes of actors do not uniquely determine outcomes. Just as peacemakers may fail to make peace, so troublemakers may fail to make trouble. From attributes one cannot predict outcomes, if outcomes depend upon the situations of the actors as well as on their attributes.'[11]

Which, of course, is true enough as far as it goes. But it might equally well be said, first, that one cannot predict outcomes from actors' situations in isolation from their attributes, and second, that prediction (of any sort) depends upon a level of epistemic stability that is, as we shall see, precisely what some realists (and some others) would deny is present and in any event misses the real point of what makes those realists who emphasize the 'tragic necessity' that underlies international politics argue in this manner.

Earlier realists were not so sanguine. For them, the academy was no more secure against the pitfalls of a monkish rationalism than the political world. Rheinhold Niebuhr, Arnold Wolfers, Walter Lippmann, and a number of lesser figures would all have argued thus.[12] Perhaps the two most interesting classical realists in this context, however, are Henry Kissinger[13] and Hans Morgenthau. While all of the above, I think, repay considerable attention, on this occasion—for reasons both of content and of space— I shall focus on Morgenthau both because I think his arguments against rationalism and scientism are the most interesting and because he provides me with a particularly good opportunity to compare the realist approach to such matters with the alternative I want briefly to sketch.

5.2. **Morgenthau and 'tragic necessity'**

Hans Morgenthau certainly believed that human experience in the world of affairs was tragic and that we needed to confront this truth if we wished to develop a sound basis for conduct either in our own lives or those of our polities. This view was implicit in everything he wrote from his early writings on international law to his later writings on Vietnam and on the uses of American power. His sense of the tragic aspects of human existence waxed and waned, sometimes his view was much darker than at other times, but he never altered this basic position. In one place above all others, *Scientific Man versus Power Politics*,[14] it is seen to be the central plank of his critique of liberalism, rationalism, and what he calls 'dogmatic scientism', which is the basis on which he erects his own account of politics, especially international politics, in his subsequent work. This view might then be said to be the foundation stone on which Morgenthau's hugely influential version of realism was based.

All of the contributors to this book of course consider realist thinking an important aspect of international political thought—we would hardly be contributing to it if we did not—and many are clearly convinced realists, of one sort or another and so the general question of the character and role of this claim cannot fail to be important to us. As we have seen, it does not appear that realism *requires* an underlying belief in the fundamentally tragic character of human existence, as Morgenthau seems to suggest. So we are pushed to ask whether Morgenthau's version of this claim offers us something that non-tragic realism does not? And, moreover, even if we grant this, is Morgenthau's way of understanding this necessarily the best way? What happens if one abandons the notion of the 'tragic' character of human existence? Must one revert to the liberalism or utopianism Morgenthau so passionately criticized? And, in any event, are these the only options for us in these chilly early days of the twenty-first century?

To attempt to deepen our understanding of these questions, let us probe Morgenthau's version of what Ned Lebow has called 'the tragic vision of politics' a little more deeply.[15] While his influence in the academy undoubtedly stems in the first place from his magisterial *Politics Among Nations*,[16] Morgenthau's deepest investigation of the tragic aspects of politics came not here but in his first English language book, *Scientific Man versus Power Politics*. As is now well known, thanks in large part to Christoph Frei's biographical research,[17] *Scientific Man versus Power Politics* emerged from both Morgenthau's immersion in the European jurisprudential debates that had dominated his intellectual life in the late 1920s and early 1930s and then his confrontation with American thought during his first nine years in the United States. Morgenthau had come to believe that American ideas, indeed in important respects the American mind itself, gave systematically wrong answers to the most fundamental of questions, those questions which (as Frei has shown) Morgenthau had taken over from his reading of Nietzsche and Kant: What may I hope for? What can I know? What is man? As a result, American thought is characterized by Morgenthau as being in the advanced state of a disease, 'an intellectual, moral and political disease' with its roots in 'basic philosophical assumptions'.[18] The essence of this disease, Morgenthau felt, was an 'historical optimism' that was rooted in the belief that human beings could always master any problem, thanks to their capacity for rationality. This belief, however, systematically neglects what, for Morgenthau is the central reality of the human condition. As he puts it towards the end of the book, 'suspended between his spiritual destiny which he cannot fulfil and his animal nature in which he cannot remain, (man) is forever condemned to experience the contrast between the longings of his mind, and his actual condition as his personal, eminently human tragedy.'[19] For Morgenthau this is a theme to which he returns again and again in this book and which echoes and re-echoes across the rest of his work. Human beings are necessarily and always imperfect and can *never* overcome this.

From this fundamental assumption Morgenthau never varied and in *Scientific Man,* he develops from it a twin critique. One prong of the assault was on the belief, which stems from ignoring the reality of the human condition, that knowledge can be acquired, deployed, and used in a scientific manner to resolve *any* potential problem. This was the problem he called 'dogmatic scientism'. As a number of commentators have pointed out,[20] Morgenthau's move to Chicago in 1943 brought him into contact with the leading representatives of the fledgling 'science of politics' and indeed the wider community of social scientists (sociologists and economists prominently among them) who held an unshakeable belief in historical optimism and a progressive view of science and politics. Morgenthau emphasized, both in *Scientific Man* and elsewhere, his complete repudiation of these views (though in *Scientific Man* his explicit opposition to the 'School of Merriam' was muted since his position at Chicago was hardly assured).

The other prong to Morgenthau's critique was a critique of liberalism itself. It is perhaps in this realm, more than any other that Morgenthau's old jurisprudential foe Carl Schmitt, had an influence on him, though, of course, Nietzsche and Weber are also prominent influences.[21] As Frei points out, what irritates Morgenthau most of all is the liberal 'repudiation of politics'; the attempt to replace the necessarily messy clash of interests and power that is the political realm with something else; Morgenthau's examples include legalism, moralism, pacifist liberalism, and democratic nationalism. Morgenthau seeks to recall for liberals the centrality of an autonomous political sphere; if they forget this, they forget everything that the history of liberal thought and practice should have taught them. Morgenthau, unlike Schmitt was no opponent as such of a liberal society, quite the contrary; but liberals, he believed, had to see the reality of their predicament squarely and that, fundamentally, meant confronting the tragic in all its forms: the 'tragic sense of life, the tragic presence of evil, the tragic antinomies of human existence' and so on and so on. This does not mean that there is no *sense* of the good in politics but rather 'there is no *progress* toward the good, noticeable from year to year, but undecided conflict which sees today good tomorrow evil prevail'.[22]

It is this sense of the tragic that Morgenthau carries with him into his detailed analysis of international politics in *Politics Among Nations* and, indeed, much later as well. There was, as many have noted, an ambivalence about Morgenthau's invocation of the tragic, he sometimes did not heed its call himself. As he confesses over twenty years later, in the prologue to his collection of essays *Truth and Power*: 'I find my faith, suggested by some of these essays, in the power of truth to move men … to action the more curious since almost 25 years ago, I launched, in *Scientific Man versus Power Politics*, a frontal (and, as it turned out, premature) attack against these and other illusions.'[23] Nonetheless, Morgenthau held fast to the assumptions outlined in *Scientific Man* and repeated on many occasions subsequently: 'we came to realize now, through political experience, what some of us had concluded before by way of philosophical reflection, that power positions do not yield to arguments, however rationally and morally valid, but only to superior power.'[24] And that, ultimately is the truth of the tragedy of the human condition, a truth it was the job of intellectuals, Morgenthau believed, to proclaim. 'What Jakob Burckhardt has said of Historians', Morgenthau reminds us, 'is true of all intellectuals: They aim to make us not clever for one day but wise forever' and thus the role of the intellectual is to remind those who work in the world 'of the brittleness of power, of its arrogance and blindness, of its limits and pitfalls, (of) how empires rise, decline and fall, how power turns to folly, empires to ashes'.[25] The hope of a rational, incremental, constructive, progressive approach to politics that was the glory and the hope of nineteenth and twentieth century progressive politics is doomed to futility, Morgenthau tells us again and again, for precisely these reasons; it is inevitable, and, because we recognize it but can never avert it—and here the difference from realists like Waltz is at its starkest—it is truly tragic.

5.3. **Necessity, but not tragedy? Oakeshott's response to Morgenthau**

But the question remains, I think, if it is unavoidable, in what sense is it 'tragic'? Tragedy, let us remember, was originally understood as an aesthetic response to human conduct rather than a characteristic condition of that conduct itself. These remarks are partly inspired by some remarks of Michael Oakeshott's found in his review of *Scientific Man versus Power Politics*, which appeared first in the *Cambridge Journal* in 1947, and which offers us, I think, a rather different way of developing the insights that tragic realists like Morgenthau unquestionably have. So before I develop these thoughts along my own lines, let me summarize the position Oakeshott adopts on Morgenthau's book.

Oakeshott was broadly sympathetic to *Scientific Man versus Power Politics*. He wrote approvingly of the main argument of the book (though not without some rather arch sideswipes at Morgenthau's style) and in fact picks up clearly the main target of Morgenthau's critique, especially in the context of international politics. As he remarks,

perhaps it is in the sphere of international relationships that the project of a science of politics [that Morgenthau was criticizing] has made itself most clear...From Grotius to the United Nations a continuous attempt has been made to demonstrate Bentham's proposition that 'nations are associates not rivals in the grand social enterprise' and to elaborate the principles of a science of peace...And Professor Morgenthau is an acute guide for anyone wishing to follow the trail of this enterprise. He does not distinguish between real moral achievements (such as they are) from rationalist aspirations and projects but he knows an illusion when he sees one.[26]

Oakeshott moves from this point to an exposition of Morgenthau's reasons for rejecting historical optimism. Morgenthau's argument about the inevitably fragmented character of human action, the *animus dominandi* and so on is, Oakeshott thinks, the strongest argument Morgenthau makes. As Oakeshott says, 'it is central to the book and it owes something to both

Augustine and to Hobbes: since the faith that is being condemned is the modern successor to that of Pelagius, the argument which exposes it is a new anti-Pelagianism.'[27] Oakeshott puts Morgenthau's argument here as follows:

the assumption of rationalism is that the conflict which springs from the human animus dominandi can be resolved and the animus itself expelled . . . but this, if we have followed Professor Morgenthau's argument is absurd: the animus is inherent in the nature of man and human activity and nothing whatever can abolish it.

He adds that he 'does not to offer any criticism of this argument. Its main principles belong to a tradition of European thought many centuries old; and if it is no more, it is at least a cogent criticism of the Neo-Pelagian assumptions of scientism.'[28]

This, however, leads on to the most fundamental difference between Morgenthau and Oakeshott. Where Morgenthau suggests we should understand the tragic sense of life and the role that it can play, Oakeshott says,

this is all very well; we know what he is trying to say, but it is an unfortunate way of expressing it. Human life is not tragic, either in part or in whole: tragedy belongs to art, not to life. And further, the situation [Morgenthau] describes— the imperfectability of man—is not tragic, nor even a predicament, unless and until it is contrasted with a human nature susceptible to a perfection which is, in fact, foreign to its character, and rationalism rears its ugly head once more in any argument which assumes or asserts this contrast. To children and to romantic women, but to no-one else, it may appear tragic that we cannot have Spring without Winter, eternal youth or passion always at the height of its beginning. And only a rationalistic reformer will confuse the imperfections which can be remedied with the so-called imperfections which cannot, and will think of the irremovability of the latter as a tragedy. The rest of us know that no rationalistic justice (with its project of approximating people to things) and no possible degree of human prosperity can ever remove mercy and charity from their place of first importance in the relations of human beings and know also that this situation cannot properly be considered either imperfect or a tragedy.[29]

It is worth pointing out that while appreciative of the review in general this point was one that Morgenthau in private correspondence with Oakeshott refused to concede. The Tragic, he insisted, 'is a quality of existence, not a creation of art'.[30] And this difference, I want to suggest, opens out an important and extremely interesting disagreement between Oakeshott and Morgenthau that is worth pondering.

5.4. The anti-Pelagian imagination in IR: Realistic but not realist?

The exchange between Morgenthau and Oakeshott is revealing in a number of ways. It is revealing in the first place in displaying the extent of the agreement between them. And this, given the many obvious differences— of age, temperament, general philosophical orientation, and experience— is remarkable enough. It is clear that, in broad terms, Oakeshott accepts the general thrust of Morgenthau's argument in *Scientific Man*, which after all parallels much of the case he himself makes in several of the essays in *Rationalism in Politics* and accepts also the general outlines of what Morgenthau thinks that his argument implies when it comes to the character of politics. To this extent, Morgenthau and Oakeshott are allies in criticizing the progressivist, scientistic character of the assumptions that drive modernity—which, for Morgenthau, were especially prevalent in the American mind.

It shows also the extent to which thinking about IR is intimately connected to more general philosophical and historical assumptions and traditions and therefore, the obvious fact, that one cannot understand IR without understanding the assumptions on which such thinking is based. Both Morgenthau and Oakeshott insist on that and it is one of the major failings of 'scientism', for them, that it fails to recognize this reality, indeed seeks to escape from it—as much political science and IR scholarship has sought to do ever since, and still does. In this sense, the 'discoveries' of so-called 'constructivist' scholarship in IR theory would not only not come as a surprise to Morgenthau but he would regard many versions of it (and certainly the currently most influential versions of it) as hardly moving much beyond scientism, and certainly not realizing the full extent of the interdependence of our experience in the world and our understanding of it. Oakeshott of course would go still further. Oakeshott's debt to philosophical idealism, especially to Hegel and Bradley is, of course, well known. For Oakeshott, we cannot penetrate behind 'understanding' to something 'real', the world is—and can only be—a world of understandings and cannot be anything else.

Does this mean, then, that we should see Oakeshott as a kind of a 'realist', albeit one who—like Morgenthau—would have very little sympathy with the current manifestations of this tradition? The answer to this is, I think, no; for what Oakeshott represents is not 'realism' but a sensibility that, while close to realism in some respects, in fact points in a very different direction.

Oakeshott himself hints at a name we might give to this sensibility when he suggests that Morgenthau's scepticism about progress and scientism is a good response to the 'neo-Pelagian assumptions of scientism'. Oakeshott shares these views, but—as the exchange over the 'tragic' character of human existence makes clear—he understands their implications in a profoundly different way to Morgenthau. Oakeshott is sceptical about tragedy as a public category partly for philosophical reasons (it was part of Oakeshott's conception of philosophy, of course, that different modes of human experience—as for example practical life and aesthetics—could not directly blend with one another[31]) but also because he thought that it simply misstated the reality. Human beings, and human actions, are simply what they are.

The greatest problem of modern political thought, Oakeshott thought, was the increasingly dominant attempt—or rather attempts for there are many different versions of it—to make them something else. It is in this respect that Oakeshott agreed with Morgenthau about the problems and the errors in rationalism and scientism—both attempts to do this—and their baleful consequences for modern thought. But Oakeshott was equally sceptical about the idea that this situation was in any sense 'tragic', for *seeing it as* 'tragic' would, he felt, push people to the opposite failing of overstressing the seriousness of the problems we face, of overstressing their novelty and their particularity.

Here, Oakeshott's permanent interest in myth, and stories that become myths, is especially helpful. In particular, his interest in the story of the Tower of Babel is very suggestive. Oakeshott's *oeuvre* contains two essays on the Babel myth, both profoundly interesting. In his retelling of the Babel myth in *On History*, Oakeshott clearly targets Nimrod and the tower builders as 'scientists' in his and Morgenthau's sense—that is to say rationalists—and their chief failing is a desire to claim heaven for themselves, without recognizing that this is, in fact, an impossibility.[32] But the *manner* of the telling of the story is central also. What for Morgenthau would have been a tragic tale, becomes, in Oakeshott's hands, almost a comedy, or, if not a comedy, then a story of human wilfulness with many comic overtones.

Oakeshott, I think, refused to see the story as a 'tragedy', for he believed it to be a basic aspect of human conduct and, as such, at least to some degree, unavoidable. To see it as tragic 'romanticizes' it, and in the process it seeks to join the world of practice and the world of the poetic together in ways that violate the central tenet of Oakeshott's general philosophy—the modal distinctiveness of the different worlds of human experience. Only if we can be content to be what we are, understanding the inevitable fragmentary character of our experiences and the tensions and dissonances of human life and conduct, may we properly enjoy ourselves, and our lives. As he put it in an early essay (the basic assumptions of which, I think, he always held to),

the religious man . . . seeks freedom . . . from all embarrassment alike of regret for the past and calculation on the future . . . memento vivere is the sole precept of religion and the religious man . . . has the courage to know what belongs to his life, and with it, steps outside the tedious round of imitation by which the world covers up its ignorance of what it is alive for . . . The world has an immortality which it preaches an immortality found in some far distant perfection of the race . . . in the worlds view, human life is an insignificant episode, brief as a dream, it is only the hoarded achievements of men which are real and substantial . . . but (for the religious man) the only immortality which fascinates him is a present immortality; so far as is possible he lives as an immortal.[33]

The sensibility that Oakeshott is here expressing owes a good deal to the aesthetic worldview that he imbibed as a young man (the echoes of Walter Pater are obvious)[34] but as a number of scholars have now remarked, it also owes a good deal to Oakeshott's reading of several other figures in intellectual history and two are particularly important, Augustine and Montaigne. Oakeshott once remarked, in a private letter to Patrick Riley, that he thought these two were 'the two most remarkable men to have lived'[35] and Oakeshott's sympathy with them is both obvious and profound. It is not, of course, that Oakeshott agrees with particular philosophical positions they might have held, rather that they all express a similar sensibility. Oakeshott himself suggests in his remarks about Montaigne in *On Human Conduct*[36] that Montaigne is Augustine 'come again to confound both Gnostics and Pelagians' and as Wendell Coates Jr. has noted in his thoughtful study *Oakeshott and his Contemporaries*,[37] much the same is true of Oakeshott himself in his own times.

The essence of this sensibility—let us call it anti-Pelagian—is scepticism about the ambitious claims made for and by human agents and, especially, the attempt to surrender self for something else; the future, the party, the race, or whatever. From this sensibility flows most of Oakeshott's characteristic positions in political philosophy; his emphasis on individuality, his acceptance of pluralism and diversity, his account of civil association as the form of political association best suited to individuals understood as he understands them and his account also of the threats to civil association.

In his review of *Scientific Man*, Oakeshott makes clear that Morgenthau's criticisms of positivism, scientism, and the like are similar to his own. But in dissenting from Morgenthau's assertion that scepticism about progress must rest on the 'tragic' character of human life, Oakeshott is speaking in the accents of the anti-Pelagian imagination he shares with Augustine and Montaigne. For Morgenthau's tragic view is, in fact, a mirror image of the views about progress that it opposes, for the rosy future of the scientistic progressives is mirrored in Morgenthau by the nostalgia for a better ordered past. While Morgenthau is right to challenge the assumptions they make, the assumptions *he* makes are equally open to challenge, at least from someone who thinks, as Oakeshott did, that the danger of Morgenthau's tragic vision (and we might add, those more recent attempts to revive it) is that it still makes 'the world' the standard. 'Realism' in IR, is still for those who share the anti-Pelagian imagination, a child of the world; to be sure a chastened child, one aware of the problems and pitfalls that lie in store for the world's children, but a child of the world for all that.

Realists would argue, of course, that the world of international politics *is* a harsh world and those who do not respect its laws, will perish by them. To them Oakeshott has a ready answer: 'that the world should wreak its vengeance on those who deny its view, is only to be expected,' he writes, 'but the world's vengeance harms none but the children of the world. And those who have cultivated a contempt for the world have discovered the means of banishing it.'[38] Augustine and Montaigne could not have put it better.

There is, then, a way of denying the claims of progress and scientism that does not collapse into realism, and a way of denying the claims of realism that does not require us to accept the illusions of progressivism. Of course, the reading of politics—and international politics—that the anti-Pelagian imagination requires needs to be spelt out in much greater detail[39] and most especially, of course, it would require a much greater elaboration—and a proper defence—that I have not offered in this essay.

Let me close, however, by simply suggesting two implications of accepting an anti-Pelagian view in the context of thinking about international politics. It would, to begin with, imply a scepticism every bit as robust as that of Morgenthau and Oakeshott about the manner in which we seek to understand international politics. We cannot have a 'science' of international politics (any more than we can have a 'science' of politics) simply because politics (and international politics) are realms of human conduct where the voice of science is merely inappropriate. Oakeshott's view, expressed most forcefully in his essay on 'The Study of Politics in a University', was that the voices that we need to chiefly understand in politics—and I would add, in international politics also—are those of history and philosophy.[40] Any attempt to understand international politics and then to interpret it must therefore start with them. The challenge of this view to the dominant ways of thinking and writing about international politics in the academy (especially in the United States—though hardly only there) does not really require much elaboration.

A second implication—though clearly one which Morgenthau himself did not share for much of his career[41]—is that there is simply no direct carry over of theoretical reflection into practical politics. Oakeshott's insistence on this point is one which even some of his admirers have found fault with,[42] on the ground that he does not always seem to practise what he preached. But this, I think, is to misstate the real point of Oakeshott's claim. Oakeshott admits that a philosophical or an historical understanding will sometimes have the affect that we will be less likely to fall victim to what in *Rationalism in Politics* he refers to as the 'corruption of our consciousness'. In other words, the kind of understanding he thinks we can have of the world does enable us to see more clearly the character of that world and thus resist false attempts to portray the world in a different light. What it cannot do, however—and what I am suggesting he is right to suggest it cannot do—is to *become* 'practice'; to become, of itself, an engagement in the world or give rise to such an engagement. That belief is even more dominant in contemporary thinking about international relations than the 'scientisitic' assumptions criticized above. It is shared, for example, by most so-called 'positivist' political scientists and by many of their post-structural, critical theoretic and constructivist critics. Thus, what I am here calling the anti-Pelagian sensibility runs counter to one of the most general assumptions made about scholarship in IR (and indeed elsewhere in the social and political sciences)—that it can have a direct and positive impact of the world of practice, that it can help build a better world. Such an ambition has been at the heart of modern IR scholarship since the creation of the Woodrow Wilson chair in 1919 and has shaped many different theoretical traditions, realist as much as idealist, post-structural as much as positivistic. On the view I am representing here, however, it is at best a delusion, at worst, folly; a view expressed best, perhaps, in the couplet with which Okeshott ends the second of his explorations of the Babel myth:

> Those who in fields Elsyian would dwell
> Do but extend the boundaries of Hell[43]

To many, I do not doubt, these views will seem to verge on the nihilistic, in their abandoning any of the guarantees that it is thought 'science' or 'knowledge' can bring to practice. To those I am tempted to reply, with Oakeshott, that 'If this suggests that [international] politics is nur fur die *Schwindel-freie*, that should depress only those who have lost their nerve.'[44] A modern anti-Pelagian will acknowledge, with the realist, the intractability of the practical world but refuse the realists accommodation to the logic of that world, and rather seek to understand it from the outside, as it were. Such an individual might also accept, with many who seek to reform the world, that sometimes reform will occur and that sometimes it should be welcomed, but they would also refuse the claim that such reform either would be or should be necessarily permanent and that somehow the world of human conduct will itself change. And again, they will stand outside the logic of the world. And that, perhaps, is the point with which we might close. The world of IR will look very different when viewed through the lens of the anti-Pelagian imagination: not because many of the features of the world will be unfamiliar, but because the logic of how they are understood and what follows from that understanding will be very different. And at bottom, the difference is a moral one; the anti-Pelagian imagination offers a world viewed from the perspective of a different scale of values. That is its opportunity—and its challenge.

NOTES

1. This is a revised version of a paper prepared for the Morgenthau centenary conference held at Gregynog Hall, Powys, 9–11 October 2004. Parts of it were also given as the Henry Tudor Memorial Lecture at the University of Durham in February 2005 (and later published, in a rather different form, as 'Tragedy or Scepticism? Defending the Anti-Pelagian Mind in World Politics', *International Relations*, 19: 3 (2005), 321–8. I am grateful to a number of people for helpful discussions of the themes of this essay. My friend and colleague Mitchell Rologas, whose fine thesis on Morgenthau I was privileged to supervise, first brought to my attention the correspondence between Morgenthau and Oakeshott in the aftermath of the latter's review of *Scientific Man versus Power Politics*. Discussions over a couple of years with him, Chris Brown, Mervyn Frost, John Gray, Stephen Halliwell, Ian Hall, Renee Jeffery, Ned Lebow, Andrew Linklater, James Mayall, Terry Nardin, Noel O'Sullivan, David Owen, Tracy Strong, and Mike Williams persuaded me that there was an interesting argument to be made about the substance of their disagreement and helped me to refine it. I would also like to thank all the participants at the Gregynog workshop for all their very helpful comments on the original version and, especially, Mike Williams for organizing the event and for his toleration (and insistent prodding) during the process of revision.
2. See Robert Keohane, 'International Institutions: Two Approaches' in *International Institutions and State Power* (Boulder, CO: Westview, 1997), 158–79.
3. For particular favourites among a large list, see Michael Joseph Smith, *Realist Thought From Weber to Kissinger* (Baton Rouge, LA: Louisiana State University Press, 1986); Joel Rosenthal, *Righteous Realists: Political Realism, Responsible Power and American Culture in the Nuclear Age* (Baton Rouge, LA: Louisiana State University Press, 1991); and Alastair Murray, *Reconstructing Realism: Between Power Politics and Cosmopolitan Ethics* (Edinburgh: Keele University Press, 1997).
4. This phrase is, of course, Martin Wight's. See his essay 'Why is there no International Theory?' in H. Butterfield and M. Wight (eds.), *Diplomatic Investigations* (London: George Allen and Unwin, 1966), 17–34.
5. Richard Ned Lebow, *The Tragic Vision of Politics: Ethics, Interests and Order* (Cambridge: Cambridge University Press, 2003); John Mearsheimer, *The Tragedy of Great Power Politics* (New York: Norton, 2002).
6. The extent of Thucydides' influence on realist scholarship is considerable, though whether Thucydides himself can be considered a 'realist' of any sort himself is far more contestable. I incline to the view that political realism as a self-conscious tradition of thinking is, in fact, a creature of the late nineteenth and early twentieth century and so none of the usual suspects to be found in standard texts on

realism—Thucydides, Augustine, Machiavelli, Hobbes—can be seen as a realist on this view, though to say this does not, of course, deny their influence on those who can be so described. The most impressive and judicious treatment of Thucydides' political thinking that I know of, Clifford Orwin's *The Humanity of Thucydides* (Princeton, NJ: Princeton University Press, 1994) argues convincingly (to me) that Thucydides is not a realist in the modern sense, which does not deny some quite close affiliations.

7. For the best recent treatment of Hamann see, Isaiah Berlin, *The Magus of the North: J. G. Hamann and the Origins of Modern Irrationalism* (New York: Farrar, Strauss and Giroux, 1994).
8. Randall Schweller, 'Fantasy Theory', *Review of International Studies*, 25: 1 (1998), 147–50.
9. See Kenneth Waltz, *Theory of International Politics* (Reading, MA: Addison-Wesley, 1979). The argument follows and, in many respects develops the last part of his equally justly celebrated *Man, The State and War* (New York: Columbia University Press, 1959), though his general philosophical orientation has changed more than somewhat.
10. Waltz, *Man, The State and War*, 236.
11. Waltz, *Theory of International Politics*, 60–1.
12. For discussions of these figures see Smith, *Realist Thought*, Rosenthal, *Righteous Realists* and Murray, *Reconstructing Realism*. Wolfers arguments can perhaps best be seen in *Discord and Collaboration: Essays on International Politics* (Baltimore, MD: Johns Hopkins University Press, 1962).
13. The tragic character of international political life was a central element in Kissinger's thought at least from his undergraduate dissertation at Harvard, entitled *The Meaning of History*, and played an important, if often underestimated, role in his first and most influential book, *A World Restored* (London: Weidenfeld and Nicolson, 1957).
14. Hans J. Morgenthau, *Scientific Man versus Power Politics* (Chicago, IL: University of Chicago Press, 1946).
15. Lebow, *The Tragic Vision of Politics*.
16. First edition 1948. There were another five later editions the last of which co-edited by Morgenthau's long time friend Kenneth Thompson.
17. See Christoph Frei, *Hans J. Morgenthau: An Intellectual Biography* (Baton Rouge, LA: Louisiana State University Press, 2001).
18. Morgenthau, *Scientific Man*, 6.
19. Ibid. 221.
20. Frei, *Hans J. Morgenthau*, 190–4; Smith, *Realist Thought*, Ch. 6, Rosenthal, *Righteous Realists*. See also Chapter 2 of Mitchell Rologas, *Hans Morgenthau: Intellectual in the Political Sphere* (unpublished Ph.D. thesis, University of St Andrews, 2001).
21. In addition to Frei, see especially Williams, *The Realist Tradition* Chapter 3 on this point. For an excellent discussion on the vexed relationship—both personal and intellectual—of Schmitt and Morgenthau see also William Scheurman's

contribution to this volume, and also Scheuerman, *Carl Schmitt: The End of Law* (New York: Rowman and Littlefield, 2001).

22. Morgenthau, *Scientific Man*, 205 (emphasis added).
23. *Truth and Power: Essays of A Decade* (New York: Praeger, 1970), 5.
24. *Truth and Power*, 5.
25. Ibid. 28.
26. Oakeshott, *Religion, Politics and the Moral Life*, ed. Tim Fuller (New Haven, CT: Yale University Press, 1996).
27. Oakeshott, *Religion*, 104.
28. Ibid. 105.
29. Ibid. 107–8.
30. Morgenthau, letter to Oakeshott 22 May 1948. *Morgenthau papers*, B44.
31. For the two most developed (and subtly different) versions of this argument see Oakeshott, *Experience and Its Modes* (Cambridge: Cambridge University Press, 1933) and 'The Voice of Poetry in the Conversation of Mankind' in *Rationalism in Politics* (London: Methuen, 1962), 197–247.
32. *On History and other essays* (Oxford: Blackwell, 1983).
33. See Oakeshott, *Religion, Politics and the Moral Life*, 37. The Essay is entitled 'Religion and the World'.
34. See, for example, the artful presentation of a similar sensibility in Walter Pater, *Marius the Epicurean* (London: Penguin, 1996).
35. The remark is quoted in Paul Franco's excellent *Michael Oakeshott: An Introduction* (New Haven, CT: Yale University Press, 2004), 23. I would like to thank Patrick Riley also for a fascinating conversation around these topics when he was a participant in the 2004 Paton symposium at St Andrews.
36. See *On Human Conduct* (Oxford: The Clarendon Press, 1975), 240–1.
37. See Wendell Coates Jr., *Oakeshott and His Contemporaries* (London: Associated University Presses, 2000), 28.
38. *Religion, Politics and the Moral Life*, 37–8.
39. Which—unsurprisingly—I am currently trying to do in a book entitled *Dealing in Darkness? The Anti-Pelagian Imagination in Political Theory and International Relations*.
40. In *Rationalism in Politics*, 184–214.
41. Though he explicitly regrets that and criticizes himself for it in the Introduction to *Truth and Power*.
42. See for example the discussion in the conclusion to Franco, *Oakeshott: An Introduction*.
43. See Oakeshott, *On History*.
44. See *Rationalism In Politics*, 60.

6 The balance of power in *Politics Among Nations*

Richard Little[1]

Although Morgenthau is regularly identified as the father of modern realism, and the precursor of neoclassical realism, there have been few systematic attempts to unpack the theory that is embedded in his central text *Politics Among Nations*.[2] The more prevalent tendency has been to ransack the text, looking for quotations that expose a reductionist view of politics. Donnelly, for example, draws on selected quotations to identify Morgenthau as a biological realist. Morgenthau's writings, however, are more subtle and complex than is often appreciated, so it is impossible to pigeonhole him in this way.[3] I offer a more pluralistic and sympathetic reading of *Politics Among Nations* that attempts to overcome the confusion and inconsistency that is frequently associated with Morgenthau's approach.[4] To this end, two main moves are made. First, I approach the text from the perspective of the balance of power—identified as the central concept in his theory. Second, I try to demonstrate that Morgenthau's approach to the balance of power is more pluralistic than is generally recognized—conflating two distinct dynamic processes. One associates the balance of power with the unintended outcome of great powers engaged in a mechanistic drive for hegemony. The other dynamic is associated with a complex set of social, ideational, and material factors that ameliorate the effects of the first dynamic by helping the great powers to maintain an equilibrium that promotes their collective security and common interests. In practice, Morgenthau makes little attempt to separate these two dynamics. It is argued here, however, that distinguishing these dynamics eliminates some of the incoherence and confusion associated with Morgenthau's approach to international politics.

Acknowledging that there are two different balance of power dynamics, moreover, makes it easier to identify and assess the overall thesis that runs through *Politics Among Nations*. Morgenthau argues that the conditions needed to sustain a stable balance of power were eroded in the nineteenth and twentieth centuries. As a consequence, the cold war international system was more dangerous and unstable than at any time since the emergence of the modern state system. But Morgenthau concludes that the cold war system contained the potential for developing a stable international system that would promote common security. Unlike Waltz,[5] however, who reached a similar conclusion, Morgenthau did not relate this potential to the structure of the system, but to the strength of diplomacy and the wisdom of statesmen. Although Morgenthau stresses the importance of structural factors, his approach is much more open and flexible than the one adopted by the structural realists who succeeded him. Nevertheless, the idea of structural transformation is central to Morgenthau's argument and his analysis reveals that there have been two major transformations in the modern international system—an assessment that shares some common ground with contemporary constructivist theorists.

The chapter is divided into four parts. The first explores the two dynamics associated with Morgenthau's conception of the balance of power. The second outlines the essential characteristics of the balance of power that emerged, from 1500 to 1789. The third part then traces the first major transformation in the international system precipitated by the French Revolution and its impact on the balance of power. The fourth examines the second structural transformation that occurred at the end of the First World War and how it affected the balance of power. The chapter concludes by suggesting that Morgenthau's theory assumes that changing beliefs can transform the nature of international politics, anticipating the position now adopted by constructivists.

6.1. **Competing balance of power dynamics**

Morgenthau views the balance of power as a 'natural and inevitable outgrowth of the struggle for power' that is 'as old as political history itself'.[6] It follows that independent balance of power systems have operated for most of human history in Asia, Africa, and America.[7] But he also associates the balance of power with 'systematic theoretic reflection' and identifies it as a European phenomenon that began to emerge in the sixteenth century. Embedded within *Politics Among Nations*, therefore, are two interconnected dynamics that are intimately associated with the balance of power. He depicts the first dynamic in mechanistic terms and it generates an unstable and dangerous world. The second essentially social dynamic ameliorates the effects of the first and helps to produce a more stable and self-consciously managed international system.[8] The essential features of these two dynamics are outlined here and subsequent parts then examine how Morgenthau traces the interaction of these two dynamics over the past 400 years.

When Morgenthau views the balance of power as a universal phenomenon, he assumes that statesmen have always been acutely conscious of their own power base and the power possessed by their neighbours. But he also insists that power is an extraordinarily difficult phenomenon to measure. This is primarily because power is such a complex concept, embracing both material factors, such as the number of troops and weapons available to the state, as well as intangible factors, such as troop morale, national character, and the quality of a government and its diplomacy. Morgenthau argues, therefore, that any attempt to assess the balance of power involves 'a series of guesses, the correctness of which can be ascertained only in retrospect'.[9] Since the size of any potential miscalculation cannot be known, at the time, Morgenthau insists that statesmen have no alternative, as a consequence, but to attempt to maximize their power position. Morgenthau, therefore, arrives at the same position as the offensive realists, such as Mearsheimer,[10] who also argues that great powers seek to maximize their power potential. Morgenthau identifies an automatic law that if one state increases its power capabilities in order to pursue an imperial policy at the expense of a rival, then there will be a 'proportionate increase in the power of the other'. By the same token, if a state is in danger of being overwhelmed by its neighbour, then it will identify other states that are similarly threatened and form alliances. It follows that states can use their own power, in conjunction with the power of other states, in an effort to counter the power of enemy states. But Morgenthau also acknowledges that if this dynamic operates in isolation, then international politics is reduced to the 'primitive spectacle' of 'giants eyeing each other with watchful suspicion', constantly expanding their military strength and contemplating pre-emptive strikes that will eliminate their opponents.[11] Morgenthau insists, therefore, that a reliance on power to counter the power of other states in the international system is 'crude and unreliable'.[12] It effectively reduces the international system to a Hobbesian state of nature. In such an environment, all talk of a restraining balance of power is ideological, employed by states that wish to preserve a power advantage possessed at that particular moment. States, Morgenthau argues, profess an interest in preserving an equilibrium in order to disguise their real interest in establishing or maintaining a hegemony.[13]

The starting point for the second dynamic, therefore, is the recognition that philosophies which are based on a lust or struggle for power have proved to be 'impotent and self-destructive'. From Morgenthau's point of view, the strength of the European tradition is that there have been self-conscious attempts to 'regulate and restrain' the power drives that otherwise would tear society apart. Rules and norms supplement or are superimposed onto the relations among states in a way that generates limitations on 'the mechanics of power politics'.[14] According to Morgenthau, this development was the product of the mutual recognition that European states were not monadic units operating in an anomic environment but components of a European republic. Morgenthau argues that in the eighteenth century, princes 'took moral and political unity for granted and referred as a matter of course to the "Republic of Europe"'.[15] He readily acknowledges that war persisted as almost a permanent feature of European international politics in the seventeenth and eighteenth centuries, but he insists, nevertheless, that princes operated within established rules of the game that were designed to preserve the overall stability of the European republic.[16]

Morgenthau is quite clear that a constitutional government illustrates most effectively how the balance of power can restrain political actors.[17] What happens under these circumstances is that the constitution deliberately sets out to ensure that power does not reside in one location, but is distributed in such a way that the power of one sector of government can be checked by another. The closest approximation to the creation of a constitutional government occurs during the establishment of a peace agreement following a major war. In this context, the idea of an equilibrium or a balance of power provides the basis for discussion amongst the participants. According to Morgenthau, the competing states had to 'restrain themselves by accepting the balance of power as the common framework of their endeavours'.[18] Despite the general acknowledgement that power is an extraordinarily difficult concept to measure, there was broad agreement in the eighteenth and nineteenth centuries that the main ingredients of power were territory, population, and armaments; and these factors provided a starting point for negotiations.[19] Morgenthau notes that the 'particular moment in history which serves as point of reference for a policy of the status quo is frequently the end of a war when the distribution of power has been codified in a peace treaty'.[20]

A clear illustration of the restraints built into the system, according to Morgenthau, occurred in the aftermath of Britain's war with the American colonies in 1783 when, despite the defeat by an overwhelming coalition, there was no attempt to crush Britain, by, for example, eliminating their Canadian possessions.[21] Although the dynamics of power politics can show through in times of war, the dynamics of restraint are almost invariably in evidence during the subsequent peace negotiations. At successive peace negotiations, for example, the great powers recognized that European stability depended upon the survival of the individual states that constituted the German Empire, and they endeavoured to consolidate a structure that would ensure this outcome. As Morgenthau acknowledges, however, this involved a significant reduction in the number of units within the German Empire in 1648 and a further reduction in 1815.[22] But in both cases, the reduction was endorsed by a European consensus. Morgenthau's overall model presupposes, therefore, that there is an interaction between these two dynamics, such that, in theory, there should be a progressive erosion of the power politics dynamic with the persistence of the restraining dynamic. The consensus on which the restraining dynamic rests should become stronger across time. Morgenthau argues that during the eighteenth century this moral consensus acted as a feedback mechanism 'strengthening the tendencies towards moderation and equilibrium'. As a consequence, 'under normal circumstances' this development would, according to Morgenthau, make the task of 'overthrowing the system of the balance of power a hopeless undertaking'.[23] But, in practice, circumstances are never normal. Instead, Morgenthau shows how the relative influence of these two dynamics has shifted during the development of the modern state system.

6.2. **The consolidation of a European balance of power 1500–1789**

Although Morgenthau acknowledges that the balance of power associated with power politics can be traced back to the origins of civilization and the emergence of state systems, he is primarily interested in the modern state system, which he traces back to the start of the sixteenth century, when theorists first started self-consciously to conceptualize the balance of power and develop policies based on this conceptualization. It is from this juncture that it becomes possible to observe, in conjunction with the power politics dynamic, a new balance of power dynamic whereby states attempt to manipulate the distribution of international power in order to establish and maintain a stable state system. By privileging this second dynamic, therefore, Morgenthau departs from the familiar periodization of international history that dates the emergence of the modern international system from 1648 when the Treaty of Westphalia brought the Thirty Years' War to an end. He argues that what is significant about the balance of power system that operated over this 300 year period is that it prevented the emergence of a universal monarchy and that from 1648 to the first partition of Poland in 1772, it ensured the survival of all the members of the system.

Nevertheless, he accepts that the end of the Thirty Years' War did usher in what he calls the 'golden age' of the balance of power. He justifies this assessment on two grounds, first, that this was the time when most of the literature on the balance of power was published, and second, that this was the era when princes most explicitly drew on the balance of power to guide their foreign policy.[24] But underpinning these two factors, Morgenthau also argues that this was the era when conditions were most favourable to operating a balance of power. In developing this argument, however, Morgenthau assumes that this period was very different from the era that emerged in the wake of the French revolutionary wars. So for Morgenthau, the first major transformation in the modern state system occurred much later than is generally presupposed. This position, however, is very much in tune with recent literature that challenges the assumption that the modern state system can be dated from 1648 and his position anticipates a number of the arguments that have been advanced to support this contention.[25]

Morgenthau's starting point is that in the first phase of the modern international state system, international politics had very distinctive characteristics. In particular, foreign policy was dynastic rather than national in character. As Morgenthau notes 'identification was with the power and the policies of the individual monarch rather than with the power and policies of a collectivity, such as the nation'.[26] It follows that during this period international politics were constituted by inter-dynastic politics based on the very close links that existed amongst the royal dynasties that ruled Europe at that time. These dynasties formed an international aristocracy that extended across Europe and formed a cosmopolitan or international society. Morgenthau identifies 'constant, intimate contact' based on 'family ties, a common language (French), common cultural values, a common style of life, and common moral convictions'.[27]

Morgenthau links several important features to the nature of inter-dynastic politics. First, members of the diplomatic and military services who were drawn from the aristocracy did not regard themselves as state officials, but as 'employees' of a dynastic family. And because they were part of a cosmopolitan society, Morgenthau also notes that an Austrian ambassador sent to France, for example, 'felt more at home in the court of Versailles than among his own nonaristocratic compatriots'. Under these circumstances it is unsurprising to find that diplomatic and military personnel 'fluctuated to a not inconsiderable degree from one monarchical employer to another'.[28] But below this closely knit aristocratic international society that extended across Europe there existed a much more fragmented society where loyalties were often much more parochial.

A second feature of inter-dynastic politics was the 'commercialization of statecraft'. Given that diplomats were part of a cosmopolitan, aristocratic, and inter-dynastic society, it was considered perfectly acceptable for a government to provide a diplomat from another court with a pension and also for foreign diplomats to receive payment for their role in helping to conclude a treaty. Morgenthau argues that these payments provided diplomats with a 'powerful incentive' to expedite negotiations and to 'blunt the edge of international controversies and confine the aspirations for power of individual nations within relatively narrow limits'.[29]

A third feature of inter-dynastic politics that affected the conduct of foreign policy was the existence of a supranational code of morality.

Morgenthau argues that it was 'in the concept and the rules of natural law that this cosmopolitan society found the source of its precepts of morality'.[30] In other words, the members of this cosmopolitan aristocracy were all Christians who accepted that they had no alternative but to observe a Christian code of conduct. It follows that in pursuing foreign policy, Christian princes were constrained by a common set of moral precepts. Morgenthau insists that these princes experienced a very strong and personal moral obligation to observe these precepts, so that 'individual members of this society, therefore, felt themselves to be personally responsible for the compliance with those moral rules of conduct; for it was to them as rational human beings, as individuals, that this moral code was addressed'. This emphasis on personal responsibility then accounts for the importance that was constantly attached to the 'honour' and 'reputation' of the European rulers, which could be endangered if they violated the common moral code in the conduct of foreign policy. The existence of 'a moral consensus' kept the limitless desire for power in check.[31]

Traces of these features managed to survive to the onset of the twentieth century, but Morgenthau insists that it was after the Thirty Years' War and before the French Revolution that their impact was most felt, and they play a significant role in explaining why this was the golden age of the balance of power. Yet these features were present before and during the Thirty Years' War and so other factors are brought into play by Morgenthau. In the first instance, he depicts the Thirty Years' War in terms of a power struggle between two coalitions of states, both possessing imperialistic or hegemonic ambitions. But such a struggle, he argues, represents the 'most frequent configuration within a balance-of-power system'.[32] It is possible, therefore, to portray the war as a particularly complex phase in a power struggle that had been going on since the end of the fifteenth century between the kings of France, the Habsburg rulers of the Holy Roman Empire, and Spain. What was different about the Thirty Years' War was that it displayed a 'ferociousness and intensity not known to other ages'.[33] Morgenthau attributes the ferocity of the war to the determination of competing religious groups to universalize their moral code and impose their beliefs on others. He argues that it took nearly a century of 'almost unprecedented bloodshed, devastation, and barbarization' to convince the contestants 'that the two religions could live together in mutual toleration'.[34] The religious conflict, therefore, helped to fuel the ongoing power political dynamic that operated amongst the competing political units.

What was particularly important about the Treaty of Westphalia, therefore, was that it brought an end to the sixteenth-century principle whereby a German prince could determine the religion of his state, and it thereby marks an important stage in the separation of religion and politics in the history of the modern European state system. But, according to Morgenthau, Westphalia also attempted to establish a balance of power that would check the ambitions of the key parties that engaged in the war.[35] With the removal of religion as a source of contention, after the peace of Westphalia, Morgenthau presupposes that the dynamic associated with power politics was very largely suppressed. Foreign policy is now depicted as the 'sport of kings, not to be taken more seriously than games and gambles played for strictly limited stakes'. Rulers, it appears, are no longer influenced by the dynamic that pushes them to maximize power. Instead, they are seen to be participating in a 'game' where the goal is to maintain an equilibrium, with an even distribution of power between two competing sets of alliances. In fact, Morgenthau effectively reduces the balance of power to a game of alliances.[36] During this era, princes would 'desert old alliances and form new ones whenever it seemed to them that the balance of power had been disturbed and that a realignment of forces was needed to re-establish it'. This is clearly a very different strategy from endeavouring to maximize power.

Morgenthau, however, undermines the importance that he attaches to international morality when he argues that the movement by princes in and out of alliances to maintain the balance of power was 'impervious to moral considerations', such as good faith and loyalty, although he goes on to say their posture needs to be regarded as 'amoral rather than immoral'. He justifies this position by suggesting that a diplomatic move that 'looks in retrospect like treachery' needs, in the context of the time, to be seen as an 'elegant maneuver' that has been executed 'according to the rules of the game, which all players recognise as binding'.[37] Sofka contests this analysis.[38] He argues that it was not the rules of the game that constrained the behaviour of the European states in this era, but rather their inherent weakness. From this perspective, there were no rules of the game. Morgenthau does not make it easy to defend his position at this juncture, because he fails to identify the rules. But more recent literature in IR is moving in this direction, acknowledging that many states in Europe had not yet emerged as depersonalized political units with clearly defined boundaries.[39] Teschke stresses the importance of viewing international relations at this time from the perspective of inter-dynastic politics.[40] Succession crises, in particular, constituted an integral part of the international fabric, with dynastic marriages providing a crucial mechanism for the acquisition of territory and the expansion of wealth. Teschke's approach presupposes that international politics at that time were structured by inter-dynastic family relations. Dynasties on mainland Europe used their dynastic connections to expand their territory, but in order to maintain good relations; they sustained a dynastic equilibrium through a process of mutual absorption of territory.[41]

This assessment is certainly compatible with Morgenthau's notion of international relations as an international game. Teschke, however, establishes a sharp distinction between what he calls a 'dynastic predatory equilibrium' and 'the balance of power', which he associates with the process of active balancing that Britain began to pursue in the attempt to prevent territorial expansion on the continent.[42] Morgenthau also agrees that Britain had a distinctive role to play in the European balance of power system which he identifies as the 'holder' of the balance of power, or the 'balancer'. Like Teschke, he accepts that Britain adopted a policy that aimed to 'counter any imperial-hegemonic ambition' on mainland Europe. But he also acknowledges that Britain's aim was to 'keep Europe divided in order to dominate the continent'.[43] His position on dynastic expansion, however, is more ambivalent than Teschke's. He acknowledges the importance of mutual compensation and notes how this principle was enunciated at the Treaty of Utrecht in 1713, when most of Spain's European and colonial possessions were divided up between the Habsburgs and the Bourbons. However, whereas Teschke sees the partition of Poland as just another example of dynastic expansion, Morgenthau wants to argue that it represents a violation of the rules.[44] As a consequence, he argues that the partition marks the end of the classic balance of power period,[45] because he insists that an aim of the balance of power was to protect the independence of all states. Teschke argues, by contrast, that one of the main effects of 'predatory dynastic equilibrium' was for small states to be absorbed by large ones and he asserts that this accounts for the 'dramatic decline in the number of European sovereign actors between 1648 and the nineteenth century'.[46] By contrast, Morgenthau insists that the balance of power system succeeded in preserving the existence of all members of the modern state system from 1648 to 1772, when the partitioning of Poland started.[47]

6.3. **The first tranformation of the international system 1789–1919**

Although Morgenthau treats the first partition of Poland as an early sign that power political balancing was coming to the fore again, for the first time since the Thirty Years' War, the events surrounding the French Revolution and the Napoleonic Wars provided further evidence of the emergence of untrammelled power politics. He associates the revolution with the rise of nationalism, which was to become a dominant force throughout the nineteenth century and represented a fundamental and ultimately fatal challenge to the dynastic world. The state ceases to be regarded as the property of a monarch and his dynastic family and we observe national power and national policies 'replacing identification with dynastic interests'.[48] Inevitably, however, this development also marks the onset of a 'gradual decline of the cosmopolitan aristocratic society and of the restraining influence of its morality upon foreign policy'.[49] The first fatality of this development, according to Morgenthau, was the balance of power, because neither the French revolutionary leaders nor Napoleon were in any way constrained by the need to maintain an equilibrium that reflected and preserved a European inter-dynastic order. As a consequence, the dynastic rules that governed this order collapsed and they were replaced by a power political drive by states to survive. Fear of Napoleon's expansionist aims eventually produced a winning coalition that ushered in a new attempt to construct a stable equilibrium in Europe.[50]

Although the winning coalition achieved unconditional victory, Morgenthau shows that the attempts to restore order and establish a new balance of power generated contradictions and proved initially to be extremely problematic. The problems arose because the new order laid out at the Congress of Vienna was based on two contradictory principles. The first was the inviolability of frontiers, and the second was dynastic legitimacy.[51] The two principles pulled in opposite directions. The first heralded a new and very different order from the one that existed before the French

Revolution, with the long-established ties between dynasties and territory finally broken. The second, on the other hand, looked to the past and attempted to restore the status quo that the French Revolution had destroyed. Morgenthau is clear that during the course of the nineteenth century it was the new order that slowly but surely overtook the old order, confirming his view that the French Revolution marked the start of a new epoch in history.[52] However, Morgenthau is also clear that elements of the aristocratic and dynastic order persisted through to the twentieth century, and that there were determined efforts made after the Napoleonic wars to sustain this order.

These efforts reflected the importance attached to dynastic legitimacy at the Congress of Vienna and they also underpinned the establishment in 1814 of the Holy Alliance by Russia, Austria, and Prussia. The ostensible aim of the Holy Alliance was to ensure that the agreements made at the Congress were maintained, although the unstated aim was to prevent the occurrence of revolution anywhere in Europe.[53] This unstated aim, however, had the effect of dividing Europe rather than helping to consolidate a consensus around a new balance of power based upon an agreed distribution of territory. Moreover, the problem became intractable when the original signatories of the Holy Alliance formally agreed in a circular, signed in 1820 at the Congress of Troppeau, never to recognize the right of any people to circumscribe the power of their king. Such an agreement, Morgenthau argues, was bound to lead to 'intervention into the internal affairs of all nations where the institution of the absolute monarch seemed to be in danger'.[54] British statesmen, however, considered that such a move undermined how they conceived of the newly established status quo. They were only interested in defending the territorial settlement agreed at the Congress of Vienna and, in addition, precluding any member of Napoleon's family from coming to the French throne. However, the offer by Russia to support collective intervention in the future by sending troops into Central and Western Europe was not seen to be an attractive option by its Holy Alliance partners and so this early attempt at what Morgenthau identifies as international government, based on great power consensus, unravelled almost immediately.[55]

Morgenthau argues, moreover, that the French Revolution and the Napoleonic Wars had initiated so much change in the international system that the survival of the old order would have required 'the continuous use of armed force in order to protect and restore absolute monarchies and their possessions throughout the world'. The use of force would have been continuous and essential according to Morgenthau because of the conflict between the principles associated with dynastic legitimacy and those linked to nationalism and liberalism. Morgenthau is also clear that the dynastic order could not survive against the opposition of both Britain and 'the conception of justice adhered to by the majority of the people living under the rule of the Holy Alliance'. From the time of Canning, he argues, British foreign policy promoted a new liberal order in Europe and the British used the national and liberal movements developing in Europe 'as weights in the scales of the balance of power'.[56]

During the nineteenth century in Europe, Morgenthau observes a slow transformation away from government by the aristocracy towards a system of 'democratic selection and responsibility of government officials'. Nevertheless, until almost the end of the nineteenth century, the conduct of foreign policy remained in the hands of aristocratic rulers in most countries. It was only in the twentieth century that officials were 'legally and morally responsible' not to a monarch but to a collectivity.[57] Morgenthau, however, is very equivocal about some of the consequences of this development. Nothing has replaced the international aristocratic society that was superimposed on divergent national societies and whose moral code served to restrain the behaviour of dynastic states. This moral consensus survived only as a 'feeble echo' in the nineteenth century, although he accepts that it was strengthened by 'the humanitarian climate of the times'.[58] In other words, the Enlightenment and the political theory of liberalism did precipitate an 'increase in the humaneness and civilized character of human relations'. Moreover, Morgenthau also associates this development with 'the rise of the commercial classes first to social and then to political importance during the nineteenth century'.[59] This was important because the commercial classes were strongly opposed to war and international anarchy and they viewed them as 'irrational disturbances of the calculable operations of the market'.[60]

Morgenthau locates his discussion of the balance of power that emerged after the Napoleonic Wars against this background and argues that it was very different from the previous balance of power system. Although he fails to elaborate on how the rules of the game shifted from the eighteenth to the nineteenth century, some of the changes are made reasonably explicit in his text and others can be inferred from his analysis of the period. First, he is clear that inter-dynastic politics gave way to international politics.[61] Despite determined attempts, during the nineteenth century, to maintain the position of absolute monarchies in Europe, the principle of national self-determination 'became one of the cornerstones upon which successive generations... tried to enact a stable political structure'.[62] This development had significant consequences for the balance of power. It meant that the kind of compensation schemes that were agreed in the eighteenth century could no longer be sanctioned, and, as a consequence, national frontiers became relatively fixed. It became difficult to use balance of power arguments to resist national unification.

A second fundamental change in the nineteenth century relates to the emergence of international government. Morgenthau cites Friedrich Gentz who argued after the Congress of Vienna that the balance of power system had been superseded by 'a principle of general union, uniting the sum total of states in a federation under the direction of the major powers'. In other words, this was 'government by the great powers' and the principle that was guiding the great powers was 'the maintenance of peace on the basis of the status quo'.[63] Effectively, the great powers agreed at the Congress of Vienna to preserve the balance of power that was defined by the territorial settlement established in 1815. It followed that any changes to that settlement would have to be sanctioned by a great power consensus. This is essentially what happened after the Belgians revolted in 1830 and demanded independence from the United Netherlands, which had been established at the Congress of Vienna. Morgenthau argues that the great powers assumed responsibility for reaching a political settlement between Belgium and Holland, thereby avoiding a major war that could easily otherwise have ensued.[64]

Although Morgenthau acknowledges that the Concert of Europe was an important mechanism for maintaining the balance of power, he also recognizes that there were other factors that were, inexorably, bringing about changes in the balance of power system in ways that could not be regulated by the Concert of Europe. The first, as noted above, relates to the impact of national self-determination within Europe. The unification of both Germany and Italy during the nineteenth century was justified on the basis of this principle. Although these unifications precipitated a massive change in the balance of power established in Vienna, neither move was either opposed or sanctioned by a great power consensus. In other words, although Morgenthau does not make this point explicitly, the principle of national self-determination effectively trumped the norms associated with the inviolability of international boundaries and stability. Morgenthau recognized, however, that the unification of Germany created an intractable problem for the European balance of power that could only be solved by the political reconstruction of Europe.[65] He also acknowledged that traditional balance of power methods failed to manage this problem, and he identifies what has become the European Union as a 'revolutionary departure from the traditional methods by which inferior powers have tried to counter a superior one'.[66] But in assessing the future success of the European Union he insists it is necessary to examine the distribution of power amongst its agencies as well as the distribution of power that exists between these agencies and the governments of the constituent states.[67]

A second factor that lay beyond the control of the Concert of Europe was the geographical expansion of the system. The Congress of Vienna effectively treated Europe as a closed system made up of five equal powers, but this was an unequivocal fiction.[68] During the course of the nineteenth century, therefore, states outside of Europe began to play an increasing role in the definition and operation of the European balance of power. What we observe over the next century according to Morgenthau is 'the gradual extension of the European balance of power into world-wide system'.[69] He views the 1823 Monroe Doctrine as a particularly crucial development, with the United States arguing that they would ensure that the existing balance of power in the Western hemisphere remained unchanged. President Monroe accepted the existing interests of Europe in the area, but insisted that the United States would resist attempts by the Europeans to repossess those states that had established their independence.[70] This position was endorsed by Britain in a speech by Canning in 1826 when he famously and bombastically declared that he had 'called the New World into existence, to redress the balance of the Old'.[71] The effect of the positions adopted by the United States and the UK was to extend the inviolability of frontiers established at the Congress of Vienna to the Western hemisphere.

The expansion of the European system, however, had other significant consequences for the European balance of power. Morgenthau distinguished between peripheral areas that either lay on the boundaries of Europe (in particular, the Balkans), or where the interests of the Europeans were marginal, and what he euphemistically calls empty spaces, although he does acknowledge elsewhere that this 'political no-man's land' was, in fact 'other people's land'.[72] In both cases, however, he observes that the European concert and European diplomacy were able to operate with conspicuous success in these regions, in the sense that the Europeans were able to resolve their differences peacefully. This 'success' was attributable to the fact that policy of compensations could be so easily applied. Morgenthau notes, for example, that Africa was 'the object of numerous treaties delimiting spheres of influence for the major colonial powers'.[73] Because there was so much 'empty space' there was 'always the possibility of compromise without compromising one's vital interests'.[74] Countries as different as Ethiopia and Persia were effectively and 'peacefully' partitioned by the European great powers; and Morgenthau accepts that this practice was 'organically connected with the balance of power'.[75]

Morgenthau compares these moves to the partition of Poland,[76] but in doing so he fails to note that he saw the partition of Poland as intimating a breakdown in the balance of power or to recognize that the techniques that the Europeans used in these empty spaces had been effectively eliminated within Europe itself because of the importance attached to the principle of national self-determination. In other words, in Europe it was the consolidation of nations rather than the partition of states that was taking place. This line of argument reinforces Keene's position that throughout the nineteenth century it is necessary to distinguish between a European and an extra-European international order.[77]

Morgenthau, however, does recognize that these developments inside and outside of Europe were having structural consequences for the European balance of power. As the empty space outside of Europe was steadily taken over by the Europeans, so the scope for compromise through compensations was being reduced. At the same time, there was no potential for territorial changes at the centre of Europe despite the insecurities for the other European states created by the unification of Germany. Morgenthau accepts, therefore, that there were structural factors that made it more difficult to maintain the status quo in Europe. But he also insists that there was still room for manoeuvre in peripheral areas, like the Balkans, and that there was scope in 1914 for a settlement of the kind that had been reached at the Congress of Berlin in 1878. But this would have required the European states to acknowledge the peripheral nature of the conflict. From

Morgenthau's perspective, therefore, it was 'blundering diplomacy' at least in part, that precipitated the First World War, as 'a conflict at the periphery of the European state system transformed itself into a struggle that threatened to affect the overall distribution of power within that system'.[78]

6.4. **Second transformation of the international system 1919–73**

The First World War demonstrated that the European balance of power had become global in extent, but for Morgenthau it was not the war itself that brought about a transformation of the international system. It was developments surrounding the war that destroyed the established balance of power and transformed world politics. These developments are seen by Morgenthau to have 'dealt the final fatal blow to that social system of international intercourse within which for almost three centuries nations lived together in constant rivalry, yet under the common roof of shared values and universal standards of action'.[79] This second transformation, therefore, is seen to be more dramatic and significant than the one that occurred at the time of the French Revolution. After the Napoleonic Wars, it proved possible to re-establish a balance of power that still had the effect of restraining the international behaviour of states. By contrast, the central feature of Morgenthau's argument is that the changes that occurred in the aftermath of the First World War created 'a new balance of power' that was based on unrestrained power politics. Morgenthau insisted, as a consequence, that it would be 'the most dangerous of illusions' to overlook or belittle the extent of the transformation that took place in the first half of the twentieth century.[80]

For Morgenthau, perhaps the most crucial change was the mutation of nationalism. In the nineteenth century, nationalism was closely associated with the development of the nation state. As a consequence, it was still possible for states to oppose each other 'within a framework of shared beliefs and common values which imposes effective limitations upon the ends and means of their struggle for power'.[81] But Morgenthau asserted that during the course of the twentieth century, states emerged that confronted each other 'as standard-bearers of ethical systems, each of them national in origin and each of them claiming and aspiring to provide a supranational framework of moral standards which all the other nations ought to accept and within which their foreign policies ought to operate'.[82] Morgenthau acknowledges that what he calls 'nationalistic universalism' was most evident in fascist Germany but he insists that the United States and the Soviet Union also adhered to a form of nationalistic universalism that was 'only a difference in degree, not in kind'.[83] It follows that in the course of the twentieth century, contests for power 'now took on the ideological aspects of struggles between good and evil. Foreign policies transformed themselves into sacred missions. Wars were fought as crusades, for the purpose of bringing the true political religion to the rest of the world.'[84]

Nationalistic universalism is traced back to the end of the First World War, and is the central dynamic producing the second system transformation. But Morgenthau identifies other crucial developments that gave additional impetus to the transformation. First, he notes that the focal point for the balance of power shifted. Although it is possible to argue that from the end of the nineteenth century a global balance of power had emerged with the result that the First World War had worldwide consequences, Europe still provided the central point of reference.[85] But by the Second World War, this is no longer the case. With the defeat of fascism, Morgenthau argues that Europe was reduced to being 'a mere function of the worldwide balance'.[86] This global balance of power was also very different from the European balance of power. In the place of nation states competing within a common frame of reference, Morgenthau argues that what now existed were two 'moral and political systems claiming universal validity' and that they had entered into 'an active competition for the domination of the world'.[87]

These two political systems, moreover, were radically different in scale from the European nation states and he traces the difference back to the nineteenth century. Although all the major nineteenth century states became interested in expanding into what Morgenthau calls empty spaces, he nevertheless draws a major distinction between the expansion of the United States and Russia, on the one hand, and the European states, on the other. The European states entered these empty spaces by establishing overseas empires and an integral link was established between this move and the European balance of power.[88] By contrast, the United States and Russia, over a longer period, were 'absorbed by the task of pushing their frontiers forward into the politically empty spaces of their continents'.[89] And Morgenthau accepts Toynbee's[90] argument that the Americans and the Russians were able to expand their territorial base 'unobtrusively', with the result that during this period of expansion, they 'did not take a very active part in the balance of power'. The long-term consequence was that in the twentieth century, these two states were continental in scale and, from a territorial perspective, dwarfed the other states in the system.[91]

It was clear to some Europeans from the early nineteenth century that the United States would eventually 'rival or overshadow Europe'.[92] For Morgenthau, this point was reached at the time of the Second World War and since then, he argues that it has become 'obvious' that the traditional nation state is now 'obsolescent in view of the technological and military conditions of the contemporary world'.[93] What Morgenthau seems to be saying here is not that traditional nation states will disappear, but that they can no longer hope to operate as great powers, with the result that the number of states that can act as great powers in the international system is greatly reduced. Indeed, in the short-run, multipolarity had given way to bipolarity. Morgenthau argues not only that a bipolar system operates very differently to a multipolar system but that the reduction of participants has a 'deteriorating effect' on the operation of the balance of power. He holds that in a multipolar system, where the defection of one state can make a considerable difference to the overall distribution of power, even small states can have a significant role to play. By the same token, states, on the one hand, are very unwilling to operate without the support of allies, but, on the other, they can never be sure that their allies will stay on side. It follows, therefore, that because alliances are so fluid in a multipolar system, so too is the distribution of power and this means that multipolarity is associated with a high degree of uncertainty, which then encourages states to be cautious.[94]

By contrast, in a bipolar system, it is difficult if not impossible for small states to affect the distribution of power by moving from one alliance to another. As a consequence, smaller states are not in a position to restrain one of the dominant states in the system by threatening to defect from its alliance. But Morgenthau goes on to argue that small states have not only lost any ability they may have had to restrain great powers, they have also lost their own room for manoeuvre. Many states, he argued, now operate within the orbit of one or the other of the two superpowers because their 'political, military and economic preponderance can hold them there even against their will'.[95] It follows that in a bipolar system, therefore, not only is there very little systemic restraint imposed on the two dominant actors, but smaller states have much less freedom of manoeuvre than in a multipolar system. The bipolar system was further hobbled because of the absence of any actor that could play the kind of balancing role to restrain the two dominant powers. Finally, Morgenthau also argues that in the absence of a colonial frontier, where the great powers expended some of their energies, yet another source of restraint on the two superpowers is missing. What Morgenthau observed, therefore, was the United States and the Soviet Union driven by fear to engage in persistent attempts to increase either their own military potential, or that of their allies. He argues that they 'bend every effort to increase their military potential to the utmost, since this is all they have to count on'.[96]

But it is not only the nature and number of the dominant units that has precipitated such a dramatic transformation in the system. The impact of these two factors was accentuated by the fact that the two dominant states in the international system were also imbued with nationalistic universalism. The presence of nationalistic universalism, in the absence of any of the restraints that had operated in the past, moved the international system onto a completely new and, from Morgenthau's perspective, dangerous and highly undesirable plane. Because both superpowers adhered to a nationalistic universalism, the balance of power also underwent a significant transformation. In the past, the great powers acknowledged the existence of peripheral areas, where they failed to identify any crucial interests and, as a consequence, there were a range of regional and essentially autonomous balances of power. As the consequence of nationalistic universalism, however, not only is the balance of power universal in scope, but the autonomy of regional balances of power has been eroded and they are 'mere functions of the new world-wide balance'.[97] Morgenthau argues that what was the 'periphery of world politics' is now 'one of the main theatres where the struggle between the two superpowers is being fought out in terms of the control of territory and men's minds'.[98]

Nationalistic universalism, therefore, is seen to ratchet up the effects of a bipolarity defined by two superpowers, particularly 'the tendency to expand into a two bloc system'.[99] Morgenthau readily acknowledged that traditional nation states were simply too weak, on their own, to act as 'effective spearheads of the new nationalistic universalism' although he did accept that a state like China could potentially take on the mantle that was currently held by the Soviet Union.[100] But he argued that it would require a fusion of traditional nation states, like France or Germany, to enable them to enter the race to make over the world 'in their own image'. Morgenthau is very clear, however, that such a move would be catastrophic and that it was vital that supranational unions, such as the European Union, did not travel down this route because he believed that the claim by any political system to have a right to impose 'its own valuations and standards of action upon all other nations' was 'evil'.[101]

Morgenthau favoured a world where national self-determination and social justice were promoted. He believed that 'poverty and misery are not God-given curses that man must passively accept but that they are largely man-made and can be remedied by man'.[102] What he found unacceptable in the era after the Second World War was the drive to bring the uncommitted areas of the world into the orbit of either the Soviet Union or the United States at the expense of social justice and national self-determination. Rather surprisingly, therefore, Morgethau ends his discussion of the balance of power on a cautiously optimistic note. Although he acknowledged that a continuation of unrestrained competition between the United States and the Soviet Union was possible, he insisted that it was not inevitable because bipolarity was a mechanism with the potential for 'unheard of good as well as for unprecedented evil'.[103] But Morgenthau fails to discuss the putative benefits of bipolarity.[104] Instead, he cites Fénelon, a French philosopher writing at the end of the seventeenth century, who favoured a system consisting of two equally powerful states, where one of the states was interested in promoting common security. Fénelon insisted that such a state would prosper by promoting equilibrium rather than pursuing hegemony. Perhaps Morgenthau was intimating that this was a route that the United States could follow. Certainly in the 1970s the United States did endeavour to implement the basic message associated with *Politics Among Nations,* using diplomacy to reach mutually agreed solutions in the area of arms control based on a new set of rules of the game.[105]

6.5. **Conclusion**

The analysis of *Politics Among Nations* in this chapter suggests that it has potential links with the constructivist approach to international politics, although it would be unnecessarily provocative to suggest that it provides an early constructivist text. Morgenthau's theory presupposes that because of the problems of measuring power there is a mechanistic or power political dynamic that pushes great powers in a hegemonic direction, but he also acknowledges that because of what constructivists call inter-subjective beliefs, the structural dynamics associated with power politics can be ameliorated. The beliefs that emerged after the French Revolution, Morgenthau argues, transformed the nature of international politics, but continued to restrain the dynamics associated with a power political balance of power. By contrast, after the First World War he observes the emergence of new beliefs such as nationalistic universalism that accentuated the impact of power politics, and eventually pushed the superpowers to extend their influence across the globe. Morgenthau was profoundly critical of this development. But despite frequent allusions to Morgenthau's opposition to the Vietnam War, it is generally not noted that his criticisms flow directly from the analysis of nationalistic universalism in *Politics Among Nations*.[106]

The chapter also challenges the common misconception that Morgenthau's analysis of the balance of power promotes a view of international politics that is fixed and unchanging. It is simply not the case that Morgenthau saw international politics as 'a static field in which power relations reproduce themselves in timeless monotony'.[107] He identifies two major transformations over the last 300 years and argues that these transformations have occurred primarily because the dominant beliefs that underpin the prevailing rules of the game have undergone dramatic shifts. In the case of the first major transformation, the French Revolution is seen to have posed a fundamental challenge to the beliefs of the international aristocracy who had previously dominated the international system. The dynastic states that prevailed before the French Revolution, slowly but surely gave way to a system of nation states. But even as this system was consolidating, the superpowers of the twentieth century were already forming on the periphery of the European system.[108] In the aftermath of the First World War, these states not only became the dominant states in the system, but they also subscribed to very different beliefs to those adhered to by the European nation states, thereby precipitating an even bigger transformation in the system.

According to constructivists, realists account for international politics in purely material terms.[109] The analysis of *Politics Among Nations* presented here demonstrates that the realist position is much more complex than this assessment acknowledges. Morgenthau's proposition that states are driven to maximize power is mediated by the idea that power is not amenable to accurate measurement. But there is also a strong presumption running throughout *Politics Among Nations* that ideas play an independent role in international politics. Dynasticism and nationalism are not material forces, but persuasive ideas that, as Morgenthau acknowledges, have been used to legitimize very different kinds of international politics. So for Morgenthau there is a complex interrelationship between material and ideational forces. It is not at all clear, as a consequence, that he would have disagreed, in principle, with Wendt's sophisticated social theory that shows how ideas govern most of the social world we operate in, although these ideas are, in the end, constrained by 'brute' material facts. But it is never these facts that inhibit social change. This was certainly the position that Morgenthau adopted. He favoured world government, but accepted that this political outcome could not be realized until there was a transformation in beliefs. In the meantime, he favoured the promotion of an international order that rested on a balance of power that promoted common security.

NOTES

1. I wish to thank the Leverhulme Trust for my Major Research Fellowship that has funded a project on the balance of power of which this forms a part.
2. Still regarded as a key text in the realist canon, the first edition was published in 1948. The fifth and final edition for which Morgenthau was responsible was published in 1973 and references in this chapter are to this edition. A seventh edition was published in 2005.
3. Jack Donnelly, *Realism and International Relations* (Cambridge: Cambridge University Press, 2000).
4. See Inis L. Claude, *Power and International Relations* (New York: Random House, 1962), for an insightful discussion of some of the problems surrounding Morgenthau's use of the balance of power.
5. Kenneth Waltz, *Theory of International Politics* (Reading, MA: Addison-Wesley, 1979).
6. Hans J. Morgenthau, *Politics Among Nations: The Struggle for Power and Peace*, 5th edn. (New York: Knopf, 1973), 186.
7. *Politics Among Nations*, 199.
8. But not necessarily a more peaceful international system; Morgenthau accepted that during what he calls the 'golden age' of the balance of power, war was a ubiquitous feature of the system.
9. *Politics Among Nations*, 204.

10. John Mearsheimer, *The Tragedy of Great Power Politics* (New York: W.W. Norton, 2001).

11. *Politics Among Nations*, 355.

12. Ibid. 225.

13. *Politics Among Nations*, 211–13. Schroeder makes the same point, indicating that in the eighteenth century, 'Britain and Russia were not alone in saying "balance" while meaning "hegemony".' See Paul W. Schroeder, 'Did the Vienna Settlement Rest on A Balance of Power?', *American History Review*, 97 (1992), 691.

14. *Politics Among Nations*, 226.

15. Ibid. 216.

16. Sofka has challenged this assessment, arguing that the great powers were interested in hegemony rather than parity and that frequently their primary war aim was to dismember their principal rival. It was not the lack of desire but a lack of resources that prevented these hegemonic states from achieving their ambitious objectives. Sofka, in other words, highlights Morgenthau's power politics dynamic but denies the existence of any restraining dynamic. See James R. Sofka, 'The Eighteenth Century International System: Parity or Primacy', *Review of International Studies*, 27 (2001), 147–64.

17. *Politics Among Nations*, 169.

18. Ibid. 219.

19. *Politics Among Nations*, 203. Edward V. Gulick, *Europe's Classical Balance of Power* (New York: W.W. Norton [1955] 1967), 249–51, documents the detailed statistics that were made available at the Congress of Vienna to facilitate the negotiations. See also Morgenthau, *Politics Among Nations*, 179.

20. *Politics Among Nations*, 41–2.

21. *Politics Among Nations*, 215. Morgenthau draws this example from Arnold Toynbee, *A Study in History*, vol. IV (Oxford: Oxford University Press, 1939), 149.

22. *Politics Among Nations*, 340.

23. Ibid. 219.

24. *Politics Among Nations*, 189. Members of the English school have similarly argued that what is distinctive about the balance of power is the self-conscious acknowledgement that there is a need to maintain a balance of power. See, for example, Herbert Butterfield, 'The Balance of Power', in Herbert Butterfield and Martin Wight (eds.), *Diplomatic Investigations: Essays in the Theory of International Politics* (London: Allen and Unwin, 1966), and Hedley Bull, *The Anarchical Society: A Study of Order in World Politics* (London: Macmillan, 1977).

25. See, for example, Andreas Osiander, 'Before Sovereignty: Society and Politics in *Ancien Regime* Europe', *Review of International Studies*, 27 (2001), 119–45, and Osiander, *The States System of Europe 1640–1990: Peace Making and the Conditions of International Stability* (Oxford: Clarendon Press, 2001); Paul J. Schroeder, *The Transformation of European Politics: 1763–1848* (Oxford: Clarendon Press, 1994); and Benno Teschke, *The Myth of 1648: Class, Geopolitics, and the Making of Modern International Relations* (London: Verso, 2003), who all argue that the fundamental

change in international politics occurred in the wake of the French revolutionary wars.

26. *Politics Among Nations*, 106.
27. Ibid. 242.
28. Ibid. 243.
29. Ibid. 243.
30. Ibid. 245.
31. Ibid. 220.
32. Ibid. 189.
33. Ibid. 256.
34. Ibid. 542.
35. *Politics Among Nations*, 189. Osiander, *The States System in Europe*, 80–2, disputes the idea that the statesmen at Westphalia were endeavouring to establish a European balance of power. Although he acknowledges that there were references in the diplomatic correspondence surrounding the treaties to equilibrium and the balance of power, he insists that these references relate to the actions of individual states and not to the system as a whole. But because Osiander accepts that this early balance of power thinking was designed to cultivate restraint, his position is not, in fact, incompatible with Morgenthau's position.
36. Jeremy Black, *The Rise and Fall of the European Powers 1679–1793* (London: Edward Arnold, 1990), 197, also argues that alliances were the most common way that rulers sought to achieve their political goals.
37. *Politics Among Nations*, 190.
38. 'The Eighteenth Century International System'.
39. Black, *Rise and Fall of the European Powers*, 192–7.
40. Teschke, *Myth of 1648*, 233–7.
41. It is important to note that Teschke is drawing on an essentially Marxist framework and he attributes the expansionist aims of these dynastic states as stemming from domestic rather than international factors.
42. Teschke, *Myth of 1648*, 233–6.
43. Teschke, *Myth of 1648*, 260; Morgenthau, *Politics Among Nations*, 194.
44. Sofka 'The Eighteenth Century International System' also sees the Polish partition as characteristic of eighteenth century power politics. There were three partitions of Poland, in 1772, 1793, and 1795. The kingdom was not restored at the Congress of Vienna. Schroeder, *Transformation of European Politics*, 524, argues that no one at the Congress thought seriously about this possibility.
45. *Politics Among Nations*, 179.
46. Teschke, *Myth of 1648*, 237.
47. *Politics Among Nations*, 202. Presumably Morgenthau arrives at this conclusion by assuming, for example, that when Habsburg Silesia was annexed by Prussia 1740, it was simply being moved from the control of one Great Power to another. Teschke and Morgenthau's positions are not necessarily incompatible. Morgenthau notes that the number of states in the German Empire was reduced from 900 to 355 at the Treaty

of Westphalia. Napoleon then eliminated 200 of these states and at the Congress of Vienna, there were only 36 members of the German Confederation.

48. *Politics Among Nations*, 106.

49. Ibid. 248.

50. Rosecrance and Lo challenge this account and argue that European governments persistently chose to bandwagon rather than balance; see Richard Rosecrance and Chih-Cheng Lo. 'Balancing Stability and War: The Mysterious Case of the Napoleonic International System', *International Studies Quarterly*, 40: 4 (1996), 479–500. Daniel Whiteneck ['Long-term Bandwagoning and Short-term Balancing: The Lessons of Coalition Behaviour from 1792–1815', *Review of International Studies*, 27: 2 (2001), 151–68] disagrees and argues that there was a clear preference among European powers to oppose French hegemonic designs. They only succumbed to French designs after unequivocal military defeats. Schroeder, by contrast, argues that Britain, Russia, and France can all be seen to have been hegemonic powers at that time. See Paul Schroeder, *The Transformation of European Politics*.

51. *Politics Among Nations*, 216.

52. Ibid. 248.

53. *Politics Among Nations*, 216. Morgenthau argues that the Holy Alliance, as an institution, was based on three treaties, the Treaty of Chaumont, 9 March 1814, the Quadruple Alliance, signed 20 November 1815, and the Treaty of the Holy Alliance, signed 26 Sept. 1815. The Holy Alliance is considered by Morgenthau to have embraced Russia, Austria, Prussia, Great Britain, and France.

54. *Politics Among Nations*, 440.

55. Morgenthau fails to note that one of the crucial features of the Congress of Vienna was the recognition and acceptance that the international system was two-tiered, with the top tier being occupied by the great powers. Andreas Osiander insists that it must be stressed that 'this was very much a new phenomenon' and that it is anachronistic and unhelpful to refer to great powers before the nineteenth century. Osiander, *The States System of Europe*, 323. See also Gerry Simpson, *Great Powers and Outlaw States: Unequal Sovereigns in the International Legal Order* (Cambridge: Cambridge University Press, 2004).

56. *Politics Among Nations*, 443.

57. Ibid. 245–6.

58. Ibid. 444.

59. *Politics Among Nations*, 382. This position may seem to anticipate the argument developed by Teschke, but whereas Morgenthau sees the rise of the commercial classes as a general European phenomenon, Teshcke maintains that the rise of capitalist property relations was distinctive to Britain and reflects a path-dependent history that has to be traced back to the feudal era. But Teschke, like Morgenthau, places Britain at the centre of the transformation of Europe from a dynastic to a liberal capitalist system.

60. Whereas Teschke sees an inextricable link between economic and geopolitical relations, Morgenthau draws a sharp distinction and this may account for his failure

to examine the significance of mercantilism for the dynastic era. For Teschke, by contrast, mercantilism is seen to underpin inter-dynastic relations.

61. Schroeder (*The Transformation of European Politics*, 578) also notes that dynastic succession disputes ceased to be an international problem after 1815.

62. *Politics Among Nations*, 220.

63. Ibid. 438–9.

64. Ibid. 444.

65. Ibid. 233.

66. Ibid. 511.

67. Ibid. 512–13.

68. Schroeder depicts Britain and Russia as hegemonic and relatively secure states, thereby possessing radically different security objectives to Prussia, Austria, and France. He argues that what effectively happened in 1815 was that Russia and Britain were in a position to say to the other Great Powers 'Our world spheres of influence are strictly ours; yours are European and therefore must be shared with us', Schroeder, 'Vienna Settlement', 689; see also Schroeder, *The Transformation of European Politics*.

69. *Politics Among Nations*, 190.

70. Ibid. 43–4.

71. *Politics Among Nations*, 190–1. Canning was reacting to the decision by France to intervene into Spain in line with Holy Alliance objectives.

72. *Politics Among Nations*, 444, 349.

73. Ibid. 179.

74. Ibid. 349.

75. Ibid. 180.

76. Ibid. 180.

77. Keene's central point is that the European order was based on the mutual recognition of state sovereignty. Beyond the boundaries of the European order, however, the Europeans attempted to impose a very different kind of order, where sovereignty was divided and the Europeans accorded themselves a right to intervene in order to promote 'civilization'.

78. *Politics Among Nations*, 349–50.

79. Ibid. 338–9.

80. Ibid. 254.

81. Ibid. 252.

82. Ibid. 253.

83. Ibid. 110.

84. Ibid. 108.

85. The importance of seeing the First World War from a global perspective is generally acknowledged, although Bourke argues that David Stevenson is the first international historian to provide a 'truly global history of the conflict'. See Joanna Bourke, 'New Tales from the Trenches', *The Independent*, Review Section, 3 September (2004), 23; and David Stevenson, *1914–1918: The History of the First World War* (London: Allen Lane, 2004).

86. *Politics Among Nations*, 201.

87. Ibid. 254.

88. As noted earlier, this phase of imperialism was significantly affected by the process of mutual compensations.

89. *Politics Among Nations*, 348.

90. *A Study of History*, 302.

91. *Politics Among Nations*, 348. Morgenthau fails to note that whereas the United States did effectively move into empty spaces, because so many of the indigenous population were killed by disease, most of the local inhabitants survived the process of Russian imperialism. For an illuminating discussion of why the impact of imperialism could be so very different, see Alfred W. Crosby, *Ecological Imperialism: The Biological Expansion of Europe 900–1900* (Cambridge: Cambridge University Press, 1986). The implications of the difference, however, were huge, because with a longer time perspective it becomes much more apparent that Russian expansion had a lot more in common with European imperialism than with American expansion.

92. Schroeder, *Transformation of European Politics*, 574.

93. *Politics Among Nations*, 331. This line of argument was first developed by Herz in *International Politics in the Atomic Age* (New York: Columbia University Press, 1959), although he later retracted and argued that traditional nation states could operate as effective political units in contemporary world politics. See Herz, 'The Territorial State Revisited', *Polity*, 1: 1 (1968), 12–34.

94. *Politics Among Nations*, 341–2.

95. Ibid. 343.

96. Ibid. 355.

97. Ibid. 201.

98. Ibid. 350.

99. Ibid. 353.

100. Ibid. 331.

101. Ibid. 331.

102. Ibid. 352.

103. Ibid. 355.

104. Waltz, *Theory of International Politics* provides one of the most rigorous attempts to account for the stability of bipolarity.

105. See Adler's perceptive constructivist account of how an American epistemic community played a crucial part in creating a shared understanding with the Soviet Union about these rules of the game. Emanuel Adler, 'The Emergence of Cooperation: National Epistemic Communities and the International Evolution of the Idea of Nuclear Arms Control', *International Organization*, 46: 1 (1992), 101–45. Morgenthau, however, believed that as long as the military competition between the United States and the Soviet Union persisted, arms control would be, at best, precarious. *Politics Among Nations*, 406.

106. For an assessment of Morgenthau's opposition to the Vietnam War, see, for example, Martin Griffiths, *Fifty Key Thinkers in International Relations* (London: Routlege, 1999), 40.

107. Stanley Hoffmann (ed.), *Contemporary Theory in International Relations* (Englewood Cliffs, CA: Prentice-Hall, 1960), 30.

108. This dynamic was explored in some depth by Dehio; see L. Dehio, *The Precarious Balance: Four Centuries of the European Power Struggle*, trans. by Charles Fullman (New York: Vintage Books, 1962), and *Germany and World Politics in the Twentieth Century*, trans. by Dieter Persner (New York: W.W. Norton, 1967). See also the discussion and empirical analysis of Dehio's work in William R. Thompson, 'Dehio, Long Cycles, and the Geohistorical Context of Structural Transition', *World Politics*, 45: 1 (1992), 127–52.

109. See, for example, Wendt, *Social Theory of International Politics* (Cambridge: Cambridge University Press, 1999); and Stefano Guzzini, *Realism in International Relations and International Political Economy: The Continuing Story of a Death Foretold* (London: Routledge, 1998), and 'The Enduring Dilemmas of Realism in International Relations', *European Journal of International Relations*, 10: 4 (2004), 533–68.

Hans J Morgenthau, realism, and the rise and fall of the Cold War

Michael Cox

Historians will no doubt continue to argue about how and why the Cold War came to an end, when exactly it concluded, and who or what played the bigger part in bringing it to a peaceful resolution. What is not in dispute is the huge impact which the collapse of the communist project had upon the wider international system. Gorbachev may have earlier vowed that he would redefine the East–West relationship. In reality he did much more, and whether as a result of Soviet economic decline, a shift in ideas, imperial overstretch, or a simple failure to understand the consequences of his own actions, set off a series of chain reactions that did not just place the competition on a new footing but brought it to an end for ever. As a result, the West not only found itself in the distinctly odd position of having no enemy to fight, but of pushing at new open doors in those parts of the world where they had been previously closed. The consequences worldwide were huge, first for the United States itself which emerged in triumphant mood, then in the Third World where the language of national liberation very rapidly gave way to the politics of structural adjustment, and finally in Europe where policies now had to be devised whose primary purpose was not to keep the 'Germans down and the Russians out' but to bring the two parts of a once divided Europe together.[1] Optimists could of course claim—and naturally did—that all this could only be to the good. Others were less sanguine. Indeed, according to one of the more famous of the new post-Cold War pundits, we would soon all be missing the certainties of the old system. Liberals may be celebrating at the moment, argued Chicago political scientist John Mearsheimer. But over the longer term, the world order in general, and the European continent in particular, would soon be experiencing difficult times. A new world disorder beckoned.[2]

This sense of unease about the future was inevitably reinforced by persistent worries about something else—namely the very obvious fact that nearly all of the so-called experts had failed to predict one of the great turning points of the twentieth century. Naturally, there were those who pushed such worries to one side, on the less-than-convincing grounds that getting this mere 'data point' wrong proved very little.[3] Others though were not so certain. After all, an enormous amount of time had gone into thinking about the Cold War. Careers had been made writing about it. An academic sub-discipline in the shape of Sovietology had even been constructed in order to understand the intentions and capabilities of the West's main enemy.[4] But at the end of the day, hardly anybody anticipated what happened between 1989 and 1991. Indeed, rather than pointing to serious change, the majority of writers believed the Cold War would persist for the foreseeable future. Thus, it was assumed that the USSR would remain in Eastern Europe, that Germany would (and possibly should) remain divided, and that the USSR would remain the expansionary threat it had always been. In fact, even after the fall of the Wall, several well-informed people—including President Bush himself—were still talking as if there was an 'East' and a 'West' and that the USSR would likely persist.[5] It might be unfair, but it is certainly great fun, to see how many well-respected analysts got the end of the Cold War wrong. As the doyen of Cold War history later noted, if events in general, and big events in particular, are tests of the validity of different theories, there is little doubt that most theories were found wanting when it came to explaining the disintegration of the communist project after 1989.[6]

Nowhere perhaps was this failure felt as intensely, or debated more frequently, than in the discipline of IR.[7] Here, there was much gnashing of teeth as it became obvious to many in the field that they had either been asking the wrong questions or providing the incorrect answers. One school of thought however came under the heaviest bombardment of all: realism.[8] The attack was sustained, and for some at least, almost irresistible. Realism, it was now regularly argued by its many critics, had revealed its intellectual poverty in the most brazen manner possible: by failing to anticipate what actually occurred to the international system between 1989 and 1991. Nor was this failure accidental. Given its own methodology, it could have very little to say (and did not) about the significant changes taking place within the Soviet system itself; and because of its materialist bias, ignored completely the impact that a set of highly revisionist ideas was having on the Soviet leadership after 1985.[9] Perhaps more damning still, realism—according to its critics—appeared to be attached to the Cold War as a particular kind of bipolar system that had brought some form of stability to the world.[10] Hence, its incapacity to predict the system's demise occurred not just for intellectual reasons alone (that might have been forgivable), but because of something far more disturbing: its identity with, and effective defence of an order whose structures it should have been analysing rather than rationalizing, and one of whose principal agents— the USSR in particular—it should have been dissecting in an altogether more detached fashion than it seemed to be doing between 1947 and 1989.

The attack upon realism as a result of its apparent failure to anticipate the end of the Cold War began a long process that left realism and realists on the intellectually defensive.[11] It also created the space—some might say a vacuum—that constructivism in its various guises very rapidly occupied.[12] Whether or not this helped or hindered IR, or indeed was even based on an accurate understanding of realism and its predictive capacities, is not an issue I want to engage with here.[13] Rather, what I want to do is something quite different: namely, explore the complex relationship between realism as a set of ideas and the Cold War itself. Here, my purpose is not to defend realism in all its manifestations, let alone rediscover its presumed 'hidden' history.[14] Instead, it is to show that the relationship between realism and the Cold War system was far more complicated and nuanced than has been suggested by opponents. This, I would suggest, is true in general.[15] However, I want to suggest that it is perhaps especially true in the case of Hans J. Morgenthau, the writer most responsible for having launched realism as an academic discourse after the Second World War, and whose views have often been read as providing a theoretical rationalization for American power. As I will try to show this particular view is based on a very one-sided reading of his work.[16] Indeed, through a close examination of his ideas (ideas that have often been more 'cited' than 'read'[17]), I will seek to demonstrate that the close identity often assumed between realism as a set of scientific truths and those who happened to wield power is at best too simple, and at worst seriously misleading. Morgenthau may have tried to 'talk truth to power'. Indeed, he was even employed for a while as a consultant to the Truman administration.[18] Yet the relationship between himself and the US foreign policy elite was never an easy one, and as time went by he increasingly found himself preaching to those who simply did not want to hear what he had to say. Moreover, this gap opened up long before the 1960s.[19] In fact, as we will see, important differences had been simmering beneath the surface for a very long time indeed.[20] These took shape in the late 1940s as the Cold War began to assume an apparently permanent form, continued throughout the early 1950s, and persisted for the rest of the decade. Certainly, if Morgenthau was a mere mouthpiece for Cold War policies as later critics have implied, then this was not something that occurred to Morgenthau, let alone to an increasingly irritated American establishment.

To chart the path that led Morgenthau the would-be insider to critical outsider, I have divided this chapter into three broad parts. As my primary purpose is to look at Morgenthau and the Cold War, it makes sense in the first section to outline his views on the US–Soviet competition. At one level, these were decidedly tough-minded. Indeed, the argument that Morgenthau's brand of realism helped shape the Cold War stems in large part from his uncompromising approach to the problems facing the United States in the post-war period. Morgenthau's primary intellectual purpose of course was never in doubt: to point out to all those who cared, or dared, to listen that conflict between states in general—and the United States and the USSR in particular—was not merely a function of their very different domestic characters, but the almost natural consequence of their position in the world at the end of the Second World War. This did not mean the relationship could not be managed. Nor did it mean that there was no room for diplomacy. However, as he made clear in his core text, *Politics Among Nations*, statesmen should be under no illusion. The world was full of traps for the unwary. The Russians were a serious foe. They had started the Cold War. And it was America's purpose in international affairs to make sure they did not win it.

This brings us then to the second part of the chapter and what to some at least must look like an obvious contradiction: the fact that Morgenthau, the realist defender of American power, felt no compunction in attacking American foreign policy when it deviated (as it more often than not did in his view) from the path of realist righteousness. His critique derived from many sources. These included an early fear that an extended Cold War between the United States and the USSR would be unsustainable over the longer term—one prediction he clearly got wrong;[21] and a more deeply held conviction that in spite of its many fine virtues, the United States was simply not equipped (if anything was particularly ill-suited) to lead the world through the post-war era. This, he argued, stemmed in part from problems rooted deep in American history, in part from the way in which domestic politics constantly distorted the foreign policy process, and in part from a profound inability to pursue a balanced strategy in a complex world undergoing revolutionary change. In fact, for a realist who according to later critics was deeply attached to the status quo for its own sake, Morgenthau displayed a remarkably acute understanding of the fact that change was both inevitable and necessary. This did not make him into a radical. On the contrary, there was something deeply conservative about his views.[22] Yet he was clear about one thing: that if America stood in the way of change, as it increasingly seemed to be doing in the Third World during the Cold War, this could only damage its interests.[23] Indeed, for someone so apparently preoccupied with the tragedy of great power politics,[24] it was in the end to be his attitude towards events on the 'periphery' that compelled him to confront what he saw as the increasingly dysfunctional character of US foreign policy.[25]

This leads lastly to Morgenthau's most celebrated critique of all: that which he directed against America's growing involvement in the Vietnam War. As the record shows, his opposition began early and stemmed from a simple proposition: that America had no need to get involved in South-East Asia in the first place. As he repeated, almost *ad nauseam*, the central task of the United States in the world arena was to balance the power of the Soviet state in much the same way, and for essentially the same set of reasons, as Britain had balanced France before 1814 and America had confronted Nazi Germany before 1945. But this purpose, he insisted, would not be served by getting entangled in the affairs of a region whose fate was not essential to the US national interest, and whose instabilities could very easily lure the United States into a dangerous quagmire from which it would be difficult to extricate itself. How prescient this particular analysis turned out to be. But how problematic too for those in Washington who had taken the decision to contain communism whenever and wherever it raised its ideological head. In fact, so problematic did they find it that as the bitter debate about Vietnam intensified in the United States, Morgenthau found himself in a position which few might have anticipated twenty years earlier: of becoming increasingly alienated from those in power whom he had been seeking to influence for the better part of a quarter of a century. How and why he arrived at this crucial juncture we now seek to explain in what follows.

7.1. **Morgenthau—a man in dark times**[26]

Because Morgenthau made his name as an academic in the United States, he has often been regarded, incorrectly, as a quintessential American thinker.[27] Yet as his recent biographer has shown,[28] while Morgenthau may have become the most influential US writer on international affairs during the post-war period—Stanley Hoffman even credits him with founding a whole new discipline—he remained in many important ways a deeply European thinker whose main intellectual influences were not American at all but that significant triumvirate of influential Germans: Nietzsche, Weber, and most controversially of all, Carl Schmitt.[29] From each he took certain important ideas: from Nietzsche a profound pessimism about mankind and a scepticism about progress; from Weber a belief in the primacy of the political and the need for intellectual detachment (not to mention a theory of power);[30] and from Schmitt, amongst other things, a view of history that saw as almost inevitable (if not desirable) the long-term decline of Europe and the rise of the United States.[31] From all three he also inherited his deep and abiding suspicion of liberalism as an international project. Morgenthau may not have been illiberal himself. Still, he always drew a sharp distinction between what was feasible within the boundaries of states, and what was possible in determining relations between them. Hence, while it may have been entirely reasonable to be a liberal in terms of domestic politics, it would be near fatal to apply the same liberal principles to foreign policy.[32] This indeed is why he was so critical of liberals in the interwar period. In his view, it had been their naivety that had allowed Hitler to gain the upper hand in Europe by the end of the 1930s; and it was the same outlook that then misled Americans in what he termed their 'apolitical' dealings with the USSR towards the end of the Second World War. In one purple passage he even accused the United States of being so befuddled by liberalism and visions of post-war international 'harmony' that it quite literally handed control of Eastern and Central Europe over to the Russians in 1945.[33]

Morgenthau's views about the post-war world were thus deeply rooted in his own experiences in Germany and Europe between the two wars. Not all theories of international politics can be explained in terms of individual biography. However, in Morgenthau's case (and in the case of many influential 'American' thinkers in the post-war years)[34] it is quite impossible to appreciate his ultimately tragic, quite 'un-American', outlook without some reference to his early life and the fact that he grew up in turbulent times on a doomed continent in the midst of a profound crisis. One relatively stable world had collapsed in 1914 and left in its wake nothing but uncertainty, doubt, and, for some, genuine despair about the future. These were not easy times in which to come to maturity, especially for a sensitive young man like Hans J. Morgenthau. Reviled as a Jew in his own native town of Coburg, denied academic tenure because of his background, and finally forced into exile by the impending threat of totalitarianism in Europe, he had every reason to be pessimistic about the world.[35] He was especially sceptical of those who thought that international problems could be solved collectively or on the basis of some modern version of the League of Nations. This he felt could only lead to tears. Indeed, like another realist of the time, E. H. Carr—from whom he borrowed more than he ever let on—he had little faith in the 'efficacy of law' or the power of institutions to solve the problem of order.[36] If anything 'misplaced faith' in such things would only encourage aggression. They had not stopped Hitler. They had done nothing to prevent the Second World War. And there was no reason to think they would perform any better after the Second World War.[37]

To add to his sense of foreboding, America he felt was drifting intellectually as global war gave way to uncertain peace. Indeed, he found it impossible to hide his sense of unease, especially with those in and around the Roosevelt administration who were hoping against hope in his opinion to build a better and more secure world through some form of co-operative relationship with its wartime ally, the USSR. This, he believed, was mere fantasy. Not only did he not trust a totalitarian state, another lesson drawn from his experiences in Germany;[38] his whole outlook made it virtually impossible for him to think of great power relations in anything other than Darwinian terms. He certainly had little faith in the persuasive power of reason or moral abstractions to tame the underlying, almost irrational urge to dominate.[39] In a bleak world where power counted for nearly everything, and paper guarantees for nothing at all, it would in fact have been the height of dilettante irresponsibility not to have taken the necessary measures to restore order after 1945. No doubt if the real world had corresponded to liberal ideals, or even resembled that much fabled 'international society', then this might not have been necessary. But the real world unfortunately was not like that, especially a world undergoing huge transformative change at every conceivable level. Hence, the United States had no choice but to take those measures that would together restore order and ensure that the USSR did not take advantage of western weakness. This of course is why Morgenthau felt so comfortable with perhaps that most 'realist' of all post-war US Secretaries of State, Dean Acheson.[40] Here, after all, was someone who understood the world he felt. Indeed, in many ways, Morgenthau was a true follower of (and at times distant adviser to) Dean Acheson, a foreign policy figure whom he admired greatly, and whose constant reiteration of the notion that there could never be any discussions with the USSR until and when the United States had created a 'position of strength' was one that Morgenthau often repeated himself.[41]

Therefore, there was little room in Morgenthau's world for wishful or optimistic thinking, something he felt that too many Americans were inclined to.[42] On the contrary, given his own essentialist views on the selfish nature of man ('moved' in his view 'by a number of basic quests')[43] there was every reason to assume the worst about the way states behaved.[44] Here, he shared a common outlook with a number of other contemporaries, including Walter Lippmann a writer whom he much admired, the influential Reinhold Niebuhr whose philosophical impact on Morgenthau was great,[45] as well as the author of the doctrine of containment, George F. Kennan.[46] Kennan in particular not only supported Morgenthau for a while (in the same way that Morgenthau later supported Kennan)[47] but also influenced Morgenthau's thinking on the peculiar and contradictory character of the USSR. Naturally, Kennan had a far more profound understanding of the USSR. Nonetheless, coming at the problem from very different perspectives, the two agreed that there was no chance of Washington coming to any kind of post-war deal with Moscow. Nor was there much point in trying. Containment, therefore, was the only possible strategy. Still, it was important to know what one was containing. Here, it was vital to distinguish between Stalin's Marxist rhetoric (which like Kennan he saw as little more than an ideological fig leaf) and the USSR's true ambitions. There was no reason to trust the Russians. On the other hand, the West should take very great care in analysing Soviet aims. The fact that the USSR talked the language of communism was not insignificant. But it was not communism as such that made it a threat. Rather, it was the fact that communism had transformed Russia from a relatively backward country into an industrial power.[48] This is why it constituted a genuine and serious problem after the Second World War, and why the United States had to respond decisively and effectively, as he felt it did in what he later saw as one of the most creative (and realist) moments of American foreign policy, when America revealed—albeit for a short period of time—its true 'pragmatic genius'.[49]

Yet, as Morgenthau gloomily concluded, this moment of creativity did not last for ever. Nor did America's early advantage, and as the 1940s gave way to the 1950s, Morgenthau began to sound a series of decidedly alarmist notes. He struck the first in 1949 when the USSR exploded an atomic device (thus eliminating America's nuclear monopoly at a stroke); he hit the alarm bell again in 1955 when Moscow made a serious turn towards the Third World; and he struck it once more in 1957 when it launched Sputnik and its first intercontinental ballistic missile (ICBM). These last two developments in particular provoked an almost splenetic response. The Cold War was certainly tilting in one direction. Unfortunately, it was tilting against the United States whose leaders seemed to have been hoodwinked by their own myopic rhetoric about the supposed inferiority of the communist system. This, he argued, was short-sighted in the extreme. Indeed, if 1957 pointed to anything, it was that the Soviet system had a proven capacity that Americans had hitherto underestimated. Bewitched by their own propaganda Washington had quite simply failed to read the proverbial writing on the wall. Russians might not have been ten feet tall. But the USSR was certainly no house of cards. It had survived the armed legions of Nazi Germany. It had then recovered from the war. And here it was again, ten years later, revealing its prowess. There was no easy answer, he concluded. One thing was certain though. That unless the United States responded by rebuilding its own military capabilities—in other words once more tried to achieve what appeared to be that ever-elusive phantom known as a position of strength—there was every chance that it would lose the position of primacy it had held in the immediate post-war years. There was no time to be lost.[50]

As the late 1950s gave way to the 1960s, Morgenthau's sense of foreboding often verging on the hysterical gradually gave way to a more nuanced position; and by the early 1960s he was beginning to sound like the realist sage of old. In part, this resulted from a change in his views on the role of nuclear weapons,[51] in part from the election of a new Democratic American administration in 1960, and in part from a recognition that the USSR faced many problems of its own. He was particularly encouraged by the events of 1968, arguing that the Warsaw Pact intervention into Czechoslovakia was as much a sign of Soviet weakness as it was of its strength. 'Power' based on raw military capabilities alone, he noted, was 'bound to be precarious'.[52] But he always remained cautious. Dialogue with the USSR was feasible. Arms control was necessary.[53] Nevertheless, the United States should not be lulled into a false sense of security. There was nothing wrong in constructing a less ideological relationship with the other side. He applauded Kissinger and Nixon for trying. It was critical however not to assume that bilateral negotiation could do away with the basic laws of IR. As he noted in the mid-1970s, one could not be in 'favour of bigger and better tensions'.[54] However, the United States should be under no illusion. The USSR, like any great power, would continue to seek influence and maximize its advantage, détente or no détente; and because it was bound to do so, the United States would be called upon to redress Soviet power—not out of any moral necessity or because the USSR was seeking world domination (a position he never espoused), but rather because the American purpose now, as it had been for the larger part of the twentieth century, was to maintain a balance the power in the international system.[55]

Naturally, this did not mean that one could not think creatively about the way in which that balance could be maintained. Indeed, as the world changed, and with it America's capacity to shape global events, the United States had to think seriously about how to maintain order under conditions where old formulas born in one era at the end of the Second World War might not work so easily twenty-five years later in an age of diminishing American capabilities (significantly, Morgenthau was a very early believer in the idea of US decline).[56] Nor should one ignore the significant alterations taking place within the wider communist world. But one should always be cautious, he urged. One did not have to go along with those who regarded the new strategy of détente as a modern form of appeasement. Nonetheless, he was not prepared to abandon long-held views for something he felt was being oversold by sections of the American foreign policy establishment grown tired of bearing the burdens of world leadership. In fact, during the last decade of his life (he died in 1980), one very much senses Morgenthau being squeezed between two positions with which he always felt uncomfortable: one articulated by an anti-communist right whose fierce attacks on the strategy of measured accommodation with the USSR he regarded as being theoretically primitive, and the other pushed by those within the liberal camp who were so intent on moving beyond the Cold War that they seemed indifferent to the problem still posed by the Soviet Union.[57] Typically, Morgenthau carved out his own position between the two poles. As he made clear, he did not want to do anything to undermine those who were trying against the odds to develop a more nuanced foreign policy. On the other hand, he did not wish to become a cheer leader for everything that was being done in the name of novelty and experiment. It was one thing accepting that the US needed to bring its overextended commitments into line with its limited resources. It would be quite wrong, however, to assume that the competition could be wished away.[58]

7.2. **Morgenthau—righteous critic**[59]

This brings us then to Morgenthau's critique of American foreign policy. As must be obvious from our narrative so far, though Morgenthau remained decidedly clear in his own mind that the USSR would always remain a serious rival (towards the end of his life he warned against a new Soviet adventurism in the Middle East and the Gulf),[60] he was no simple-minded cold warrior himself. Thus, he was never convinced that the Soviet Union was driven by an overriding ideological purpose. He assumed that security was its most cherished objective. And in spite of a momentary flirtation with alarmist thinking in the late 1950s, he rarely fell for the standard Cold War argument that there was some vast international plan organized by Moscow to bring about a single world state. On the contrary, like most

American realists of the time, he not only viewed the Soviet Union as the most modern form of imperial Russia—and therefore could be dealt with as an almost normal power—but that where communism did arise (except in the very special case of Eastern Europe after the Second World War) it did so not because of some organized conspiracy based in Moscow, but because of a protest against local conditions. This, he felt, was a crucial distinction to make. Hence, if the US got the Soviet challenge right, it would in his opinion be able to pursue a balanced foreign policy; if on the other hand, it got it wrong, then the US could easily get itself into serious trouble. As he argued at the time, the first duty of American statesmen during the Cold War was to know what the US was confronting and what it was not; and it was obvious, in his view, that it was not facing a state led by revolutionary dreamers. Ruthless opponents the Russians may have been, utopians and moralists they were not.

If only the same could be said of those whose task it was to guide the United States. Here, Morgenthau noted a very obvious irony: namely, that whereas Soviet leaders seemed to be realists the same could hardly be said of their American counterparts. Indeed, at the heart of his whole critique of US foreign policy was the simple but important argument that America more often than not substituted woolly thinking (usually taking the form of grandiose crusading talk about making the world safe for democracy) for hard-headed analysis about the world as it really was. American exceptionalism took many forms, he believed. One of them, unfortunately, expressed itself in the arena of foreign policy where its inclinations were rarely if ever realist, and more often than not driven by a deep moral desire to refashion the world in its own image. The question he wondered was why. He provided several different kinds of explanation.

One dealt with the way America had come into being in the first place. Europe had matured under conditions of extreme insecurity where statesmen had no alternative but to treat foreign policy with the utmost seriousness. America on the other hand had been born security rich from day one. This meant it looked at the world through the eyes of an overconfident teenager who either refused to grow up or was unable to understand the deeper reasons for its very good fortune. Blessed by geography, surrounded by two vast protective oceans, and threatened by nothing more dangerous than Canadians, Mexicans, and fish, the United States, he felt, was almost constitutionally incapable of seeing the world through the same mature lenses as its less fortunate peers across the Atlantic. This lack of awareness was in turn reinforced by something from which the United States very directly benefited but which again Americans invariably failed to recognize or appreciate: the long nineteenth-century peace in Europe and British control of the oceans surrounding its shores. Naturally, this did not mean the United States could not act with great ruthlessness when it wanted to; witness here its conquest and subjugation of the American continent itself. Nor did it get everything wrong. Nevertheless, at the end of the day, there was something strangely inappropriate about such a nation playing a leading role in international affairs when it did not possess (and always seemed unlikely to acquire) the deeper wisdom which the European states had been compelled to attain through sheer practical necessity.[61]

To be fair, Morgenthau did not reject the whole American foreign policy tradition. In fact, he went to great lengths to point out that there had been times when the United States had possessed wisdom in abundance. Unfortunately, any true sagacity it may have once had—which he conceded it had had in the very early years of the republic—it had lost along the way. As he put it in 1951, summing up 150 years of US diplomatic history, 'the classic age of American statecraft came to an end with the disappearance of that generation of American statesmen' like Hamilton and Washington. Thereafter, he sadly concluded, it had been nothing but 'intellectual barrenness and aridity...relieved only by some sparse and neglected oases of insight....'[62] What then passed for foreign policy, he concluded, was not foreign policy at all but 'improvisation', or worse, 'the invocation of some abstract moral principle in whose image the world was to be made over'. He was especially scathing about Woodrow Wilson. Wilson, he believed, was the quintessential idealist in politics, full of good liberal advice for other people—particularly if they happened to be advocates of that dreadful idea of a balance of power—but quite incapable himself of either understanding the complexities and limits of world politics or crafting a mature American foreign policy for the long term. Instead he contented himself with fine words about a new world of freedom that sometimes upset old allies (notably the UK), weakened international order (most obviously through his promotion of the idea of self-determination), and assumed that peace could be built on the basis of brave declarations about a new diplomacy rather than a concrete set of policy measures that recognized the centrality of power.

The result was as catastrophic as it was predictable, for what emerged after the First World War was not a new world order based on careful US calculation about its interests, but a series of symbolic actions that not only did little to address the world's terrible problems but made the situation much worse by giving the impression that one could tackle threats through a series of reforms that had little or nothing to do with power relations on the ground. As Morgenthau learned through bitter personal experience, such gestures cut little ice with those intent on doing wrong.

Morgenthau hoped that America's involvement in the Second World War and its newly acquired post-war responsibilities would help cure the United States of its childish inclinations, quite literally turn it from the youthful Price Hal into the mature Henry the Fifth. Indeed, one of the more obvious reasons for writing *Politics Among Nations*—aside from the more mundane one of making some serious money—was to help instruct the educated American public (including its policymakers) in the true ways of the world; and for a very brief moment it looked as if the US had, after a 150-year detour, returned to the true path of realism. Admittedly there were signs of the old ideological impulses, including, most obviously, Truman's announcement in March 1947 of waging a global crusade against communism. But this, Morgenthau hoped, was a mere bump along the road. Saner voices were bound to prevail. Sadly, however, this is not how things turned out, and as the Cold War intensified and the international situation deteriorated after 1949 and 1950, the moral, and increasingly hysterical, voice of America once again began to drown out the voices of those (like Kennan) who had hitherto pursued a more balanced course.

To make matters worse, domestic politics in the shape of Senator McCarthy began to insert itself more and more into the foreign policy debate. In his view, and that of other kindred sprits at the time, this was little short of disastrous. Most immediately, it made rational discussion about US foreign policy impossible by forcing moderates onto the defensive. More seriously, it tended to reinforce the already strong American inclination of discussing international relations as if it were some giant international morality play, with the forces of good represented by the United States situated on one side of the barricade, and the forces of evil represented by the USSR, Red China, and communism standing on the other. This, he felt, was not only dubious analytically; it was also potentially dangerous from a policy perspective. Morgenthau might not have always kept a level head when it came to thinking about the USSR. But it was one thing to be momentarily alarmed by the growth of Soviet power, as he most evidently was during the second half of the 1950s. It was quite another to assume that the whole world was now confronted by the equivalent of a worldwide pandemic that could only be combated by the United States going global. Such an undifferentiated approach, he reasoned, not only challenged the balanced logic upon which realism was based. It also threatened to turn the United States into the world's counter-revolutionary policeman. This, he believed, was bound to have undesirable results, especially in that one part of the world where the Cold War would in the end be decided: namely, in the Third World.[63]

First and foremost, it would place the United States on the defensive by compelling it to dance to a tune played by others rather than one of its own composition. It would also draw it into situations where it could easily be manipulated by undemocratic elites who only had to cry 'communism' in order to receive large-scale US backing. This, he argued, would not only weaken US credibility by making it appear overly reactive but also draw it into conflicts it could just as easily have ignored. It might also transform it into the bastion of reaction everywhere. Indeed, if it looked to many in the Third World (as it was bound to) that the United States was not simply engaged in the containment of the USSR but in the support of what they (and Morgenthau) regarded as an unsustainable status quo, this would be politically disastrous, for it would place the United States in the strategically dangerous position of underwriting unpopular regimes that might one day be overthrown. More seriously still, it would hand Moscow a major weapon in the wider Cold War by making it, and not the United States, look like the champion of progressive change. On this Morgenthau was adamant. America, he believed, had to win the hearts and minds of peoples once exploited by the European colonial powers. However, it could not achieve this by defending the indefensible, especially in an age of revolutionary change.

Morgenthau of course was no bleeding heart liberal when it came to thinking about the Third World and its future. He had little time for many of its more anti-western leaders, many of whom he regarded as little more than demagogues. And he never espoused the fashionable Third World notion of dependency. The only way forward for the former colonial countries he believed was to become more closely associated with the West.

Nor was he opposed to a little subversion in those places—like Cuba— where, he believed, there was something at stake. Morgenthau was no anti-imperialist. What concerned him though was not the measured use of American power where necessary, but rather its indiscriminate expenditure, especially in situations where the United States might not have a vital interest. Herein lay the big difference between himself and those who advocated what he saw as an irresponsible globalism. For Morgenthau, there simply had to be some objective way of knowing how to act and where; and of deciding when to act and for what precise purpose. For those whom he criticized with increasing bitterness, all of these subtle calculations looked like so much academic nitpicking. No less than the great globe itself was under threat they argued; thus America had to respond accordingly from South America to Africa, from the Middle East to the far corners of the Asian continent. For Morgenthau such recklessness, bordering on the strategically promiscuous, was likely to come back to haunt the US. One day Americans would be compelled to pay a very heavy price indeed for having failed to act with greater circumspection. As we now know it did not have to pay that price in the 1950s, in an era of *Pax Americana*. However, the day of reckoning did in the end arrive, in the shape of Vietnam.

7.3. **Vietnam: America's 'Sicilian expedition'**

Though Morgenthau made his reputation as a successful academic, public intellectual and popular writer long before the 1960s, it was to be his critique of US policy towards Vietnam that thrust him into the political limelight. It was not a role he necessarily sought. Nor did he always feel entirely comfortable with some of the more radical allies with whom he was later compelled to work alongside. Yet by sheer persistence married to an integrity that was then rare in the American academic community, he very quickly emerged as one of 'America's main critics of the Vietnam War'.[64] Nor was he some late convert to the anti-war cause. As has been scrupulously documented elsewhere, he began to articulate a position long before it was fashionable or politically safe to do so.[65] In fact, at least a decade before most Cold War liberals and their establishment allies had begun to question American intervention in South-East Asia (even then it took the disaster that was 1968 to convince them to come out against the war), Morgenthau had already been building a reasoned case against American foreign policy.[66]

For Morgenthau, the specific issue of Vietnam could not be isolated from the problem of the US role in Asia more generally. Here, Morgenthau argued for a middle path between intelligent engagement and indiscriminate intervention. As a keen supporter of the United States he had no trouble of course in supporting a close American relationship with Japan and South Korea. Nor did he oppose the firm containment of communist China. What concerned him was less America's ability to contain China as a state—China after all was light years behind the United States in terms of capabilities—and more a fear that it would seek to deal with the revolutionary threat posed by the Maoist regime in much the same way as it had successfully dealt with the USSR in Europe after the Marshall Plan: by trying to build the Asian equivalent of NATO.

This was a theme he returned to time and again. In Europe, he argued the United States had been confronted by the very direct presence of the Soviet Union whose ambitions it had sought to contain (successfully in his view) by building a close military partnership with its principle allies. In Asia, this approach could and would not work—in part because the threat was never really military in character (thus military alliances were beside the point), and in part because one of the principle causes of disorder in the region was the very European powers with whom the United States happened to be allied. As Morgenthau was quick to point out, whereas a close relationship with friends in Europe made a good deal of sense on the old continent, it made a good deal less in those parts of the world where the Europeans were seen as being part of the problem rather than contributing to the solution. Moreover, to act as if answers drawn from one set of circumstances made very much sense in another could only end in political tears. As he later noted, what had been a great success in advanced Europe after the Second World War could easily turn (and ultimately did) into a 'dismal failure' when applied to Asia.[67]

Morgenthau also raised an even more difficult issue for US foreign policymakers dealing with Asia: namely how to adjust to a dynamic revolutionary process whose primary driving force was not communism as such but a nationalism directed against the West. This was a conundrum like no other, and Morgenthau, typically, asked the tough questions and came up with what to many must have sounded like a deeply radical answer. There was no getting away from the problem: revolution was a 'foregone conclusion' in Asia he felt.[68] The United States could thus adopt one of three positions towards it—ignore it entirely (impossible), oppose it completely (unsustainable), or move with the times (the position he actually advocated). This, however, was not a course of action likely to recommend itself to a Washington elite who saw the hand of the USSR in nearly everything going on in the Third World. They were even less likely to go along with an even more revisionist thought occasionally advanced by Morgenthau: namely, that the success of communism in some states on the periphery did not necessarily challenge America's interest. As Morgenthau always insisted, it was not an ideology that represented the real threat to international order in the post-war period but one very large, militarily capable state in the form of the Soviet Union. Communist revolutions in backward Asian countries might work to Russia's benefit. But then again they might not. In fact, as the example of Yugoslavia had already proved (and the split between the USSR and China later showed) communists who came to power under their own steam could just as easily turn out to be a liability rather than an asset for Moscow.

Morgenthau's bold thinking on Asia and the Asian revolution did not of course win him very many friends in a United States grown used to viewing communism through a simplified monolithic lens. Nor did it do much to influence official thinking on Vietnam, a country which he visited for the first time in 1955. From the outset he was none too impressed with Washington's performance. Having too readily committed itself to the dictator Diem (a classic example if ever there was one of a ruler and regime that managed to survive by constantly playing the communist card) the United States went on to commit one predictable mistake after another, finally culminating in the large-scale escalation of 1965. In the process, America was also compelled to be increasingly 'economic with the truth'. Thus, instead of admitting that it faced an all-Vietnamese insurgency, it insisted that the war was the result of a North Vietnamese attack upon the integrity of the sovereign state of South Vietnam. To hide the fact that it had little or no chance of winning, it then talked up its own successes while all the time claiming that victory lay just around the corner. Finally, to make matters worse, it tried to sell the whole thing on the basis of a bad theory that asserted—without ever having to prove—that if one domino fell in Vietnam they were bound to fall everywhere else as well.[69]

Unsurprisingly, by the middle of the 1960s Morgenthau found himself opposed to a war waged in what he regarded as an insignificant country by a foreign policy establishment who should have known better. However, none of this made the slightest difference; and as the war intensified, the more bitter the debate about it became at home. This had serious consequences for Morgenthau himself. Up until now at least he had been something of a lone voice whose various warnings had appeared in small circulation magazines like *The New Republic.* Now he was to become an important voice in an increasingly public debate. As a result, he began to draw down fire upon himself, partly from those on the political left who believed his critique did not go far enough, and partly (and more significantly) from enemies in the pro-war establishment who saw him as providing just a little too much respectable cover for those of a more critical persuasion. The Johnson administration even set up an operation of its own (suitably entitled 'Project Morgenthau') in an effort to discredit his position, while pro-war advocates within his own professional association made sure that he never became president of the American Political Science Association.[70] Morgenthau responded in typically robust fashion, most obviously by going on to the offensive himself. In May 1965, for instance, he was a key speaker at the first national teach-in on the war organized in Washington; a month later he participated in a live televised debate with one of the doyens of the Johnson administration, McGeorge Bundy. He also introduced a distinctly non-realist note into his critique. Hitherto he had attacked the war on the largely instrumental grounds that involvement in Vietnam was not only misconceived and unnecessary (the loss of Vietnam in his view would not have made one jot of difference to the balance of power) but was also doing more damage than good to America's prestige in the world. Now he inserted an increasingly moral tone into what he said. The war, he now began to argue in ways 'seemingly at odds with his realist perspective', was not merely unwise and ill-advised but unjust, genocidal, and possibly even motivated by a racist disdain for Asians.[71] Nor was this a momentary lapse. Indeed, not long after the war had come to an end, he was talking quite openly of the war not just as a war that betrayed the fundamentals of realism—one that bore 'very slight relation to reality' to use his own words—but as being 'the prototype of an unjust war', one moreover that had betrayed America's core idealism![72]

Morgenthau's new found edge was at least one tiny seismic measure of the profoundly disturbing impact that Vietnam was to have upon American intellectual discourse in the late sixties and seventies. As Morgenthau later conceded, the war did not just provoke a debate about foreign policy but caused profound social and political disintegration within the United States itself.[73] This is one of the reasons why Morgenthau often sounded so sympathetic to the new left. They were less threat and more symptom of diseased times, he believed, and as such should be treated with a degree of tolerance. Yet there were limits. Engaging with the new left was one thing: accepting their analysis of the war or their radical (and in his opinion utopian) answers to the world's problems was something else altogether. It was perfectly reasonable to critique American foreign policy. It was not reasonable however to think that the US was the principle source of the world's main problems. Furthermore, if there was a lesson to be learned, it was not that the international order had to be refashioned, but rather that American leaders would have to act in the future with less arrogance than they had displayed hitherto. This would not have made the war worthwhile. Nothing ever could. But if it produced a more balanced, nuanced, American approach to international politics in an age of revolution, then at least some good might have come of the whole sorry debacle in South-East Asia.

7.4. **The lessons of Morgenthau**

I began this essay with the end of the Cold War and the attack launched against realism because of its apparent failure either to explain or to anticipate the system's peaceful collapse between 1989 and 1991. I continued by then suggesting that the relationship between Morgenthau's realism and the Cold War raises a series of difficult questions for those who assume a simple identity between realism and US foreign policy after 1947. I will end now with some brief reflections and ask what, if anything, students of IR can learn from engaging with Morgenthau's analysis of the Cold War.

The first thing they should learn perhaps is to take greater care when making sweeping generalizations about the relationship between a certain theoretical discourse and real world events. As I hope to have shown here— and as others have shown elsewhere—the relationship between realism as a set of ideas and the 'real world' after 1947 was never straightforward.[74] At one level the critics are right: realism obviously did aim to provide some sort of road map for those in power. To this extent the truth it expounded was the truth of a very particular kind. But to serve power well, it also had to do far more: namely, warn those with power about the problems that would inevitably arise if they deployed the power they had without due care and attention. Hence, by definition it had to be critical. It also had to be objective, to tell the 'truth', even when the truth hurt or made the bearer of bad tidings deeply unpopular with those who did not want to hear what was being said to them.[75] No doubt critical theorists will argue (and have done for some time) that this still means that realism—even in the capable and informed hands of a Morgenthau—was and remains problem-solving; that at the end of the day it was and remains compromised by its very purpose of trying to be useful to those in the policy-world. There may be something to this. Still, those who have adopted this line must explain why Morgenthau, the founding father of American realism, managed to say so much that was obviously not acceptable to those in power. They must also come to terms with the fact that the source of this tension was the same realism which they believe made it impossible for him to be critical in the first place. Morgenthau may still not be critical enough for some analysts. On the other hand, he was not quite the establishment mouthpiece his opponents have sometimes made him out to be.

The second issue raised here relates to the evolution of IR as a field after the Cold War. Many of those who attacked realism in the wake of the quite unexpected end of the Cold War, did, without doubt, score a number of powerful hits against an edifice that had once seemed impregnable. They also did much to reinvigorate the discipline. However, they did so in such a way that seemed to cast realism (quite unnecessarily) in the role of enemy 'other' that had to be dealt a death blow before the discipline could move forward again.[76] This, I would suggest, has had some very unfortunate consequences. Most obviously, it has meant that the history of realism in the Cold War has not been very well studied in all of its complexity. Indeed, what has passed for its history amongst some writers at least has been more straw man than the real thing. Second, the constant attacks on realism have also had the unfortunate result of marginalizing certain ways of thinking about international politics. Some no doubt will say this is all to the good. However, it has had its downside, the most obvious one being the almost total neglect of various kinds of materialist explanation. It is no coincidence of course that those discourses in IR, that have been most popular since the end of the Cold War, have been precisely those that have stressed ideas and subjectivity rather than brute facts such as power. There will be those who will applaud such a move. However, it does leave IR open to the serious charge that it has little to say about a world in which power still remains unequally distributed and where policymakers themselves continue to think about the international system in largely realist terms. Indeed, it is no coincidence that as IR has apparently retreated from realism, the 'discipline' (if discipline it should now be called) has virtually become a no-go area for practitioners and policymakers themselves. Again, this may be no bad thing. Detached after all is what true academics are supposed to be. But it is one thing being detached. It is something else altogether when one becomes so far removed from 'reality' that one looks to be living on another planet.

This brings us then to what Morgenthau might have said about the world after the end of the Cold War itself. There is no way of knowing, to be sure. However, one suspects that he would have been more than a little concerned about two things. First and most obviously, he would have been less than impressed with the renewal of interest in international liberal thinking during the 1990s. It is certainly difficult to think of him being much taken with democratic peace theory or the notion that globalization and international institutions taken together would be able to eliminate the underlying urge to power among states. One also must assume that he would have been more than a little worried too about the obvious lack of balance in the new international system. As Richard Little argues in his own chapter to this book, Morgenthau's own theory of the balance of power was by no means consistent. That said, he still believed that it was necessary to the maintenance of some form of global equilibrium, and that without it, all sorts of problems would likely flow, including (as we have witnessed over the past few years) a growing tendency by an apparently unchecked hegemon under conditions of unipolarity to assert itself more forcefully.

In fact, as Mearsheimer has argued, precisely because Morgenthau was in the last analysis a thinker who 'valued prudence' and feared 'big-stick diplomacy', he would have had great difficulty in coming to terms with the recent imperial turn in US foreign policy. It is certainly hard to think of Morgenthau being a fan of George W. Bush.[77]

Which leads us lastly to the Iraq War, without doubt the most crucial foreign policy decision taken by the United States since the end of the Cold War. Again one can only speculate. Nonetheless, given Morgenthau's more general concern about US interventions in the Third World, it is difficult to think of him supporting the decision to take military action against Saddam.[78] Wars should not be entered into lightly he believed; quite the opposite: they should only be undertaken if there was either no other choice or there was a direct threat to the United States itself. One should not fight wars of choice, as many realists (often citing Morgenthau in their defence) have insisted upon since 2002. Indeed, one of the more interesting developments since Bush assumed office is a renaissance of interest in Morgenthau, brought about in large part because one of his core arguments—that states should only undertake actions abroad that were clearly in their national interest—is one that seems to fit the Iraqi case so well.[79] If nothing else, this renewed engagement with one of the doyens of realism seems to prove that there is still a good deal of life left in a set of ideas whose obituary has so often been written in the past.[80] Even so, realists were no more successful in convincing Bush and his team about the dangers of going into Iraq, than Morgenthau was in trying to persuade Kennedy and Johnson about the serious implications of becoming embroiled in Vietnam. As Morgenthau found out then—and his successors are discovering now—one can try and talk 'truth' to power, but there is no guarantee that the powerful will listen.

NOTES

1. The most useful collection of historical essays on the end of the Cold War remains Olav Njolstad (ed.), *The Last Decade of the Cold War: From Conflict Escalation to Conflict Transformation* (London: Frank Cass, 2004). For an IR perspective see Nick Bisley, *The End of the Cold War and the Causes of Soviet Collapse* (Basingstoke: Macmillan, 2004).

2. John Mearsheimer, 'Back to the Future: Instability in Europe after the Cold War', *International Security*, 15: 1 (1990), 5–56.

3. Robert Keohane, 'International Relations, Old and New', in R. E. Goodin and H. D. Klingerman (eds.), *A New Handbook of Political Science* (Oxford: Oxford University Press, 1996), 463–4.

4. Michael Cox (ed.), *Rethinking the Soviet Collapse: Sovietology, the Death of Communism and the New Russia* (London: Pinter/Cassell, 1998).

5. Egbert Jahn, 'The Future of Europe, Eastern Europe and Central Europe', in Ronald J. Hill and Jan Zielonka (eds.), *Restructuring Eastern Europe: Towards a New European Order* (Aldershot: Edward Elgar, 1990), 203–18.

6. John Lewis Gaddis, 'International Relations Theory and the End of the Cold War', *International Security*, 17: 3 (Winter 1992/3), 5–58.

7. See Pierre Allan and Kjell Goldmann (eds.), *The End of the Cold War: Evaluating Theories of International Relations* (Dordrecht: Martinus Nijhoff, 1992).

8. See Brian C. Schmidt, 'Realism as Tragedy', *Review of International Studies*, 30 (2004), 428–31 especially.

9. Robert D. English, *Russia and the Idea of the West: Gorbachev, Intellectuals and the End of the Cold War* (New York: Columbia University Press, 2000).

10. Kenneth N. Waltz, *Theory of International Politics* (Reading, MA: Addison Wesley, 1979).

11. Jeffrey W. Legro and Andrew Moravcsik, 'Is Anybody Still a Realist?', *International Security*, 24: 2 (1999), 5–55.

12. Richard Ned Lebow and Thomas Risse-Kappen (eds.), *International Relations Theory and the End of The Cold War* (New York: Columbia University Press, 1995).

13. For a robust defence of realism see William C. Wohlforth, 'Realism and the End of the Cold War', *International Security*, 19: 3 (1994/5), 91–129.

14. Sean Molloy, *The Hidden History of Realism: A Genealogy of Power Politics* (New York: Palgrave, Macmillan, 2006).

15. Kjell Goldman, 'Introduction: Three Debates about the End of the Cold War', in Pierre Allan and Kjell Goldman (eds.), *The End of the Cold War*, 9–10.

16. See, for example, Jim George, *Discourses of Global Politics: A Critical (Re)Introduction to International Relations* (Boulder, CO: Lynne Rienner, 1994).

17. Michael C. Williams, *The Realist Tradition and the Limits of International Relations* (Cambridge: Cambridge University Press, 2005), 82.

18. Morgenthau recalled much later that 'after publication of *Politics Among Nations*, I became well known in academic and government circles in the United States, and from 1949 to 1951 I was active as a consultant to the State Department and more particularly to the Policy Planning Board. This was primarily through the attention George Kennan paid me.' Cited in Kenneth Thompson and Robert J. Mayers (eds.), *Truth and Tragedy: A Tribute to Hans J. Morgenthau* (New Brunswick, NJ and London: Transaction Books, 1984), 372.

19. 'Until 1965 it was relatively easy for the Department of State and Department of Defense to claim Morgenthau as one of their own.' Marcus Raskin, 'The Idealism of a Realist', in Thompson and Mayers (eds.), *Truth and Tragedy*, 87.

20. As one admirer notes, as early as 1951, following publication of his *In Defense of the National Interest*, many began to see in Morgenthau a 'voice of rationality' ... 'amidst the Cold War hysteria'. See Richard J. Barnet, 'In Search of the National Interest', in Thompson and Mayers (eds.), *Truth and Tragedy*, 153.

21. 'A nation can try to obtain its international objectives in three ways: it can go to war; it can bring overwhelming power to bear upon its opponents; or it can negotiate for a settlement. Spokesmen in our government have sometimes believed in a fourth way: the cold war with a minimum of relations between East and West and with the issue of peace and war hanging in the balance, lasting perhaps for a generation. This possibility is so extremely unlikely as to be no real possibility at all.' Hans J. Morgenthau, *In Defense of the National Interest: A Critical Examination of American Foreign Policy* (New York: Knopf, 1951), 139.

22. Alfons Sollner, 'German Conservatism in America: Morgenthau's Political Realism', *Telos*, 72 (Summer 1987), 161–77.

23. Hans J. Morgenthau, 'A Political Theory of Foreign Aid', *American Political Science Review*, 56: 2 (1962), 301–9.

24. For example John J. Mearsheimer, *The Tragedy of Great Power Politics* (New York: W.W. Norton, 2001).

25. As Richard Little notes in his chapter (quoting Morgenthau) it was the 'periphery of world politics' during the Cold War that was to become 'one of the main theatres, where the struggle between the two superpowers' was 'being fought out in terms of control of territory and men's minds'. Hans J. Morgenthau, *Politics Among Nations; The Struggle for Power and Peace*, 5th edn. (New York: Knopf, 1973), 355.

26. This subtitle is derived from the study written by Hannah Arendt, a contemporary close to Morgenthau whose work influenced him enormously. See her *Men In Dark Times* (London: Jonathan Cape, 1970).

27. Greg Russell, *Hans J. Morgenthau and the Ethics of American Statecraft* (Baton Rouge, LA: Louisiana State University Press, 1990).

28. Christoph Frei, *Hans J. Morgenthau: An Intellectual Biography* (Baton Rouge, LA: Louisiana State University Press, 2001).

29. On the German philosophical influences on Morgenthau see Tarak Barkawi, 'Strategy as Vocation: Weber, Morgenthau and Modern Strategic Studies', *Review of International Studies*, 24: 2 (1998), 159–84, and Hans-Karl Pichler, 'The Godfathers of Truth: Max Weber and Carl Schmitt in Morgenthau's Theory of Power Politics', *Review of International Studies*, 24: 2 (1998), 185–200.

30. See Brian C. Schmidt, 'Competing Realist Conceptions of Power', *Millennium*, 33: 3 (2005), 532.

31. See Martti Koskenniemi, *The Gentle Civilizer of Nations: The Rise and Fall of International Law, 1870–1960* (Cambridge: Cambridge University Press, 2001), 460.

32. In an important (but little referred to) work that he wrote in 1940 for the American Philosophical Society, Morgenthau argued that a 'liberal foreign policy' when applied to 'the international scene where the conditions are largely absent to which liberalism owes its victories in the domestic field' would jeopardize 'the very survival of liberalism in the domestic field'. Cited in Jonathan Haslam, *No Virtue Like Necessity: Realist Thought In International Relations Since Machiavelli* (New Haven, CT: Yale University Press, 2002), 194.

33. Fifteen years after the end of the Second World War Morgenthau observed: 'Had the United States been aware of the nature of the political world that it was to enter at the end of the Second World War, it would have bent every effort . . . to keep the Red Army as far east as possible. Had it done this, West Berlin would not have become an island in a red sea, Czechoslovakia would not be a Russian satellite, and the Red Army would not stand a hundred miles from the Rhine. The United States did not do this because it was so anxious to live in an apolitical environment of security and reasonable harmony.' *The Purpose of American Politics* (New York: Knopf, 1960), 131.

34. See Robert Jervis, 'Hans Morgenthau, Realism, and the Scientific Study of International Politics', *Social Research*, 64: 4 (1994), 854.

35. This is brought out in Gregory Eckstein, 'Hans Morgenthau: A Personal Memoir', *Social Research*, 48: 4 (1981), 642, 648 especially.

36. See Hans J. Morgenthau's critical but still highly favourable review of Carr's work, 'The Political Science of E.H. Carr', in *World Politics*, 1: 1 (1948), 127–34.

37. Richard Ned Lebow, *The Tragic Vision of Politics: Ethics, Interests and Orders* (Cambridge: Cambridge University Press, 2003), 222–3.

38. On the impact of Germany's collapse in the 1930s on his later thinking see J. Honig, 'Totalitarianism and Realism: Hans J. Morgenthau's German Years', *Security Studies*, 5: 2 (1995), 283–313.

39. On the importance of the irrational in politics see Morgenthau's *Scientific Man versus Power Politics* (Chicago, IL: Chicago University Press, 1946).

40. On Morgenthau's admiration for Dean Acheson see Vojtech Mastny (ed.), *Power and Policy in Transition* (Westport, CT: Greenwood Press, 1984), 1.

41. Hans J. Morgenthau, 'The Mainsprings of American Foreign Policy: The National Interest versus Moral Abstractions', *American Political Science Review*, XLIV: 4 (1950), 833–54.

42. See Jervis, 'Hans Morgenthau, Realism, and the Scientific Study of International Politics', 854.

43. Hans J. Morgenthau, 'Justice and Power', *Social Research*, 41: 1 (1974), 163.

44. Morgenthau is recorded as saying: 'You see, for Marx, what we call human nature is a product of society. But I would say, society is a product of human nature.' He continued: 'If you look at the Old Testament or Greek mythology, you see the same attributes in man that we see in him today.' Quoted in Hans J. Morgenthau, *Political Theory and International Affairs*, ed. Anthony F. Lang, Jr. (London: Praeger, 2004), 65–6.

45. Morgenthau called Niebuhr 'the greatest political philosopher of his time'. See his 'The Influence of Reinhold Niebuhr in American Political Life and Thought', in Harold R. Landon (ed.), *Reinhold Niebuhr: A Prophetic Voice in Our Time* (Greenwich, CT: Seabury Press, 1962), 109. According to Tjborn L. Knutsen, Niebuhr provided the 'moral foundation for the new realist approach' to world politics after the Second World War. Morgenthau then 'drew out the International Relations implications of Niebuhr's writings'. See his *A History of International Relations Theory* (Manchester: Manchester University Press, 1997), 241.

46. See Michael Cox, 'George F. Kennan: Requiem for a Cold War Critic, 1945–1950', *Irish Slavonic Studies*, 11 (1990–1991), 1–35.

47. It was through Morgenthau that Kennan was able to deliver a series of lectures at the University of Chicago (Morgenthau's university) that were later published under the title *American Diplomacy, 1900–1950* (Chicago, IL: University of Chicago Press, 1951).

48. See his comment on 'Russian Power' in his 1957 essay 'The Fortieth Anniversary of the Bolshevist Revolution', in his edited collection, *The Impasse of American Foreign Policy* (Chicago, IL: University of Chicago Press, 1962), 139–42.

49. *The Purpose of American Politics*, 132.

50. For a fine analysis and critique of Morgenthau's views on war in the late 1950s see Campbell Craig, *Glimmer of a New Leviathan: Total War in the Realism of Niebuhr, Morgenthau and Waltz* (New York: Columbia University Press, 2003), 98–101 especially.

51. See Greg Russell, 'Science, Technology and Death in the Nuclear Age: Hans J. Morgenthau on Nuclear Ethics', *Ethics and International Affairs*, 5 (1991), 115–34.

52. Hans J. Morgenthau, *A New Foreign Policy for the United States* (London: Pall Mall Press, 1969), 76.

53. Hans J. Morgenthau, 'The Pathology of American Power', *International Security*, 1: 3 (1977), 6.

54. Morgenthau, 'The Pathology of American Power', 12.

55. Hans J. Morgenthau, 'Changes and Chances in American–Soviet Relations', *Foreign Affairs*, 49: 3 (1971), 429–41.

56. See his 'The Pathology of American Power' for his views on US decline after the 1960s.

57. Significantly, Morgenthau berated the Vietnam War critic William J. Fulbright in 1970 for being 'dangerously naïve concerning the threat posed by the Soviet Union and Communist China'. Quoted in Randall Bennett, *Fulbright: A Biography* (New York: Cambridge University Press, 1995), 577.

58. Over twenty years after publishing his classic *Politics Among Nations*, Morgenthau was still repeating the old mantra that: 'The United States has one primary national interest in its relations with other nations; the security of its territory and institutions', *A New Foreign Policy for the United States*, 241.

59. Subtitle adapted from Joel Rosenthal, *Righteous Realists: Political Realism, Responsible Power and the Nuclear Age* (Louisiana State University Press, 1991).

60. See Kenneth W. Thompson, 'The Cold War: The Legacy of Morgenthau's Approach', *Social Research*, 48: 4 (1981), 676.

61. For Morgenthau's views on American history, see in particular his *The Purpose of American Politics* (New York: Knopf, 1960).

62. Morgenthau, *In Defense of the National Interest*, 3–4.

63. For scholarly confirmation of Morgenthau's assessment of the importance of the Third World, see Odd Arne Westad, *The Global Cold War: Third World Interventions and the Making of Our Times* (Cambridge: Cambridge University Press, 2005).

64. Kenneth W. Thompson, *Masters of International Thought: Major Twentieth Century Thinkers and the World Crisis* (Baton Rouge, LA: Louisiana State University Press, 1980), 86.

65. Jennifer W. See, 'A Prophet Without Honour: Hans Morgenthau and the War on Vietnam, 1955–1965', *Pacific Historical Review*, 70: 3 (2000), 419–47.

66. It is thus inaccurate to suggest that Morgenthau only jumped political ship and discovered the Vietnam War in 1965 or 1966, only after the New Left had escalated their own protests. See Robert Buzanco, *Vietnam and the Transformation of American Life* (Oxford: Blackwell, 1999), 96–7.

67. See his 'We are Deluding Ourselves in Vietnam', *New York Times Magazine*, 18 April 1965.

68. Quoted from Morgenthau's 1955 essay 'The Revolution We are Living Through', in *The Impasse of American Foreign Policy*, 249.

69. See Hans J. Morgenthau, *Vietnam and the United States* (Washington, DC: Public Affairs Press, 1965), 38–42.

70. Richard Ned Lebow in his *The Tragic Vision of Politics: Ethics, Interests and Orders* (Cambridge: Cambridge University Press, 2003), 240.

71. Jennifer W. See, 'A Prophet Without Honour', 442–3.

72. See Hans J. Morgenthau, 'The Lessons of Vietnam', in John H. Gilbert (ed.), *The New Era In American Foreign Policy* (New York: St Martin's Press, 1973), 15, 17.

73. Morgenthau, 'The Lessons of Vietnam', 18.

74. See also Michael C. Williams, 'Why Ideas Matter in International Relations: Hans Morgenthau, Classical Realism and the Moral Construction of Power Politics', *International Organization*, 58: 4 (2004), 633–66.

75. As Kenneth Thompson has noted of Morgenthau: 'It mattered not whether the statesman whose policies he discussed was friend or foe.' Cited in Mastny, *Power And Policy in Transition*, 1.

76. For an excellent defence of classical realism against some of its would-be postmodern critics, see William Bain, 'Deconfusing Morgenthau: Moral Inquiry and Classical Realism Reconsidered', *Review of International Studies*, 26: 3 (2000), 445–64.

77. John Mearsheimer, 'Hans Morgenthau and the Iraq war: Realism versus Neo-Conservatism'. http://www.opendemocracy. Accessed on 19 May 2006.

78. According to one analyst, George W. Bush ignored Morgenthau's basic principles of foreign policy on nine counts when it came to Iraq. See Karl E. Meyer, 'Weighing Iraq on Morgenthau's Scale', *World Policy Journal*, 20: 3 (2003), 89–92.

79. Tim Dunne and Brian Schmidt, 'Realism', in John Baylis and Steve Smith (eds.), *The Globalization of World Politics: An Introduction to International Relations*, 3rd edn. (Oxford: Oxford University Press, 2005), 177–9 especially.

80. Stefano Guzzini, *Realism in International Relations and International Political Economy* (London and New York: Routledge, 1998).

8 Hans Morgenthau and the world state revisited

Campbell Craig

A basic paradox runs through Hans Morgenthau's conception of the world state, at least in his writings after 1955 or so.[1] His realist critique of international idealism is at its most devastating when it comes to existing plans and hopes for the construction of world government; yet at the same time Morgenthau suggests that the advent of nuclear weapons has made the nation state obsolete and world government necessary for human survival. The sentiment he most ruthlessly dismisses becomes the sentiment required to prevent species extinction.

In his 1965 *World Politics* article 'Hans Morgenthau and the World State' James Speer II discerned this paradox, attributing it to deep inconsistencies in Morgenthau's political philosophy. This chapter affirms Speer's pioneering analysis. But it goes beyond it, attempting to explain the reasons for Morgenthau's inconsistency by placing his paradoxical conceptions of the world state within a historical context. Morgenthau's odd attitude towards the world state did not arise only from a general intellectual confusion that can be understood abstractly, without reference to time or place. It arose primarily from his struggle to contend philosophically with the advent of the thermonuclear revolution in the late 1950s and early 1960s, from his inability to reconcile his core ideas with radically changing material circumstances. The likely consequences of thermonuclear war led Morgenthau towards conclusions that seemed to demand a renunciation of traditional state-centred realism and an advocacy of an immediate world state. As an American scholar with an immense, hard-earned intellectual influence by the middle of the 1950s, however, Morgenthau was not in an easy position to renounce the foreign policy worldview that defined his international reputation. This chapter is an account of the intellectual struggle that ensued.

8.1. The impossibility of a world state in Morgenthau's realism

During the late 1940s Morgenthau advanced a bleak vision of international politics to his new American audience. Hoping to shock his readers out of their long-standing optimism about world politics, Morgenthau developed a political philosophy in his book *Scientific Man versus Power Politics* and a praxeology of foreign policy and International politics in his book *Politics Among Nations* that presented a pessimistic vision of human nature and its manifestation at the international level. Man is a power-hungry creature who satisfies his cravings via the rapacious state. International relations constitute the collision of these rapacious states, in the form of amoral diplomacy or, eventually, actual warfare. A foreign policy developed by 'scientific' men aiming to reform and ameliorate these collisions is doomed to failure, as this simply makes their states easier to conquer by other states that remain brutal and militaristic. Morgenthau pressed these points home at length, with thorough reference to the history and practice of foreign policy, in his epochal work *Politics Among Nations*, the first edition of which was published in 1948.[2]

The comprehensive, even exhaustive nature of *Politics Among Nations* allowed Morgenthau to convey his ideas to several different target audiences. Some of the writing seemed aimed at aspiring diplomats, some at undergraduates new to the subject, some at American policymakers. But at the heart of the book, as of all classic texts, was a basic intellectual argument, made again and again, in various guises.

American statesmen and scholars had been trying to reform international politics since the eighteenth century. Many such reforms, and in particular those advanced in the twentieth century, were based upon the presumption that the anarchical ferocity of international politics could be ameliorated—much as the crudeness of the American political system at home had been reformed and improved after the Civil War.

In dismantling this presumption, Morgenthau drew upon the core idea already advanced by other realists such as E. H. Carr and Reinhold Niebuhr,

that the anarchical nature of international politics made it less susceptible to reform and improvement than the hierarchical nature of domestic
politics.[3] Working from this general proposition, Morgenthau postulated
a simple binary for great power foreign policy. A great power has two
choices in facing its destiny. It can accept the reigning political condition
and adopt a balance-of-power foreign policy; this entails an acceptance
of international anarchy and, therefore, of eventual major war. Or, it can
attempt to abolish international politics, not by improving and reforming
its existing nature but by creating a genuine world state—to put it another
way, by eliminating international anarchy. The alternative between balance
of power and a serious world state was the only one any great power hoping
to survive should consider. Halfway measures—such as the existing UN
Security Council—were ineffective, representing not only an unwillingness
to face up to the demands of international politics but also courting real
danger, in so far as a nominal world state such as the UN might encourage
states to drop their guard.[4]

Morgenthau pointed to this danger because he had good reason to
worry that Americans would gravitate towards such halfway measures in
their post-war foreign policy. The United States had historically rejected
balance-of-power politics, in part because of American cultural rejection
of European political amorality, but also because of the poor performance,
to say the least, of this diplomatic tradition during the first half of the
twentieth century. Morgenthau, like many other observers, believed that
this sentiment would tempt Americans to pursue some kind of alternative
to the old world system responsible for the carnage of 1914–45, a suspicion
confirmed by the widespread popularity of the United Nations Organization in early post-war America.

As we shall see, Morgenthau was himself not totally unsympathetic to
this American view, particularly in an age of total war. But in 1948, he
believed that a world state was absolutely unattainable, especially in a world
dominated by the United States and the Soviet Union. Taking his role as
public intellectual seriously, Morgenthau concluded that it was necessary
to emphasize this opinion to his more idealistic compatriots, to focus
intensively upon the impossibility of world government, lest they become
enchanted with world government, pursue it in lieu of a balance of power,
and end up committed to a toothless international organization vulnerable
to the domination of a cynical and militaristic state.

Morgenthau's case against the world state in the first edition of *Politics Among Nations* was based upon both conceptual and practical grounds. A world state was presently an impossibility first because there existed no transnational community to speak of that would pledge its allegiance to a global government rather than national ones. National states possessed what Morgenthau, borrowing from earlier political philosophers, defined as three essential attributes of a genuine state: a monopoly over organized violence; loyalty from its citizens that outweighed other sectional or ethnic loyalties; and the ability to provide some degree of impartial justice to all citizens, in the absence of which they would transfer their loyalty to other sections or groups.

Any world state that might be conceived of in 1948 could not possibly claim such attributes. For a world state to undertake the vast task of seizing war-making weaponry from all national states, it would have to persuade large sections of the world's population that it deserved their loyalty rather than their previous national government, and that it could provide them with a reliable form of justice that their previous nations could not. On the probabilities of this happening Morgenthau writes:

Under the present moral conditions of mankind, few men would act on behalf of a world government if the interests of their nation would require a different course of action. On the contrary, the overwhelming majority would put the welfare of their own nation above everything else, the interests of a world state included. ... The odds are to such an extent in favor of the nation that men who might be willing and able to sacrifice and die that the world state be kept standing do not even have the opportunity to do so in the world as it is constituted today.[5]

Morgenthau's initial rejection of the world state is both compelling and methodologically inconsistent. His iteration of the obstacles to its formation is so formidable that it is difficult for the reader to avoid being swept away by it. He partakes of John Stuart Mill's 'three-part' test for the possibilities of political action: any world state must take possession of all three of the necessary state functions to succeed, yet under 'present moral conditions' the advocates of such a state are nowhere close even to seizing one of them. To create a world state, planetary revolutionaries would have to attract the loyalty of a large percentage of the world's population, persuade them that they would be able to provide reliable justice beyond what their original nation could provide, and then use this mandate somehow to take control of all large states and their weaponry. In 1948, it was not difficult for Morgenthau to assess that the odds of them even beginning to achieve one, much less three of these objectives were almost zero. The practical case against the world state that Morgenthau accumulates is formidable.

At the same time one sees immediately in Morgenthau's argument a blurring of description and prescription. It is one thing to argue that there are fundamental, or even structural, obstacles to the formation of a world state, as Morgenthau sometimes implies, and quite another to observe that in contemporary circumstances people are unlikely to back such a state. Writing a century earlier, Marx might well have conceded that peoples in certain nations had almost no chance of achieving a successful revolution given their present moral condition, but this should not have led him to highlight the impossibility of revolution, as this would have diluted his message and thereby affected that condition. Was Morgenthau's primary aim to arrive at logical conclusions about the modern implications of international politics, or was it to assess only what was realistically attainable? To follow the former path one may run the risk of appearing eccentric or radical, but to follow the latter means downplaying what one thinks is right in favour of what happens at that moment to be politically feasible.

Morgenthau was caught, as have been many scholars interested in influencing policy, in a dilemma between philosophical consistency and public relevance. Writing at a moment of acute importance, when a wrong turn taken by the United States would have led to consequences he thought dire, he chose to play down the logic of world government and highlight its dangers. Central to this decision was his perception of Stalin's Soviet Union, a regime he regarded as absolutely cynical and hence a poor partner in any quest for global government.[6] The possibility of world government was so low and the risks of a failure so high that the world state notion he put forward in *Politics Among Nations* was effectively speculation, even as it logically followed from his argumentation.

During the 1950s Morgenthau cultivated his reputation as one of the nation's leading commentators on foreign policy and international politics. He began to contribute articles and columns to newspapers and popular magazines, and he published two more editions of *Politics Among Nations*, now the dominant text in university courses. Towards the end of the decade, clearly aiming to make his name nationally as the 1960 election approached, Morgenthau published several volumes, including three collections of essays and yet another edition of *Politics Among Nations* that appeared in time for the presidential campaign.

Before 1960, Morgenthau chose not to highlight his early musings about the possibility of a world state, despite the fact that the advent of a Soviet atomic, and then thermonuclear, arsenal made the attainment of such a state much more desirable than it had been in 1948. If a world state was the only logical means of permanently preventing great-power war, then surely it took on fundamentally greater importance now that great-power war threatened the very survival of the West, if not the species. Yet despite his clear recognition of the implications of thermonuclear weaponry, expressed as early as 1954 in an article for the *Bulletin of Atomic Scientists*,[7] Morgenthau veered towards a hard-line Cold War stance; towards, in other words, a conviction that the United States could deal with the Soviet Union only according to a militaristic version of the balance of power, and its attendant risk of major war.

His increasingly aggressive approach to the Cold War manifested itself in two kinds of argumentation. First, he took a generally critical line with respect to the Eisenhower administration's war-avoiding policies during the 1956–59 period. Morgenthau attacked the administration's passive response to the Soviet invasion of Hungary in late 1956 and its concurrent decision to side with the Soviet Union and against its traditional allies Britain, France, and Israel in the Suez crisis, despite the fact that both of these actions surely reflected the flexible and undogmatic approach to foreign policy he had long been championing in *Politics Among Nations*. In 1957 he joined the cry of alarmism after the Soviet Sputnik test, comparing it to Pearl Harbour, and calling for a massive American re-militarization programme to prevent the Soviet attainment of Cold War supremacy.[8]

As Speer notes, perhaps the culmination of Morgenthau's disenchantment with American foreign policy and the possibility of a world state can be found in an essay published in the volume *Dilemmas of Politics* in 1958. Here, he questions whether world government could ever prevail over the permanent lust for power he had emphasized in *Scientific Man versus Power Politics*, and whether it could resolve 'the conflict between the Soviet Union and the United States by peaceful means'. The solution to this rivalry, he added, 'under present conditions, does not lie in world government but in facing squarely concrete problems ... such as American security as against Russian security, the unification of Germany, peace in the Middle East'.[9]

Even more startling than his increasing alarmism and unilateralism was Morgenthau's temporary embrace of nuclear strategy. The advent of the Soviet arsenal, together with Eisenhower's development in the late 1950s of a reactive strategy of Mutual Assured Destruction, had led many American scholars and defence specialists to argue that the United States must develop strategies of limited nuclear war, whereby the nation could avoid, in a moment of Cold War crisis, a dismal choice between capitulation and total nuclear war—or as the presidential candidate John Kennedy put it in 1960, 'Holocaust or Humiliation'.

Eager to find an interesting solution to Cold War stalemate that might attract the attention of the Democratic Party, Morgenthau followed this trend. In another *Bulletin of Atomic Scientists* article he asserted that the 'United States must prepare for, and fight if necessary, a limited atomic war, with the atomic ingredient carefully adapted to the challenge to be met—strong enough, at the very least, to avoid defeat, but not so strong as to provoke all-out atomic retaliation.' In a *New Republic* piece written several months later, in late 1956, he went further, declaring that the claim that the prospect of thermonuclear war made the use of force unthinkable 'has no merit', and that indeed such fatalism 'actually increases the risk of atomic war, for it is tantamount to impotence before the threat of force'.[10]

Morgenthau's flirtation with nuclear strategy was a shocking deviation not only from the Nietzschean political philosophy expressed in *Scientific Man versus Power Politics*, but also, as we shall see, from the more coherent anti-nuclear stance he cultivated after 1960. Moreover, Morgenthau's endorsement of a more 'concrete' antagonism vis-à-vis the Soviet Union, an antagonism to be enhanced by inflexible foreign policies and a greater risk of nuclear war, suggested a willingness to jettison the idea of a world state. His essay in *Dilemmas of Politics* clearly implies that he had given up on the possibility, even though the growing thermonuclear arsenals in the hands of both superpowers simply increased the necessity of a world state, as he had defined that necessity. In every way Morgenthau appeared by the end of the 1950s as a scholar who had foregone his more detached, philosophical, and cosmopolitan view of international politics in favour of a militaristic nationalism resembling that of conservative Democrats like Henry Jackson, Stuart Symington, and John Kennedy.

8.2. **The thermonuclear revolution and Morgenthau's return to the world state**

As is always the case in the actual history of ideas, Morgenthau did not decide one day to drop one approach to international politics and adopt another as if he was trading in for a new car. During the late 1950s and early 1960s, he gradually recognized that the thermonuclear revolution—the development of arsenals and delivery systems so destructive that great-power war had become unsurvivable—had rendered his realist understanding of international politics obsolete. Naturally enough, the withering Cold War crises of this period pushed him further in this direction. A salient aspect of his new approach to international politics was his renewed embrace of world state logic.

Morgenthau was one of several American scholars and leaders who began to discern in the late 1950s that the logic of nuclear strategy began to break down once one thought clearly about how an actual war between the United States and the Soviet Union might end short of total nuclear exchange. The problem for him, as for his fellow analysts, was that this realization led to conclusions that were politically unacceptable in the sphere of American foreign policy during the late 1950s. If a war between the United States and the Soviet Union could only result in total devastation, then the only solution to this was either to abandon the struggle against the Soviet Union—to commit Cold War surrender—or to pursue the kind of world state that could permanently prevent great-power nuclear war. No other alternative could reliably solve the fundamental dilemma of thermonuclear war. Yet to advocate either of these solutions was, for an intellectual in Cold War America, to follow a sure path to political marginalization, an end to any chance of influence. Calling for Cold War surrender was not exactly a viable option for Morgenthau, or indeed any citizen; more to the point, advocating a world state at this time (and, for the most part, even today) carried with it the odour of naivete and unconsidered idealism that Morgenthau had been fighting against since his arrival in the United States. Intellectuals who followed the implications of the thermonuclear revolution to their logical conclusion faced a future of political irrelevance.

This dilemma twisted the thinking of many lesser intellectuals in the late 1950s. As we have seen, it threatened to do so to Morgenthau himself, but as the decade came to an end he began to edge away from political advocacy and back towards philosophical analysis. Elements of this decision began to appear in his writings and lectures of 1958 and 1959.

The germinal problem for Morgenthau, as it was for all would-be nuclear strategists, was the feasibility of limited war between two nuclear super-powers. In 1955 and 1956 Morgenthau, as we have seen, advocated the development of a limited nuclear war strategy, despite its apparent incompatibility with his understanding of international politics. By early 1958, he abandoned this position, at least rhetorically. In a lecture at Dartmouth College in February, he argued that the strategy of limited nuclear war faces the dilemma of 'distinguishing between strategic and tactical weapons, a dilemma which has confused the writers of military doctrine since the time of Clausewitz'. Limited nuclear war, he concluded, would too likely escalate into total war.[11] But his concurrent published writings contradicted this view.

In a March 1958 article in *Current History*, Morgenthau concluded that the United States needed a 'capability to fight local wars with conventional weapons and without resort to all-out atomic weapons'. He continued with this argument in December, lamenting that 'we are unprepared to fight a limited war', and warning that 'we are moving quickly into a zone of mortal danger created by the military superiority of the Soviet Union'.[12] These warnings indicated that Morgenthau was maintaining his belief in a limited war to defend Europe, in direct contrast to the opinions he expressed at Dartmouth. Which was his true attitude? Since 1955 he had been trying to formulate a military strategy that could allow the United States to prevail over the Soviet Union in Europe without unleashing a total nuclear war, but at the same time was suggesting, if not in his published writings, that any such strategy was hopeless. Faced with this classic dilemma, Morgenthau began to turn away from strategic writing altogether. Great-power war in the nuclear age, he was beginning to believe, was simply a problem his realism could not solve. Instead, Morgenthau turned towards a more radical conception of international politics that departed from his original realist worldview.

Following classical political philosophy, Morgenthau had postulated in his early writings that a primary function of the nation state, in terms of its utility to the citizen, is protection. The state may also serve as a vehicle for power lust, but its irreducible purpose is to defend its society from external attack and conquest. In the nuclear age, the state can no longer provide this function. The nuclear-age state 'must rely upon its psychological ability to deter those who are physically able to destroy it', Morgenthau wrote in the June 1957 issue of the *Yale Review*, because no state can physically prevent such destruction. The collapse of this protective function signalled the end of the predominance of the nation state. 'Nationalism', he concluded, 'has had its day.'[13] In *The Purpose of American Politics*, a publication of a series of lectures given at Johns Hopkins in 1959, Morgenthau continued with this theme. The thermonuclear revolution had obviated 'the elemental task of any political organization: to safeguard the biological survival of its members'.[14]

Any doubts about whether the nation could still protect its population from a general nuclear war disappeared from Morgenthau's writing after 1960. 'Qualitatively speaking', Morgenthau wrote in a review of Reinhold Niebuhr's *The Structures of Nations and Empires*, this vulnerability to total destruction 'is the only structural change that has occurred in international relations since the beginning of history'. All-out nuclear war, he informed the readers of the 1961 *Encyclopedia Britannica*, is 'likely to destroy all belligerents and thus to eliminate the very distinction between victor and vanquished. No possible end can justify it; it is an instrument of mass murder and suicide.'[15]

The question remained, however: was such a total nuclear war inevitable following the onset of armed hostilities between the two superpowers? Morgenthau continued to dance around this central problem. In a 1959 *Commentary* article he discusses the ongoing Berlin crisis at length without even attempting to elaborate on whether a war over that city was possible; he simply evaded the question. In *The Purpose of American Politics* he clings to the possibility of limited war, stating, in contradiction to his 1958 Dartmouth lecture, 'the capability for limited war, atomic or conventional, might actually be used in support of the national interest, as the circum-stances would require'. Yet in a March 1961 address at the University of Maryland he was not so evasive, bitterly attacking the 'scientist' view that nations could be manipulated to strategic ends. Could the United States survive even a major nuclear war, as the writer Herman Kahn was arguing? It could, Morgenthau allowed, only if we accepted Kahn's vision of human society as 'a primitive ant colony.'[16]

This withering comment belied the fact that Morgenthau himself had remained evasive about limited war in his published writing. Even as he was attacking the idea of winnable nuclear war in public addresses, he equivocated on the subject: in his 1959 *Commentary* piece, *The Purpose of American Politics*, and in the third edition of *Politics Among Nations*, which was also released in 1960, he steered clear of the question. Following the election of John Kennedy, Morgenthau began to write more directly.

'If a nation cannot resort to nuclear weapons without risking its own destruction', Morgenthau asked in 1961, 'how can it support its interests in a world of sovereign nations which is ruled by violence as the last resort?'[17] Here, pithily, was the big question, and one more genial to Morgenthau's way of thinking than the strategic issues he avoided confronting. Morgenthau pushed further, however, envisioning the sources of a world state.

In a 20 September 1959 piece in *The New York Times Magazine*, 'What the Big Two Can, and Can't Negotiate', Morgenthau introduced an interesting proposition. The article's subject was negotiation between the two Cold War superpowers, and Morgenthau naturally identified conflicts between the two sides that were not negotiable, and ones to which they both would have a common interest in adhering. One common interest, Morgenthau notes almost in passing is the 'common fear of atomic destruction', which 'ought to neutralize the United States' and Russia's fear of each other'.[18] This of course was not an unimportant point, for if the United States and Russia no longer feared one another, the other questions of Cold War negotiation would fall by the wayside, not to mention the realist presumption that mutual fear between the two superpowers could not be eliminated by concerns about war. What could Morgenthau have meant by this?

In his 1961 address at the University of Maryland, Morgenthau elaborated. Nuclear power, he said, 'requires a principle of political organization transcending the nation state and commensurate with the potentialities for good or evil of nuclear power itself'. He continued:

For all-out nuclear war is likely to obliterate the very distinction between victor and vanquished and will certainly destroy the very objective for which such a war would be fought. . . . It is at this point that the realistic and utopian approaches to politics in general and to international relations in particular merge.[19]

The utopian approach to IR, as we have seen, separated into two categories: the (futile) quest for international organization; and the quest for an actual world state. In another piece in *The New York Times Magazine*, published in October 1961, Morgenthau saw in the United Nations an 'opportunity to point the world in the direction of replacing national sovereignty with supranational decisions and institutions, for the fundamental argument in favor of the United Nations is the incompatibility of national sovereignty with the destructive potentialities of the nuclear age'. Yet, as he had suggested in his earlier writing, the United Nations could only provide direction; to attain true supranational control over nuclear war, a world state would be necessary.[19] In his *Encyclopedia Britannica* essay, Morgenthau shows how such a state might emerge. His discussion is worth quoting at some length. The immediate dilemma of Cold War conflict suggests a higher principle of international organization, which might eliminate 'local threats to peace' and cool off the Soviet–American rivalry. The larger dilemma of total nuclear war, he wrote,

suggests the abolition of international relations itself through the merger of all national sovereignties into one world state which would have a monopoly of the most destructive instruments of violence. Both kinds of solutions are supported by the awareness of the unity of mankind underlying the inevitable fragmentation of international relations.

However inarticulate and submerged, this awareness has never disappeared even in the heyday of nationalism, and it has been sharpened by the threat of nuclear destruction facing all mankind. These solutions are also supported by the longing to give that unity a viable political form . . . through theoretical schemes and practical measures to transform international relations into a supranational political order. This longing, in times past mainly a spiritual or humanitarian impulse, in the nuclear age has been greatly strengthened by the desire, innate in all men, for self-preservation.[21]

Morgenthau's suggestion here cannot be easily dismissed as an inconsequential detour from his realist worldview, a lament that anyone might have made in the dark days of 1961. He is not, in a weak moment, acknowledging that the utopian school was right all along; he is arguing, rather, that the prospect of thermonuclear war has caused the utopian and realistic approaches to merge. This argument, moreover, is not simply asserted, as was his claim about a 'diplomatic revolution' in 1956; it is based upon his perception that humanity's instinct for self-preservation, central to all realist explanations of world politics, can now regard the threat to its survival not the conquest of other states, as was the case before the atomic age, but the very prospect of great war. Here, in other words, is the social motivation, previously lacking, that can generate the political pressure necessary to create a genuine world state—a new leviathan that can protect its citizenry from external threat.

Morgenthau recognized that a realism which countenances great-power war in the thermonuclear age defies its core justification as an ideology of survival. For a time, he tried to make great-power war fit into his original conception; by 1961 he altered his realism to account for a technology that made great-power war unjustifiable. Interested in developing a more scientific analysis of international politics and the nuclear age, Morgenthau initially sought to use his insight into the revolutionary implications of nuclear weapons as a means of developing a new theory. He first introduced this idea in a 1959 volume edited by William Fox, titled *Theoretical Aspects of International Relations*. A theory of international politics is 'not an easy thing' to write, Morgenthau notes, because the quest to look beyond the moral claims of nations and discover pure reality behind them makes the theoretician 'suspect of being indifferent to all truth and all morality'. Yet such a quest, he continues, 'has become paramount in an age in which the nation, deeming itself intellectually and morally self-sufficient, threatens the human race itself with extinction'. A great theory of international politics, he was suggesting, might prove to be the one way for reason to solve the nuclear dilemma, for 'the mind of man' to master 'that blind and potent monster which in the name of God or history is poised for universal destruction'.[22]

Morgenthau was less optimistic by 1961. His address at the University of Maryland attacked the 'pretence' of modern theory for creating 'the illusion that a society of sovereign nations ... can continue the business of foreign policy and military strategy in the traditional manner without risking its destruction'. The collapse of Western civilization after a nuclear war, he said, signifies the point where 'the theoretical understanding of international relations reaches its limits'. Any new theoretical understanding must begin with the problem of nuclear war, not only with its effect 'upon the structure of international relations' but also the 'intellectual, political, and institutional changes which this unprecedented revolutionary force is likely to require'.[23]

Morgenthau never attempted to devise such a theory. By the early 1960s he was getting near retirement, preoccupied with public affairs, and unfamiliar with contemporary theoretical methodology. In the end, though, his disinclination to pursue a serious theory of international politics was based upon core philosophical grounds. For Morgenthau, international politics not only derived from basic elements of human nature that could be characterized in normative terms; it was also conducted for human objectives that could be so classified. In other words, he regarded the objective of survival in a dangerous world as a normative good, as something all political entities ought to pursue. His realism was based upon a certain conception of human nature, but equally based upon the assumption that realism served a particular goal. Thus Morgenthau, in his 1961 address, could ingenuously propose that a new theory of IR could derive from the political transformation the thermonuclear revolution 'is likely to require'. For him, theories are devised to serve normative ends.

The thermonuclear revolution forced Morgenthau to abandon his attempts to develop a rationalistic theory of international politics and a blueprint for American foreign policy. Facing conceptual breakdown, he returned to the pessimistic and ironic European political philosophy of his roots.[24] Such was the tone at least in his most brilliant treatise on nuclear war, a piece he published in the September 1961 issue of *Commentary* called 'Death in the Nuclear Age'.

'It is obvious', Morgenthau began, 'that the nuclear age has radically changed man's relation to nature and to his fellow men.'[25] Nuclear power had made political revolution within industrial society impossible, and it had made great-power war 'an absurdity'. By making two essential forms of political violence senseless, the thermonuclear revolution had transformed the meaning of international politics. There was to be no raising the possibility of limited nuclear war in this article: for Morgenthau, nuclear war now simply meant total destruction. By total destruction, Morgenthau meant the permanent obliteration of any society involved in a nuclear war. A full-scale nuclear exchange would mean social death within all the belligerent nations, 'by killing their members, destroying their visible achievements, and therefore reducing the survivors to barbarism'. Such a calamity would have a meaning beyond the physical and political destruction of nation states and their peoples, because it would eliminate the transcendent meaning of death. Man overcomes his inevitable mortality by leaving monuments to himself, most nobly in the form of individual and collective cultural achievements that are remembered by future societies forever. Knowing this, secular man and society understand that death is not meaningless. Indeed, the act of choosing death, by seeking danger in order to attain glory—to commit 'suicide with a good conscience', as Morgenthau quotes Friedrich Nietzsche—constitutes the most heroic kind of action modern civilization knows.

The death that results from nuclear war does not permit this kind of meaning. It is unheroic—hundreds of millions dying following the 'turning of a key'—and it is not chosen by those who die. But there is far more to it than that. Not only will a total nuclear war destroy the societies that wage it, making it impossible for those societies to leave monuments to themselves, it will, by permanently putting an end to civilization, destroy the monuments left by peoples and societies since the dawn of history. 'Man gives his life and death meaning by his ability to make himself and his works remembered after his death', Morgenthau writes. 'Patroclus dies to be avenged by Achilles. Hector dies to be mourned by Priam. Yet if Patroclus, Hector, and all those who could remember them were killed simultaneously, what would become of the meaning of Patroclus' and Hector's deaths?' Heroism loses its meaning if no one exists to appreciate it:

Thus we talk about defending the freedom of West Berlin as we used to talk about defending the freedom of the American colonies. Thus we talk about defending Western civilization against communism as the ancient Greeks used to talk about defending their civilization against the Persians. Thus we propose to die with honor rather than to live with shame. Yet the possibility of nuclear death, by destroying the meaning of life and death, has reduced to absurd cliches the noble words of yesterday. To defend freedom and civilization is absurd when to defend them amounts to destroying them. To die with honor is absurd if nobody is left to honor the dead. The very conception of honor and shame require a society that knows what honor and shame mean.[26]

Within the space of a few years, Morgenthau came to conclude that his traditional realist understanding of international politics had been made obsolete by the thermonuclear revolution. He also understood that this development made the world state not only necessary but also possible. Gradually, he developed a deep philosophical understanding of the dilemma created by nuclear weaponry. But he never was able to articulate the political steps required to solve this dilemma.

8.3. **The sources of Morgenthau's world-state confusion**

During the last decade of his life Morgenthau sporadically referred to the necessity of a world state and how the thermonuclear revolution had transformed international politics. But at the same time, he continued to write about other aspects of international relations as if nothing had changed; indeed, during the 1960s and early 1970s he focused most of his attention on the Vietnam War. He wrote, very clearly, that the new weaponry available to the superpowers required a radical transformation of politics, but he did not pursue this claim, treating it in a way as if it were only a minor digression, something mentioned in passing. It constitutes a curious dissonance in his late writing.

Speer contends, in 'Hans Morgenthau and the World State', that Morgenthau's inconsistency with respect to world government ultimately stems from philosophical confusion—namely, his conflation of the lust for power and fear. Adopting a more conventional Hobbesian view, Speer argues that the 'power thrust' that Morgenthau highlights especially in his early writings is not an essential aspect of political nature but rather 'ought properly to be seen as a secondary phenomenon, that is, as a reaction to fear'. Speer suggests, correctly, that Morgenthau emphasizes power lusts over simple desires for security and protection 'because of his commitment to the organismic mystique that comes out of German Romantic Nationalism but belongs to the whole nexus of German philosophy and sociology in the nineteenth century'.[27] This commitment, Speer continues, prevents Morgenthau from taking seriously the more Lockean notion of a gradualist formation of world government. The idea of a bottom-up world federalism does not occur to him: 'the whole concept', Speer writes, 'seems alien to his thought'.[28]

Why, then, did Morgenthau raise the possibility of a world state, of the latent 'unity' of man, in the early 1960s? For Speer, these musings appear to be the consequence of Morgenthau's intellectual confusion, his inability formally to incorporate a Lockean understanding of supranational politics into his conception of international politics even though this is precisely the idea he is looking for.

If we are to examine Morgenthau's writing on its own terms, analysing its intrinsic philosophical consistency with respect to abstract problems of international politics, we can use Speer's insight to close the book on Morgenthau's muddled vision of a world state in the nuclear age. Morgenthau recognizes the essential logic of the world state as early as 1948, and a decade later he comes to understand that the apparent choice had come down to a world state or omnicidal nuclear war. Yet he remains unable to develop any mechanism by which such a state might arise, and he continues, at least in ensuing editions of *Politics Among Nations*, to emphasize the structural impossibilities of world-state formation.[29]

Morgenthau's philosophical inconsistencies explain his difficulties with the concept of the world state. But a further question might be posed: what explains his philosophical inconsistencies? Is it intrinsic, as Speer implies, or may we attribute it, at least in part, to the historical setting in which he wrote?

It is unsatisfactory to locate the origin of every idea solely in its particular historical context, if for no other reason than that such a method transforms thinkers into mere digesters of historical action. It establishes a one-way causal direction from public events to ideas, and draws too distinct of a line between them. In Morgenthau's case, however, it would be even more implausible to maintain that his ideas were intrinsic to his own philosophical contemplation, that they were unaffected by what was happening around him.[30] For Morgenthau lived and wrote during a period in which material circumstances entirely outside of his control—namely, the technological advent of the thermonuclear revolution—overturned the basic premises of his political philosophy. Indeed, he lived and wrote at a time in which material factors germane to international politics changed more radically, in the space of a decade or so, than they aggregately had over the previous several centuries. Yet this revolution, it is crucial to remember, was not some sort of obvious occurrence that was one day reported in *The New York Times*. Morgenthau, like any other American concerned with international politics and foreign policy, was forced to try to understand what the advent of megaton warheads and ICBMs meant, while at the same time watching the two superpowers come to the brink of the Third World

War in the Berlin and Cuban crises. The notion of the world state appealed to him at this time as the only logical solution to the nuclear dilemma, but he had to pose this solution against the tumult and uncertainty of the crisis years, and his continuing belief that the Soviet Union would never agree to any kind of world government. As the appeal of the world state ratcheted up towards basic issues of human survival, so did the dangers of concluding a bogus world state with the cynical Soviets. Morgenthau's traditional realism was unequipped for this kind of dilemma, and so it bounced around directionlessly, lacking completely the authoritative tone of his 1950s policy punditry.[31]

An inkling of more systematic thinking appeared in a late piece of writing, Morgenthau's brief introduction to David Mitrany's 1966 book *A Working Peace System*. Eager to endorse Mitrany's functionalist manifesto for world government, Morgenthau repeated his earlier statement that the nuclear age had rendered the nation state 'obsolete' and that the 'rational requirements of the age' call for 'an amalgamation of nation states into larger supra-national entities'.[32] He elaborated, slightly: such amalgamation would constitute a 'voluntary co-operation of a number of nations with common interests for the purpose of creating a supra-national institution after the model of the specialized agencies of the United Nations and of the European communities'.[33]

What could persuade these nation states to take such an unprecedented step? As he had written a few years earlier, it would require a growing awareness among world leaders that the nation state could no longer protect them from a nuclear war that would end everything. 'The attempts at creating a united Europe', he wrote, 'testify to this awareness.'[34]

Perhaps. But as Morgenthau would normally have been the first to point out, the development during the Cold War of transnational institutions such as the European Community or 'specialized agencies' of the UN happened beneath a structure of superpower rivalry that tolerated them only *because* they did not actually threaten this superpower. Because this was so, was (and is) it actually wise to regard such institutions as models for an actual world state? The historical logic of state formation suggests that a world state that supersedes, rather than contends with, traditional international politics ought to look fundamentally different from the pretenders of today. As Daniel Deudney argues, it is a basic mistake to presume that the world state of tomorrow will resemble the nation state or regional union of today writ larger.[35] The process of taking control of the world's entire arsenal of war-making weaponry without triggering major war will require policies and strategies different in kind than those presently used by UN officials and European bureaucrats, and will therefore foment a kind of politics unrecognizable to us now.

It is safe to say that Morgenthau would never have predicted the advent of an international political system dominated, as it is today, by one power. The prospect would have gravely concerned him, terrified as he was by 'a nationalistic universalism which identifies the standards and goals of a particular nation with the principles that govern the universe'.[36]

But he also would have recognized power when he saw it. American unipolar power is the giant elephant in the backyard, a beast that often seems to be ignored by many European thinkers and leaders who appear to think that they can develop transnational political institutions in spite of it. The way towards building a world state has changed fundamentally since Morgenthau's day. During the Cold War, it meant overcoming the mutual suspicions of the two superpowers, something that, as we have seen, Morgenthau down deep probably believed was impossible. Now, it means co-opting American power into a transnational order, a task for which Morgenthau's embrace of the world state provides much inspiration but little in the way of direction.

⬚ NOTES

1. Parts of this chapter draw upon the analysis in Campbell Craig, *Glimmer of a New Leviathan: Total War in the Realism of Niebuhr, Morgenthau and Waltz* (New York: Columbia University Press, 2003).
2. For a fuller treatment of Morgenthau's initial American writing and in particular its brutal tone see Richard Ned Lebow, *The Tragic Vision of Politics* (Cambridge: Cambridge University Press, 2003), Ch. 6; Michael Williams, *The Realist Tradition and the Limits of International Relations* (Cambridge: Cambridge University Press, 2005), Ch. 3; Joel Rosenthal, *Righteous Realists* (Baton Rouge, LA: Louisiana University Press, 1991), Ch. 2; and Campbell Craig, *Glimmer of a New Leviathan*, Ch. 3. On the development of Morgentheu's ideas before he arrived in America, see Christoph Frei, *Hans J. Morgenthau: An Intellectual Biography* (Baton Rouge, LA: Louisiana State University Press, 2001).
3. See Niebuhr, *Moral Man and Immoral Society* (New York: Scribners, 1932) and Carr, *The Twenty-Years Crisis* (New York: Harper, 1984), originally published in 1939.

4. Morgenthau, *Politics Among Nations* (Chicago, IL: University of Chicago Press, 1948), 387.

5. *Politics Among Nations*, 400–1.

6. Morgenthau's views of the USSR are implicit in the first edition of *Politics Among Nations*. They become more explicit in his 1951 book *In Defense of the National Interest*. Further treatment of his increasingly anti-Soviet position can be found in Craig, *Glimmer of a New Leviathan*, 68–71.

7. 'The Political and Military Strategy of the United States', *Bulletin of the Atomic Scientists* (October 1954).

8. See especially two articles: 'Has Atomic War Really Become Impossible?' in *Bulletin of the Atomic Scientists* (January 1956); and 'The Revolution in United States Foreign Policy', *Commentary* (February 1957).

9. James Speer, 'Hans Morgenthau and the World State', *World Politics*, 20 (1968), 216.

10. 'Has Atomic War Really Become Impossible?', and 'The Decline and Fall of American Foreign Policy', *New Republic* (10 December 1956).

11. 'A Reassessment of United States Foreign Policy', lecture at Dartmouth College, 10 February 1958, in *Politics in the 20th Century*, vol. 2, 63–4.

12. 'Russian Technology and American Policy', *Current History* (March 1958), reprinted in *Politics in the 20th Century* (Chicago, IL: University of Chicago Press, 1962), vol. 2, 149; 'The Last Years of Our Greatness?' *New Republic* (29 December 1958), 12, 13–14.

13. 'The Paradoxes of Nationalism', *Yale Review*, 46 (June 1957), 490–1, 496. For a similar argument, expressed at the same time, see John Herz, 'Rise and Demise of the Territorial State', *World Politics*, 9 (1957), 489.

14. *The Purpose of American Politics* (New York: Knopf, 1960), 308; as John Herz was also arguing at the same time: see *International Politics in the Atomic Age* (New York: Columbia University Press, 1959), esp. Ch. 1. Also see Daniel Deudney, 'Nuclear Weapons and the Waning of the Real-State', *Daedalus*, 124 (1995), 213–16.

15. Review of Niebuhr's *The Structure of Nations and Empires*, in *Christianity and Crisis*, 8 February 1960; *The Purpose of American Politics* (New York: Knopf, 1960), 12; 'International Relations', entry originally published in *Encyclopedia Britannica* (1961), reprinted in *Politics in the Twentieth Century*, vol. 3, 174.

16. Ibid. 168; 'Intellectual and Political Functions of a Theory of International Relations', address given at the University of Maryland, March 1961, published in *Politics in the Twentieth Century*, vol. 1, 70.

17. 'International Relations'.

18. 'What the Big Two Can, and Can't Negotiate', originally published in *The New York Times Magazine* (20 September 1959), reprinted in *Politics in the 20th Century*, vol. 3, 320.

19. University of Maryland address, 75–6.

20. 'The Threat to, and Hope for, the United Nations', originally published in *The New York Times Magazine* (29 October 1961), reprinted in *Politics in the 20th Century*, vol. 3, 284.

21. 'International Relations', 174–5.
22. William Fox (ed.), *Theoretical Aspects of International Relations* (South Bend: University of Notre Dame Press, 1959), 117–18.
23. University of Maryland address, 66, 71, 76–7.
24. See Frei, *Hans J. Morgenthau*, 225–6.
25. Morgenthau, 'Death in the Nuclear Age', *Commentary* 32 (September 1961), 231.
26. 'Death in the Nuclear Age', 232.
27. For the definitive treatment of Morgenthau's Germanic influences, see Frei, *Hans J. Morgenthau*.
28. Speer, 'Hans Morgenthau and the World State', 223, 225–6.
29. Morgenthau's iteration of the obstacles to a World State remains basically unchanged in all editions of *Politics Among Nations*. See, for example, the last edition (Knopf, 1985), by Morgenthau and Kenneth Thompson, 533–7.
30. For a discussion of intrinsic and extrinsic effects on the development of political philosophy, see Quentin Skinner, *The Foundations of Modern Political Thought*, vol. 1 (Cambridge: Cambridge University Press, 1978), introduction.
31. One can confirm the effect of the thermonuclear revolution upon Morgenthau's realism by examining how other realists reacted to the same problem. That two realist contemporaries—Reinhold Niebuhr and George Kennan—reacted in very similar ways and at precisely the same time convinces me, at least, that the historical context here must be seen as determinative. For Niebuhr, see Craig, *Glimmer of New Leviathan*, Ch. 4.
32. Morgenthau, 'Introduction', in Mitrany, *A Working Peace System* (Chicago, IL: University of Chicago Press, 1966), 9–10. I am grateful to Mike Williams for bringing this introduction to my attention.
33. 'Introduction' to *A Working Peace System*, 10–11.
34. Ibid. 10.
35. Daniel Deudney, *Bounding Power: Republican Security Theory from the Polis to the Global Village* (Princeton, NJ: Princeton University Press, 2006).
36. Morgenthau, 'Introduction' to *A Working Peace System*, 8.

9 Morgenthau now: Neoconservatism, national greatness, and realism

Michael C. Williams

Why should contemporary theories of IR be interested in Hans Morgenthau? This is no simple question. To intellectual historians, the answer often lies in Morgenthau's central role in the development of realism and its place in the evolution of IR as a field of study. To some contemporary realists, Morgenthau articulated principles of power politics that continue to provide enduring insights into world politics, even if they seem frequently to feel that the foundations on which he based his theory need to be replaced. For more critical observers, the answer to the question is simpler: a continuing interest in Morgenthau marks the deleterious influence of flawed realist understandings of world politics that should be left behind as fully and quickly as possible. Morgenthau's brand of realism, in this view, is both dated and dangerous: a historical relic with little to say about the challenges of contemporary world politics.

In this chapter I suggest a different answer to this question, for it seems to me that Morgenthau's relevance is greater today than it has been for decades, not because his realism provides an account of the timeless nature of a world governed by power politics, but because of the ways in which it provides a means of engaging directly with one of the most controversial recent approaches to thinking about international politics and foreign policy: neoconservatism. While realists have been among the most vocal and robust critics of many elements of neoconservative foreign policy—particularly concerning the war in Iraq[1]—contemporary realism has by and large failed to come to terms with the neoconservative challenge at its most fundamental levels. And it is here that Morgenthau's realism is perhaps most instructive today. For while neoconservatism has often drawn rhetorical power by contrasting itself to realism, realists such as Morgenthau and Reinhold Niebuhr were intimately familiar with the post-war debates over the nature and fate of liberal modernity that provide the precursors for much of today's neoconservative movement. What is more, they provided powerful criticisms of the dangerous consequences that could follow from too radical a formulation of these concerns, criticisms that have considerable resonance today. When seen in this light, an engagement with Morgenthau's realism provides a way of deepening theoretical engagement with the foundations of neoconservatism, a remarkably prescient warning about the dangerous directions in which neoconservative understandings could lead, and a way of reconnecting some of the concerns of classical realism to contemporary international political theory in ways that recover both its richness and its political relevance.

9.1. **Neoconservatism and the struggle with liberal modernity**[2]

It is, of course, difficult to characterize any broad intellectual and political movement without being accused of distortion, and neoconservatism (as its proponents rarely tire of reminding us) is a far from unified position.[3] Yet despite differences on many issues and across generational divides, there are nevertheless also fundamental similarities and continuities. Neo-conservatism can, in Irving Kristol's words, be thought of as 'a "persuasion" to use a nice old-fashioned term; a mode of thought (but not quite a school of thought)'.[4] Perhaps the most important theme underlying this mode of thought lies in its struggle with the nature of politics in modernity. Unlike some forms of traditional conservatism, neoconservatism is not anti-modernist.[5] On the contrary, one of neoconservatism's most important arguments is that conservatism must confront the intrinsically pro-gressive and forward-looking logic of political modernity. Modern politics puts a premium upon the realm of ideas, on 'ideology' in its broadest sense, because it is inseparable from competing visions of the future, the good, and how to get there. As Kristol puts it, modern politics is inescapably 'ideological in the sense that it consists of political beliefs that are oriented in a melioristic way—a "progressive" way, as one says—toward the future. It is impossible for any set of political beliefs in the modern era to engage popular sentiments without such a basic orientation. In this sense, all modern societies of whatever kind conceive of themselves to be progressive. The rare exception, an overtly "reactionary" backward-looking regime, is correctly perceived to be an absurd and transient, and usually nasty, anachronism.'[6] Ideology is thus the ground upon which modern politics is fought; it is, in Kristol's words, an intrinsic and indispensable part of the broad struggle over 'the key question: who owns the future'.[7]

Neoconservatism's stress on the importance of ideas and the direction of political culture is, therefore, a direct consequence of its understanding of modernity as an epoch in which all political programmes and positions must cast their arguments and conduct their struggles in terms of these aspirations. Yet if there is no escaping the future-oriented, progressive cast of modernity, neoconservatism is deeply ambivalent about its possibilities, suspicious of its potential directions, and positively hostile towards some of its most powerful trajectories. The focus of much of this suspicion and hostility is, of course, 'liberalism'. But neoconservatism's relationship to liberalism is more complex than is often allowed. Far from rejecting liberalism tout court, neoconservatism seeks to develop an understanding of where liberal political thought has gone wrong, veering from its original, positive contributions to human liberty and progress to a point where, in the neoconservative view, it has become an obstacle and a threat to both.

The neoconservative view of liberalism (and, indeed, of realism) can be nicely illustrated by examining briefly its approach to the place of 'interest' in political life. The classical liberal idea that people have and pursue interests is, they argue, an essential element in the analysis of modern societies; no cogent social theory can do without it. What is more, the idea of interest is also a valuable dimension of the ethical structure of modern societies. Like the thinkers of the 'new Right' such as Friedrich Hayek and Milton Friedman, neoconservatives view the idea that individuals have interests (and that they should be allowed to pursue these interests) as an important moral principle, and as a bulwark of individualism, liberty, and a market society.

But if interest is essential in the operation (and analysis) of modern societies, neoconservatives see it as an insufficient basis for a healthy and viable polity. In fact, they argue that a recognition of the limits of interest as a foundation for social order is amongst the most important dimensions of political understanding, a dimension systematically obscured by liberal-individualist ideology and which stands at the heart of the dilemmas and disorders characteristic of contemporary liberal societies. Here they part company with the new Right, as well as with the forms of liberal-ism they so strongly oppose, and develop an analysis of the pathologies of modern liberalism at three levels: the individual, the social, and the political.

At the level of the individual, the reduction of action to nothing more than the pursuit of self-interest gives rise to a destructive combination of hedonism and despair. Lacking any broader vision within which to locate their lives, liberal individuals are driven by (often base) impulses and quests for ephemeral self-gratification that ultimately renders life empty and 'meaningless'.[8] Socially, this form of individualism is destructive of communal ties and values. It yields a debased public culture in which any sense of higher values or societal ethos is trampled by the relativistic demands of liberal freedom, and where public needs are undermined by wholly private desires and driven by a frenetic consumerism and com-modification. Individual liberty and self-realization may be the honestly held and even well-intentioned goals of this form of liberalism, but its consequences are anomie and degradation. Subjectivism in values and hedonism in desires erode the individual's sense of self and the moral and social bonds necessary for the health of the social order, leaving a corrupted society lacking any viable sense of the public good.

At the level of political institutions, the dynamics of a corrupted liberal society are mirrored in a destructive and debilitating pluralism. Portraying politics as nothing more than the pursuit of individual or group interests, liberal pluralism effectively reduces the state to nothing more than a vehi-cle for the furtherance of those interests. The consequent destruction of any cogent concept of the public interest breeds cynicism in and about politics. Equally importantly, it leads to a loss of belief in the value of the political order itself, and unwillingness to defend that order against those who would destroy it. If, as Kristol puts it, the value of democracy lies solely in its capacity to allow individuals to maximize their interests, there is no compelling reason why those individuals should defend that order if their interests might be better served by its destruction. A purely technical, managerial, democratic pluralism is not, he argues, theoretically inconceivable. What is inconceivable is why anyone should care for that order at all.[9]

Self-interest alone is incapable of generating an adequate vision of political obligation, of structures of social solidarity, or of commitment to the defence of the state or democratic values. Individually and culturally, it leads to hedonism, subjectivism, and cynicism. Politically, its expression is institutional pluralism: the reduction of politics to nothing more than the competition for individual goods characteristic of narrowly defined interest-group politics that only 'generates discontent, cynicism, and "alienation" among the citizens'.[10] When politics becomes reduced to purely self-interested action by individuals or organized interest groups without a conception of the *public interest* that transcends a simple liberal plurality of interests, decline follows. Democracy, having been reduced to a technique for decision-making rather than a political value, ceases itself to be valued. Commitment to the political order—and willingness to defend it—decays.

Neoconservatism's criticisms of liberal modernity are hardly new. Indeed, as Kristol points out, 'For well over a hundred and fifty years now, social critics have been warning us that bourgeois society was living off the accumulated moral capital of traditional religion and traditional moral philosophy, and that once this capital was depleted, bourgeois society would find its legitimacy ever more questionable.'[11] By the late twentieth century, neoconservatives argue, this crisis has finally and indisputably arrived, and liberal modernity is increasingly experiencing in reality the crisis that its critics have for so long been predicting.

Increasingly lacking in legitimacy, and bereft of any compelling theory of political obligation, the main challenge—indeed the main *threat*—confronting modern liberal societies is not economic crisis, or even external challenges: it is *decadence*. As Kristol ringingly declared at the very height of the 'second Cold War': 'The enemy of liberal capitalism today is not so much socialism as it is nihilism.'[12] Without core principles that provide social meaning, cohesion, and direction, decadence is the spectre that haunts liberal-capitalist societies. Far from opposing this trend, capitalism simply treats it as another cultural phenomena to be commodified and sold within a cultural marketplace driven by hedonistic desires. What is more, with its economistic and rationalistic biases, 'bourgeois' (liberal-individualist) thought is incapable of responding to this challenge, for in fact it 'never really could believe that self-destructive nihilism was an authentic and permanent possibility that any society had to guard against. It could refute Marx effectively, but it never thought it would be called upon to refute the Marquis de Sade and Nietzsche.'[13]

The neoconservative critique of modern liberalism explains its hostility to the dominance of rationalism in contemporary social and political science—and, by extension, much of contemporary realist thinking. Although effective within certain narrowly bounded confines, rationalistic principles of political analysis are in fact manifestations of the culture of liberal rationalism. As both a principle of individual action and a tenet of social analysis, rationalist self-interest that underpins much of political science today both reflects and contributes to the 'self-destructive paradox' of contemporary liberalism that threatens the achievements and possibilities of liberal modernity itself. 'Value-free' political science is thus of little use to societies facing this crisis, since 'being "value free", as they say, [it] cannot come up with any persuasive arguments as to why they should not act in this way'.[14] As an intrinsic part of liberal modernity, rationalist social science is incapable of even seeing the crisis of modernity, not to mention rising to the challenge of meeting it.

9.2. **Resources of reconstruction and the recovery of republican virtue**

The neoconservative reading of the crisis of modern politics is certainly grave, but it is not despairing.[15] The crisis can be countered, and there are resources available to do so. The first dimension of this recovery project involves a re-examination of the legacy of liberalism. Despite its often virulent rhetorical hostility to 'liberals' and 'liberalism', neoconservatism is not hostile to the liberal tradition as a whole. On the contrary, it argues that classical liberalism did not reduce individuals to rationally self-interested agents (and society to their interactions), but continued to assert the need for a sense of individual virtue and social mores in a stable, cohesive, and economically vibrant society.[16]

Second, neoconservatives link the individualism and virtue of classical liberalism to the emergence of republican government. In this account, the political genius of the Founders of the American republic lay in their recognition that individual virtue was not an end in itself; it was part of 'civic virtue', a process of fashioning selves capable of democratic self-government.[17] The concern of republican virtue was with 'character', the kinds of individuals capable of self government, the social conditions conducive to the creation of such individuals, and the formation of individuals who *also* found their self-expression and fulfilment in the public sphere and in the pursuit of the public interest.[18] The message of the American Revolution, accordingly, is that 'a self-disciplined people can create a political community in which an ordered liberty will promote both economic prosperity and political participation'.[19] Republican virtue is not, for neoconservatives, an abstract idea: it is the core of the American idea. Seen in the light of this reconstruction, the loss of individual and public virtue is not just a source of social dislocation, nor is decadence simply a matter of conflicting tastes or mores: they are threats to democracy itself, and to United States as a political order. If this is the foundation of the Republic, then it is essential it be recovered if the Republic is to survive.

In response to this threat, neoconservatism adopts a twofold strategy. First, it seeks to rekindle individual virtue and to reconnect the individual to the community by showing how republican virtue is part of the national ideal of the Republic itself. Moreover—and this is one of neo-conservatism's most striking and most important claims—understanding the foundations of the Republic allows for an ideologically compelling, forward-looking, and outwardly oriented form of American nationalism. The project of renewing the Republic by bringing it back to its foundations will not succeed if it consists solely of a nostalgic, backward-looking patriotism. This is the path of traditional conservatism and patriotism, which is incapable of creating an effective political platform in a modern era whose defining political logic is progressive and forward looking. What is required is a commitment to *ideals*, to the meaning of the nation in a heroic sense capable of mobilizing individuals to virtuous action in the public sphere domestically, and in foreign policy internationally. To quote Irving Kristol once more: 'Neoconservatism is not merely patriotic—that goes without saying—but also nationalist. Patriotism springs from a love of the nation's past; nationalism arises out of hope for the nation's future, distinctive greatness.'[20] Nationalism is a necessary dimension of success in modern, 'progressive', ideological politics, for 'in the modern world, a non-ideological politics is a politics disarmed'.[21]

As neoconservatives are well aware, advocating the necessity of an ideological nationalism and a heroic politics of national greatness is likely to cause more than a little unease. Their resolution to the dilemma lies yet again in a return to the principles of the American republic and in an appeal to its exceptional form of nationalism. Founded upon a virtuous response and resolution to the dilemmas of liberal-modernity, the principles of the American republic underpin a form of nationalism that avoids the parochial and destructive tendencies of modern nationalism while retaining its political virtue and socially mobilizing potential. American patriotism is different because, as William Bennett puts it, it is a patriotism of ideals, not of the soil; and while it 'has become something of a cliché to talk of American "exceptionalism" ... there is no ignoring the fact that the American nation itself was founded in exceptional circumstances and on an exceptional statement of timeless principles. Put simply, the United States was the first nation ever to base its very sense of nationhood on a set of universal principles derived from natural rights, as enunciated in its Declaration of Independence.'[22] Some years earlier, William Kristol and Robert Kagan argued for what has come to be called 'national greatness conservatism' in almost identical terms, declaring that

American nationalism—the nationalism of Alexander Hamilton and Henry Clay and Teddy Roosevelt—has never been European blood-and-soil nationalism. It's true that in the absence of a real appeal to national greatness, some conservatives are tempted, a la Pat Buchanan, to turn to this European tradition. But this can't and shouldn't work in America. Our nationalism is that of an exceptional nation founded on a universal principle, on what Lincoln called 'an abstract truth, applicable to all men at all times.' Our pride in settling the frontier, welcoming immigrants and advancing the cause of freedom around the world is related to our dedication to our principles.[23]

The idea of national greatness and its necessity is a key dimension of the neoconservative vision of the American national interest. The national interest of the United States is fundamentally related to the history, values, and identity of the Republic itself, and 'every profound foreign policy debate in America's history', Robert Kagan has declared, 'has ultimately been a debate about the nation's identity and has posed for Americans the primal question "Who are we?" '[24] The answer lies in a vision of the American republic as in its essence a progressive force, a nation embodying *universal* values whose greatness resides precisely in the fact that its founding principles are not limited to the United States itself. In this way, the struggle is not to move back to the past: it is to return to the past in order to recover resources that will allow the United States to move resolutely forward into the future. The American national interest, properly understood, is—like the United States itself—exceptional. But it is not unique. It is part of an historic mission that can and should be shared by all peoples; and it would be, if only virtuous governments could rule. The culmination of this logic is, of course, the promotion of democracy as part of a 'muscular patriotism' based upon 'freedom and greatness'. Creating an international order of values is good for *both* America and the world. A policy of 'benevolent hegemony' makes sense precisely because 'American foreign policy should be informed with a clear moral purpose, based on the understanding that its moral goals and its fundamental national interests are almost always in harmony.'[25]

For neoconservatives, the resources of cultural and political renovation are thus to be found in particular strands of modern liberalism and constitutionalism, and a particular form of populism.[26] Ensuring the survival of the American republic and its virtues requires an intellectual endeavour to recover these traditions, and a cultural and political strategy to ensure their prominence. Equally importantly, it requires a political leadership that can represent those ideals and mobilize political support by allowing the society to see its 'populist' values and identity reflected in the personal characteristics and policies of the leadership itself. Neoconservatism's stress on 'character' in leadership and boldness in policy (especially foreign policy) is a product of this vision, and an important part of its lionization of Ronald Reagan and Theodore Roosevelt arises from what neoconservatives portray as their keen understanding of the need for American presidents to represent for (and to) the American people the greatness of the nation, and to demonstrate that it 'owns the future'.[27]

9.3. **Realism and the national interest**

In the neoconservative vision, the national interest cannot be reduced to an analytic concept of foreign policy or a narrowly defined material interest. It is a political principle: a symbol and requirement of the political virtue needed for a healthy modern polity. Conversely, the lack of a clear, powerful, mobilizing understanding of the national interest is a sign of societal decadence. The nihilistic and fragmenting aspects of modern urban society and culture must be countered by a reassertion of the values of the nation, and a restoration of the tradition of 'republican virtue'. Strong, socially vibrant conceptions of both the public interest and the national interest are essential if a political community is to combat the corrosive acids of modernity. A strong, morally cohesive society with a clear sense of the public interest provides a basis for the national interest, while a national interest constructed on these lines will support the creation and maintenance of such a public. As both a product and a symbol of the public interest, the national interest not only provides a guide for policy abroad: it expresses— and in the process fosters and supports—the operation of political virtue at home.

Neoconservatism's critique of realism[28] emerges from this perspective, and develops along three reinforcing lines. First, the endless debates and indeterminacy within realism over what the national interest is reflect more than just the complexities of judgment, which neoconservatives readily acknowledge. More fundamentally, they are the logical outcome of an approach to foreign policy severed from values and a deeper understanding of the national interest as a necessary expression of those values. As a result, realism suffers the fate of modern rationalism as a whole. It lacks any view beyond narrowly strategic material calculation, narrowly pragmatic judgment, or pluralist competition.[29] This is not a resolution to the problem of the national interest in modern politics: it is a *symptom* of the decline of both intellectual and political life: a mark of decadence masquerading as objectivity.

Second, a realist policy guided by traditional realpolitik alone is ironically yet profoundly *unrealistic*. Unable to connect adequately to the values and identity of the American people, a realist foreign policy will fail to generate either the commitment or the resources necessary to ensure its success. Accordingly, in an early call for a 'neoReaganite foreign policy', William Kristol and Robert Kagan drew upon this theme to insist that 'it is already clear that, on the present course, Washington will find it increasingly impossible to fulfill even the less ambitious foreign policies of the realists, including the defense of so-called "vital" national interests in Europe and Asia. Without a broad, sustaining foreign policy vision, the American people will be inclined to withdraw from the world and will lose sight of their abiding interest in vigorous world leadership. Without a sense of mission, they will seek deeper and deeper cuts in the defense and foreign affairs budgets and gradually decimate the tools of U.S. hegemony.'[30]

Finally, instead of providing security for American society, a realist foreign policy actually contributes to its decay. Lacking a clear vision of the national interest that can be explained to citizens and connected to their values, realist foreign policy is of necessity often duplicitous. But mendacious policies abroad only further erode virtue at home, and a realist policy of the national interest actually exacerbates political cynicism and social decay within the state. As a consequence, the entropic and cynical tendencies that are at the core of liberal-modernity are heightened by a realist foreign policy. Realism paradoxically encourages a division between morality and foreign policy that mirrors the liberal divide between interests and ethics, and in the process undermines both. As Kristol and Kagan put the point: 'The remoralization of America at home ultimately requires the remoralization of American foreign policy. For both follow from Americans' belief that the principles of the Declaration of Independence are not merely the choices of a particular culture but are universal, enduring, "self-evident" truths. That has been, after all, the main point of the conservatives' war against a relativistic multiculturalism.'[31]

In sum, far from protecting the state, realist theories of the national interest actually endanger it, however advantageous their manipulative actions may appear in the short term. Disconnected from values, realism cannot give any content to the national interest beyond a minimal and ultimately ineffective and debilitating pragmatism, or a corrosive cynicism. A manipulative 'realism' will only lead to decline—incapable of pulling people with it and thereby gaining the necessary resources and support, it will either fail, or will have to resort to secrecy and manipulation, thus furthering in practice the social cynicism about values that it advocates in theory. Corrosive of support abroad and eroding virtue at home, it is ultimately ineffective internationally and destructive domestically.

What is even worse, in this process realism actually deprives modern societies of one of the most effective means of mobilizing virtue and combating decadence—the idea of the national interest itself. By contrast, in the neoconservative vision the national interest can be used to counter modernity's worst dynamics. A 'moral' foreign policy reinforces those virtues and values in the citizenry of the United States, and helps get their support for pursuing the national interest which they can actually see as an expression of their values, and which they can identify with. In this way, realism removes the potential for the national interest to be used as an effective form of political mobilization and reformation in support of a virtuous polity. The national interest thus needs to be recaptured from traditional realists in both theory and practice so that it can become a substantive guide and mobilizing symbol in foreign policy, and contribute to political reconstruction at home.[32]

In their rallying cry for an 'elevated patriotism' that transcends both liberal-modernism *and* traditional conservatism, Kristol and Kagan call for a return to the heroic vision of national interest as national greatness that will offset both a debilitating liberalism and an equally debilitating traditional conservatism based on a narrow parochial patriotism at home and isolationism in foreign policy. 'A true "conservatism of the heart"', they write, 'ought to emphasize both personal and national responsibility, relish the opportunity for national engagement, embrace the possibility of national greatness, and restore a sense of the heroic, which has been sorely lacking in American foreign policy—and American conservatism— in recent years.'[33] Failing to do so will mean that 'Deprived of the support of an elevated patriotism, bereft of the ability to appeal to national honor, conservatives will ultimately fail in their effort to govern America. And Americans will fail in their responsibility to lead the world.'[34]

9.4. **Morgenthau, virtue, and national greatness**

The difficult and perhaps deteriorating situation in Iraq has no doubt damaged the neoconservative project, in some eyes fatally. But even if neoconservatism is no longer the power it was, it is important to be clear about its impact and its implications both for realism and for future debates over foreign policy in the United States and beyond. For while realism is in many eyes enjoying a renewed 'springtime'[35] as a result of its apparently vindicated scepticism concerning the invasion of Iraq, there is also little doubt that the neoconservative assault on realism has had a considerable impact on debates over precisely what it means to be 'realistic' about international politics in general, and about American foreign policy in particular. Henry Kissinger, to use only one prominent example, has argued that 'The advocates of the important role of a commitment to values in American foreign policy have won their intellectual battle', and goes on to argue for a new synthesis of 'values and interests' in debates over its future direction.[36] Francis Fukuyama, despite his recent 'realist' criticisms of many neoconservative policies, continues to develop a foreign policy that he regards as deserving of the latter name. And from the other side, Fukuyama's interlocutor and intellectual adversary Charles Krauthammer has proposed a new 'convergence' between realism and neoconservative democratic globalism, a stance he terms 'democratic realism'.[37] Realism may well be back in vogue in many quarters, but as in the past it is far from clear precisely what this means conceptually or politically, and it is often equally unclear exactly how realism is to engage with contending views, including those of neoconservatives, that are unlikely to fade completely from the political scene.

The question of what it means to be a realist, and how realists (and other schools of thought in IR) are able to engage in these debates is made even more complex by the evolution of realism within the academy. Indeed as realism, particularly in the United States, has moved ever closer towards rationalist forms of social science, it has become ever less able to engage with either the theoretical lineage or the political positions (and power) of neoconservatism and the debates over the meaning of realism that it has sparked. However, this is not true of all forms of realism; in fact, while neoconservatives have often used realism as a foil against which to define their own stances, perhaps the most sophisticated and sustained engagement with the issues articulated by contemporary neoconservatives can actually be found in the realism of Hans Morgenthau. In the remainder of this chapter, I seek to sketch some of the ways that Morgenthau's realism reveals both a direct awareness of the issues raised by neoconservatism and constitutes a partial, although in important ways limited, response to it.[38] My goal is not to argue for an uncritical return to Morgenthau's realism as a guide to today's challenges, but to suggest that through a broader engagement with his thinking it is possible to draw inspiration towards theoretically rich and politically engaged aspects of realism that have become largely lost in IR and that can provide insights for engaging contemporary controversies in new and salient ways.

Although it is too often forgotten today, once one moves beyond the more familiar parts of *Politics Among Nations* it soon becomes evident that Morgenthau (like Niebuhr) took an engagement with the dilemmas of liberal modernity as a key starting point for his political realism.[39] Indeed, his thinking evolved in the context of the most intense debates over the 'crisis of liberalism' in Weimar Germany, and as William Scheuerman and Chris Brown discuss in this volume, it can compellingly be argued that Morgenthau's early work in particular constitutes a 'hidden dialogue' with the controversial Weimar jurist (and trenchant critic of liberal modernity) Carl Schmitt—a dialogue tellingly analogous to that which preoccupied one of the intellectual godfathers of today's neoconservatives, Leo Strauss.[40]

The broader questions of politics in liberal modernity were at the heart of the critique of liberalism that Morgenthau developed in works such as *Scientific Man versus Power Politics*, and they remained central to his thinking throughout his career.[41] His criticisms of liberalism and rationalism are meant to apply to social and political life as a whole, not just to international affairs. He, too, worried consistently about the question of meaning in modernity and its consequences for individual conduct and social cohesion,[42] and was deeply concerned with (and opposed to) the reduction of liberal democratic politics to a sterile pluralism that would undermine the foundations of a democratic polity, as well as inhibiting effective foreign policy. In fact, his writings are replete with concerns that resonate with contemporary neoconservatism, from the dangers of a 'decadent liberalism', to the crisis of a technocratic or narrowly pluralistic liberal-democracy, to the challenges faced by liberal-democracies in foreign affairs—especially in conditions of emergency.[43]

Perhaps most strikingly of all, Morgenthau even called directly upon the idea of 'national greatness' as a means of understanding the 'purpose of American politics', and as a strategy for recovering and reinvigorating the values of the Republic and providing guidance for its foreign policy. In terms as ringing as any contemporary neoconservative, Morgenthau declared the uniqueness and historical importance of the American republic and its guiding purpose of 'equality in freedom'. This purpose, he argued, was extraordinary. Following the lead of one of his great political exemplars, Abraham Lincoln, he argued that 'Other nations have reflected upon their unique contribution by contemplating their past and have drawn inspiration and standards for action from that contemplation. Yet no other nation has ever decided at the very moment of its birth, by way of a rational choice among alternatives, what its unique contribution was going to be, what would distinguish it from all other nations, for the sake of what purpose it was being founded.'[44] Such sentiments may seem unlikely coming from someone so often identified with a cynical and amoral realism, but this simply shows how distant Morgenthau's actual political vision is from the remarkably narrow account that has come to dominate discussions of his realism in IR today.

Yet, while Morgenthau demonstrates a clear awareness of the fundamental political questions that underpin much of contemporary neoconservatism, and even shows a similar urge to find the resolution to these questions in an appeal to American exceptionalism, he also provides an account of the dangers of this situation that stand in opposition to the uncritical eulogies of national greatness neoconservatives. Morgenthau continually stressed that the promise of American politics also held dangers. The abstract nature of 'freedom' at the heart of that purpose was a source of great strength, a continual renewal and impulse towards a better future. But it was also a source of continual crises, as the ability to live up to these ideals both at home and abroad forced an engagement with power. In seeking to create freedom, the Republic often ended up exercising a 'brutal domination' that justified itself in terms of ideals while in systematic bad faith denying the reality of its actions and in the process risking either rejecting its purpose by retreating into isolationism or denying that purpose through an aggressive moral universalism.[45]

Similarly, Morgenthau warned that appeals to national greatness and a principled patriotism could easily contribute to a political culture prone to an imprudent and crusading foreign policy. Patriotism risked becoming identified with a bellicose nationalism, virtue with an aggressive internationalism, and each with support for military adventures.[46] Moreover, he felt that an uncritical politics of national greatness would have disastrous impacts on diplomacy, producing a policy that divided the world between true allies who recognized American virtue as well as American power, and who were willing to face up to the existential issues at stake in the struggle between a civilization of values and the renewed spectre of nihilism, and those unreconstructed regimes, decadent liberals, overly optimistic rationalists, or narrowly self-interested cynics who were cast as irresponsibly obstructive at best, positively dangerous at worst. Far from providing the basis for a robust and responsible foreign policy, Morgenthau worried that the uncritical assertion of national greatness and the *assumption* of legitimacy on the basis of an *a priori* claim to virtue actually risked undermining the legitimacy and power of the United States. Greatness, he argued, is something that must be recognized by others, not just asserted by the self: too great a regard for one's own virtue was a constant temptation to be zealously guarded against, lest it yield hubristic blindness or arrogance, deaf to the demands of prudence, leading to disaster rather than glory.

Equally importantly, the fragility of a modern identity built on a commitment only to an abstract ideal meant that conflicts or crises over that identity (over Kagan's 'primal question': 'who are we?') were an intrinsic part of American politics. When confronted with such dilemmas, he warned (as Tocqueville asserted long ago) that the tendency of American egalitarianism was to elevate conformism, to cast dissent as treason, or to repress domestic contestation by invoking the unifying spectre of domestic or foreign threats and enemies.[47] While calling for a need to recognize the attractions of 'national greatness' as an antidote to some of modernity's most corrosive dynamics, he refused to regard these ideals as adequately realized within the United States itself, and was fearful that engaging in foreign adventures would prove a tempting if ultimately illusory response to deep domestic difficulties.

A keen awareness and stinging critique of these domestic failings is yet another aspect of Morgenthau's legacy that is generally ignored today. As noted previously, a concern with decadence and hedonism, with the ascendance of private interests and the decline of the public sphere, was a part of Morgenthau's early thinking that he never left behind. Unlike many contemporary neoconservatives, however, he is unwilling to foist these ills solely upon an amorphous 'liberal culture', much less to attribute them primarily to the predations and pathologies of liberal cultural elites.[48] Morgenthau's realist focus on power (and the interests of the powerful) as central to politics provides a useful counter to so narrow a view. Instead, he points in often strikingly critical tones to broader structures of power and forms of domination—from processes of social rationalization and bureaucratization, to concentrations of economic and political power—at work modern societies, and in post-war American politics.[49] His concern is that bureaucratization, political majoritarianism, and rule by opinion polls and media manipulation have become a threat to the principle of equality and to the future of democracy in America itself. In terms of equality, these dynamics have led to ever greater domination of the state by powerful private interests and to the effective political disenfranchisement of the weakest and the poorest. At the same time, effective public policy is undermined not only by this structure of political domination, but also by the entropy of interest-group pluralism. Inequality, the loss of a public sphere of vibrant political participation and contestation, and the erosion of the capacity of the state to act effectively in support of broad social purposes, were amongst his greatest concerns.[50] He was, accordingly, deeply critical of economic and racial inequalities, and of concentrations of political and economic power, in ways that stand starkly at odds with contemporary neoconservatism's preoccupation with the 'culture wars'. Far from lionizing American national greatness as an abstract rhetoric, he called on his adopted country to examine itself critically, and to live up to its principles. 'The restoration of national purpose', as he put it, 'requires a reorientation of the national outlook, a change in our national style.'[51]

Morgenthau was thus well aware of the issues represented by neoconservatism today, and he took them very seriously indeed. However, he not only took a much more critical view of the inequities of the social and economic status quo than do most neoconservatives, but also stressed the dangers lurking in too radical a formulation and response to the dilemmas of liberal modernity. He had seen with his own eyes how charges of social decadence and calls for a renewal of political virtue could easily be transformed into an intolerant politics that not only undermined effective foreign policy formulation, but that could also threaten the health—and even the survival—of liberal-democracy itself. The experience of Weimar, where the crisis of liberalism gave rise to a radically anti-liberal politics, hovers in the background of many of his writings on both domestic politics and foreign policy. His worry was not only that an uncritical liberalism might become too weak to sustain a vibrant democracy—he was equally (and often even more) concerned that a reaction against these dilemmas, especially in a situation exacerbated by high levels of insecurity or international tensions, would lead liberal democracies to overreactions that posed at least as great a threat to their principles and liberties.

In sum, Morgenthau was consistently concerned that declarations of national virtue could become barriers to criticism and powerful weapons with which to attack critics at home for being insufficiently virtuous, decadently weak, lacking heroic zeal and fortitude, or even harbouring a suspiciously weak commitment to the American ideal itself. He feared that far from securing democracy such ideas could easily become a means for furthering the interests of already powerful actors and stifling the vibrant debate that is both the lifeblood of democratic politics and a vital contribution to successful policy.[52]

But while Morgenthau's thinking provides a powerful basis for engaging with neoconservatism, meeting its challenge also reveals important tensions and limitations in his own thinking. 'National greatness' neoconservatism, as we have seen, seeks to combat the dilemmas of liberal-modernity through a progressive vision of history and, especially, through a direct appeal to *nationalism* as a mobilizing rhetoric of a virtuous polity. Morgenthau rejects such an appeal—indeed some of his sharpest criticisms are directed against nationalism, that 'blind and potent monster' that threatens universal destruction.[53] Morgenthau certainly has good reasons to be suspicious of nationalism. But his rejection of its affective power leaves him with the fundamental problem of sustaining or reviving a virtuous and self-limiting political order when the increasingly bureaucratized and anomic conditions that he sees characterizing modern politics militate against such developments.

His primary strategies in this struggle are three. First, he seeks to revive a principled commitment to civic republicanism, and hopes that the principles of the American republic, the institutional structures of a domestic division and balance of power, and a revivified political culture will prevail.[54] Second, he consistently argues (in classically Weberian terms) that modern politics requires great leadership to both mobilize and *restrain* political commitment and virtuous action.[55] Morgenthau is well aware of the limits of these first two strategies. Although he demonstrates in his later years a quite remarkable faith in democratic politics, he is never so naïve as to believe that this potential is unproblematically positive, inevitably progressive, or imminently triumphant. Similarly, he holds that great leadership is probably even more unlikely to arise under present conditions than its already fleeting appearances in the past would lead us to hope, and the despair which sometimes characterizes his writings emerges from his understanding that a virtuous politics and responsible leadership are rare (and perhaps ever-fading), as well as a clear recognition that an appeal to the 'purpose' of American politics and great leadership are as likely to yield a politics of chauvinistic nationalism and demagogic manipulation as they are to foster civic virtue and great statesmanship.

Morgenthau also, of course, has recourse to a third strategy of limitation: the existence of an international balance of power that will act to constrain national excesses through their inevitable confrontation with opposition. Yet here, too, Morgenthau is far from sanguine. He stresses the historically bloody nature of this ultimate form of limitation. Moreover, although he argues at length that the development of nuclear weapons has changed fundamentally the role that this dynamic plays in politics he has, as Campbell Craig has shown, at best a fleeting glimpse of the political implications of this transformation.

9.5. **Conclusion**

A reading of Morgenthau that moves beyond his most well-known treatments of international politics or foreign policy such as *Politics Among Nations* and *In Defence of the National Interest* reveals a set of concerns that resonate remarkably with contemporary neoconservatism. This is hardly surprising, since his thinking emerges from a position that was acutely aware of the theoretical claims and political concerns represented by neoconservatism, both historically through his engagement with the crisis of liberalism in Weimar and through his engagement with debates over the fate of liberal politics in post-war America. While Morgenthau shared many of the concerns expressed by contemporary neoconservatism, he nonetheless also developed a powerful account and critique of the dangers that such views might hold for domestic politics and foreign policy. Recovering this aspect of classical realism provides an important counterweight to neoconservatism's castigation and caricaturing of the realist tradition. Our appreciation of Morgenthau's realism may be heightened or diminished by an awareness of these dimensions of his thinking, but they demonstrate that the concerns of realism (or at least of Morgenthau's brand of it) embrace political and philosophical concerns far wider than are generally recognized.

When reading Morgenthau, it is difficult to escape the sense of foreboding, and indeed of tragedy, that pervades much of his writings. Yet it is also impossible not to recognize the unflinching willingness to confront difficult questions, and a deep commitment to political action and ethics. In his survey of the challenges arising from too close an identification of national virtue with international politics, Morgenthau argued that these challenges placed a specific responsibility on international political theory. In fact, he argued that one of the core 'commitments of a theory of international politics'—and one of its most important political functions—was to stand in opposition to the more dangerous tendencies in modern politics. As he put it in a passage worth quoting at length: 'The difficulties which stand in the way of the theoretical understanding of international politics have grown more formidable with the ever more intensive identification of national purposes and policies with absolute truth and universal morality. . . . To look in such circumstances at one's own nation and its relations with other nations objectively, dispassionately, critically has never been more difficult, hazardous, and necessary than it is today. This presents a theory of international politics with its supreme intellectual and moral challenge.'[56]

These words seem as relevant today as they were half a century ago. Whether one accepts Morgenthau's realism or not, they provide at least one part of a legacy that contemporary thinking about international politics should be happy to embrace.

☐ NOTES

1. See John Mearsheimer, 'Hans Morgenthau and the Iraq War: Realists Versus Neoconservatives', http://www.opendemocracy; see also John Mearsheimer and Steven Walt, 'An Unnecessary War', *Foreign Policy*, 134 (January/February 2003), 51–62 and, for a survey of these arguments, Brian Schmidt and Michael C. Williams, 'Realism, Neoconservatism, and the War in Iraq' (forthcoming).

2. This section draws on parts of my analysis in 'What is the National Interest?: The Neoconservative Challenge in International Relations', *European Journal of International Relations*, 11: 3 (2005), 307–37.

3. For recent denials that 'neoconservativism' exists, see Max Boot, 'Think Again: Neocons', *Foreign Policy* (January/February 2004) and David Brooks, 'The Neocon Cabal and other Fantasies', *International Herald Tribune*, 7 January (2004) [originally appeared as 'The Era of Distortion', *New York Times*, 6 January (2004), A23]; a sharp rejoinder is Michael Lind, 'How Neoconservatives Conquered Washington and Launched a War', www.archive.salon.com/opinion/feature/2003/04/09/neocons

4. Irving Kristol, *Reflections of a Neoconservative* (New York: Basic Books,1983), 75.

5. For a treatment of conservatism in International Relations, see Jennifer Welsh, ' "I" is for Ideology: Conservatism in International Affairs', *Global Society*, 17: 2 (2003), 165–85.

6. Kristol, *Reflections of a Neoconservative*, x.

7. Ibid. 253–6.

8. Irving Kristol, *Two Cheers for Capitalism* (New York: Basic Books, 1978), 254.

9. Kristol, *Reflections of a Neoconservative*, 50.

10. Ibid. 245.

11. Kristol, *Two Cheers for Capitalism*, 65–6; see also Robert H. Bork, 'Culture and Kristol', in Christopher DeMuth and William Kristol (eds.), *The Neoconservative Imagination* (Washington, DC: AEI Press, 1995), 135.

12. Kristol, *Two Cheers for Capitalism*, 66; italics in original.

13. Kristol, *Two Cheers for Capitalism*, 68; for a very clear statement of the analogous Straussian position here, see Thomas L. Pangle, 'The Roots of Contemporary Nihilism and Its Political Consequences According to Nietzsche', *Review of Politics*, 45: 1 (1983), 45–70.

14. Kristol, *Reflections of a Neoconservative*, 64.

15. Wider readings of how émigré political thinkers sought to come to terms with this broad crisis in elements of post-war American political science are: John G. Gunnell, *The Descent of Political Theory* (Chicago, IL: University of Chicago Press, 1993); Ira Katznelson, *Enlightenment and Desolation* (New York: Columbia University Press, 2002). More broadly still, see Geoffrey Hawthorne, *Enlightenment and Despair: A History of Social Theory* (Cambridge: Cambridge University Press, 1990).

16. Kristol, *Reflections of a Neoconservative*, 149. For a broader account of the place of virtue in liberalism see David Berkowitz, *Virtue and the Making of Modern Liberalism* (Princeton, NJ: Princeton University Press, 2000) and the important studies by Albert O. Hirschman, *The Passions and the Interests* (Princeton, NJ: Princeton University Press, 1977); J. A. W. Gunn, *Politics and the Public Interest in the Seventeenth Century* (London: Routledge and Keegan Paul, 1969); and J. G. A. Pocock, *The Machiavellian Moment* (Princeton, NJ: Princeton University Press, 1975).

17. Kristol, *Two Cheers for Capitalism*. For Arendt's influence on Jeanne Kirkpatrick, see John Ehrman, *The Rise of Neoconservatism: Intellectuals and Foreign Affairs 1945–1994* (New Haven, CT: Yale University Press, 1995), 115, 117–18. This has also been a key theme of Straussian political theorists; see, for example, the divergent positions in Robert H. Horowitz (ed.), *The Moral Foundations of the American Republic* (Charlottesville, VA: University of Virginia Press, 1986) and Harry V. Jaffa, *American*

Conservatism and the American Founding (Durham, NC: Carolina Academic Press, 1984), along with the criticisms of Gordon S. Wood, 'The Fundamentalists and the Constitution', *New York Review of Books* (February, 1988), 33–40; and Shadia Drury, *Leo Strauss and the American Right* (New York: Palgrave Macmillan, 1999).

18. For an exploration of this lineage, in a huge and diverse literature, see Daniel Walker Howe, *Making the American Self: Johnathan Edwards to Abraham Lincoln* (Cambridge, MA: Harvard University Press, 1997), and in IR, Vibeke Schou Tjalve, *American Jeremiahs?: Reinhold Niebuhr, Hans J. Morgenthau, and the Realist Recovery of a Republican Peace* (Copenhagen: Copenhagen Political Studies Press, 2004).

19. Kristol, *Reflections of a Neoconservative*, 89.

20. Ibid. xiii.

21. Ibid. ix.

22. William Bennett, 'Morality, Character, and American Foreign Policy', in William Kristol and Robert Kagan (eds.), *Present Dangers: Crisis and Opportunity in American Foreign and Defense Policy* (San Francisco, CA: Encounter Books, 2000), 291.

23. William Kristol and Robert Kagan, 'Toward a Neo-Reaganite Foreign Policy', *Foreign Affairs*, 75: 4 (1996), 18–32.

24. Robert Kagan, 'A Tougher War for the U.S. is One of Legitimacy', *New York Times* (24 January 2004).

25. Kristol and Kagan, 'Toward a Neo-Reaganite Foreign Policy', 27; Bennett, 'Morality, Character, and American Foreign Policy', 303.

26. These themes are also found in Straussian approaches, however the oft-debated relationship between Strauss and neoconservativism are beyond the scope of this chapter.

27. Illustration of this pervasive theme included Ben Wattenberg, *Values Matter Most* (New York: Free Press, 1995) and Bennett, 'Morality, Character, and American Foreign Policy'.

28. For a direct critique of Morgenthau, see Joshua Muravchik, *Exporting Democracy*, (Washington, DC: AEI Press, 1991), Ch. 1.

29. As William Kristol argues, for example, although 'material interests and geographical and historical characteristics of nations' are important, 'The nature of a regime is crucial, rather than some alleged underlying, geographically or economically or culturally determined "national interest". The priority of the political order implies a morally informed American foreign policy.' 'The members of the president's foreign-policy team have all become Reaganites', *The Weekly Standard*, 8: 21 (2 October 2003) 1.

30. Kristol and Kagan, 'Toward a neoReaganite Foreign Policy', 28. In Michael Ledeen's notable phrasing: 'Whenever I hear policy-makers talking about "stability", I get the heebie-jeebies. That is for tired old Europeans and nervous Asians, not for us. In just about everything we do, from business and technology to cinema and waging war, we are the most revolutionary force on earth. We are not going to fight foreign wars or send our money overseas merely to defend the status quo; we must have a

suitably glorious objective. We are therefore not going to stick by a government that conducts foreign policy on the basis of *Realpolitik*. Without a mission, it is only a matter of time before public opinion will turn against any American administration that acts like an old fashioned European state. Just ask Henry Kissinger. That is why I find the realist position highly unrealistic.' 'Contribution to "American Power—For What?" ', *Commentary*, 19: 1(2000), 36–7.

31. Kristol and Kagan, 'Toward a Neo-Reaganite Foreign Policy', 31.
32. Or, for that matter, from its reduction to commercial interests alone, which overlooks the primacy of politics. See, for example, William Kristol and David Brooks, 'What Ails the Right', *Wall Street Journal* (15 September 1997).
33. It also, of course, provided a post-Cold War means of attempting to reunify American conservatives and the foreign policy of the Republican Party; see James W. Caesar, 'The Great Divide: American Internationalism and its Opponents', in Kristol and Kagan (eds.), *Present Dangers*, 25–43.
34. Kristol and Kagan, 'Toward a Neo-Reaganite Foreign Policy', 31–2.
35. Lawrence F. Kaplan, 'Springtime for Realism', *The New Republic* (21 June 2004), 20–3; though it should be noted that Kaplan is himself sceptical about the value of this resurgence.
36. Henry A. Kissinger, 'Intervention With A Vision', in Gary Rosen (ed.), *The Right War?: The Conservative Debate On Iraq* (Cambridge: Cambridge University Press, 2005), 53.
37. See the original statement of Fukuyama's re-positioning his 'The Neoconservative Moment' and Krauthammer's response, 'In Defense of Democratic Realism', both reprinted in Rosen (ed.), *The Right War?*, 170–200. Krauthammer's broader arguments can be found in *Democratic Realism: An American Foreign Policy for a Unipolar World* (Washington, DC: American Enterprise Institute, 2004), and 'The Neoconservative Convergence', *Commentary*, 120 (July/August 2005), 21–6. Moreover, those predicting the complete demise of the neoconservative project might do well to ponder the contrasting fates in the Bush Administration of the reports on the future of US policy in Iraq provided by Baker-Hamilton 'Iraq Survey' Group, and the American Enterprise Institute-sponsored Kagan-Keane report, tellingly entitled 'Choosing Victory' and supported by prominent neoconservatives such as Elliot Cohen.
38. This objective is of course open to easy charges of being anachronistic. However, as I hope to have shown previously, many of neoconservativism's themes have a long history and as I hope to demonstrate invoke philosophical themes and political positions that Morgenthau was more than familiar with.
39. Important recent recoveries of this dimension of Morgenthau's thinking include Christoph Frei, *Hans J. Morgenthau: An Intellectual Biography* (Baton Rouge, LA: Louisiana State University Press, 2001); Martti Koskenniemmi, *The Gentle Civilizer of Nations* (Cambridge: Cambridge University Press, 2002), 413–509; Richard Ned Lebow, *The Tragic Vision of Politics* (Cambridge: Cambridge University Press, 2003); and William Scheuerman, 'Another Hidden Dialogue: Hans Morgenthau

and Carl Schmitt', in Scheuerman, *Carl Schmitt: The End of Law* (New York: Rowan and Littlefield, 1999), 225–52. Ehrman argues for the influence of Niebuhr in neoconservatism, but fails to do so in any depth and without regard for the significant divergences between Niebuhr and neoconservatism.

40. This case is most directly made in Scheuerman, 'Another Hidden Dialogue', and in his and Chris Brown's contributions to this volume. See also the discussion in Koskenniemmi, *Gentle Civilizer of Nations*, and Michael C. Williams, 'Why Ideas Matter in IR: Hans Morgenthau, Collective Identity, and the Moral Construction of Power Politics', *International Organization*, 58: 4 (2004), 633–66, and Williams, *The Realist Tradition*. Schmitt's critique of liberalism is most clearly made in *The Crisis of Parliamentary Democracy*, trans. by Ellen Kennedy, (Cambridge, MA: MIT Press, 1988) and *The Concept of the Political*, trans. by George Schwab (Chicago, IL: University of Chicago Press, 1996). For a broad treatment see McCormick, *Carl Schmitt's Critique of Liberalism*. On Strauss and Schmitt, see Heinrich Meier, *Carl Schmitt and Leo Strauss: The Hidden Dialogue*, trans. by J. H. Lomax, (Chicago, IL: University of Chicago Press, 1995). A fine recent treatment in IR is Jean-Francois Drolet, 'The Visible Hand of Neoconservative Capitalism', *Millennium*, 35: 2 (forthcoming, 2007).

41. See also one of his last works, *Science: Servant or Master?* (New York: New American Library, 1972), that harkens back to these early concerns.

42. On Niebuhr's connection to the political debates surrounding pragmatist philosophy and the fate of the American Left, see John P. Diggins, *The Promise of Pragmatism: Modernism and the Crisis of Knowledge and Authority* (Chicago, IL: University of Chicago Press, 1994) and, more broadly, his *The Rise and Fall of the American Left* (New York: W.W. Norton, 1992). On Morgenthau's engagement with political modernity, which was informed largely by his reading of Nietzsche and Weber, see Frei, *Hans J. Morgenthau*.

43. The critique of 'decadent liberalism' is most fully pursued in Hans J. Morgenthau, *Scientific Man versus Power Politics* (Chicago, IL: University of Chicago Press, 1946), that of the increasing narrowness of democratic politics in *Truth and Power: Essays of a Decade* (New York: Knopf, 1970), and *Politics in the 20th Century*, vol. 3, 71–116, as well as in the works cited below. I have pursued some of these issues more fully in Williams, *The Realist Tradition*, 172–92.

44. Hans J. Morgenthau, *The Purpose of American Politics* (New York: Knopf, 1960), 29; for specific appeals to greatness see, 8, 293–341.

45. Morgenthau, *Purpose of American Politics*, 112.

46. See, for example, Morgenthau, 'Nationalism', in *Politics in the 20th Century*, vol. 1, 181–93.

47. See, for example, 'The Corruption of Patriotism', in *Politics in the 20th Century*, vol. 1, 390–408; *Purpose of American Politics*, 57–8, 145–8; see also the discussion in Williams, *The Realist Tradition*, Ch. 3.

48. I have examined this aspect of neoconservatism and its political power and strategies in, *Culture and Security: Symbolic Power and the Politics of International Security* (London: Routledge, 2007), Ch. 5.

49. Among many possible examples, see 'What Ails America', in *Truth and Power*, 29–39, and 'The Coming Test of American Democracy', in *Truth and Power*, 209–14, and his analysis of the 'new feudalism' in *Purpose of American Politics*, 274–92. For a recent analysis that stresses material interests in the 'culture wars' see Thomas Frank, *What's Wrong with America?: The Resistible Rise of the American Right* (London: Secker and Warburg, 2004). See also the treatment of the political uses of fear in Corey Robin, *Fear: The History of a Political Idea* (Oxford: Oxford University Press, 2004).

50. Morgenthau, *Truth and Power*, 5–9; and *Purpose of American Politics*, 197–274, which attacks (among a litany of ills) 'hedonism' and the 'decline of the public realm' as parts of the 'contemporary crisis at home'.

51. *Purpose of American Politics*, 322.

52. Worries most clearly expressed in Morgenthau, 'How Totalitarianism Starts', in *Truth and Power*, 53–4; and 'The Military Displacement of Politics' in *Politics in the 20th Century*, vol. 1, 328–35, and strikingly in relation to IR theory in 'The Commitments of a Theory of International Politics', in *Politics in the 20th Century*, vol. 1, 60–1. For contemporary examples of populist mobilization of the rhetoric of betrayal, see Ann Coulter, *Treason: Liberal Treachery From the Cold War to the War on Terror* (New York: Random House, 2003), David Horowitz, *Unholy Alliance: Radical Islam and the American Left* (Washington, DC: Regnery Books, 2004), and the analysis in Williams, *Culture and Security*, 114–17.

53. Hans J. Morgenthau, 'The Nature and Limits of a Theory of International Relations', in William Fox (ed.), *Theoretical Aspects of International Relations* (South Bend: University of Notre Dame Press, 1959), 174–5.

54. The latter concern explains in part his (often highly) qualified sympathy and support for the new left and student movements of the 1960s.

55. Again, among many examples, see 'The Integrity of Political Action' in *Politics in the 20th Century*, vol. 1, 359–60, as well as his praise of Lincoln in Hans J. Morgenthau and David Hein, *Essays on Lincoln's Faith and Politics* (Lanham, MD: University Press of America, 1983).

56. Morgenthau, Hans J., 'The Commitments of a Theory of International Politics', 60–1.

10 Texts, paradigms, and political change

Richard Ned Lebow

The contributions to this volume are indicative of the growing interest in Hans J. Morgenthau. The principal catalyst of this interest is surely the end of the Cold War and the re-thinking of IR theory it has encouraged. Morgenthau is not the only theorist to whom scholars have turned; Thucydides, Nietzsche, Carl Schmitt, E. H. Carr, and Hedley Bull, and the 'English School' more generally are all undergoing revivals. If we widen our horizons to comparative politics and political theory, we observe a similar phenomenon with respect to Émile Durkheim, Leo Strauss, and Michael Oakeshott among others.

These revivals point to the need to conceptualize the relationship between political developments and texts. It seems obvious that major political changes or transformations—and more about what a transformation is in a moment—can provide an opening to criticize current policies and the discourses that sustain them, or are thought to do so. Older texts can be important resources in this effort. They can be used to decentre dominant discourses and provide a starting point, even a degree of legitimacy, to new ones. Morgenthau has proven a useful vehicle for exposing the pretensions of American foreign policy and limitations of neorealism. In *Tragic Vision of Politics*, I argue that he is one of a number of useful resources for building theories that eschew prediction in favour of explanation, and offer themselves to policymakers as frameworks for working their way through problems.[1]

Contributors to this volume have used him for these several ends, as well as a subject of study in his own right. By examining the influence of Aristotle on Morgenthau, Anthony F. Lang, Jr., demonstrates the latter's concern for the ethical foundations of foreign policies and the essential role of prudence (*phronesis*) in successful foreign policies. William E. Scheuerman and Chris Brown explore the relationship between Morgenthau and Carl Schmitt. They make us aware that realism is at the intersection of diverse traditions and owes debts to multiple predecessors, some of them people most realists would, with good reason, prefer to distance themselves from. Scheuermann and Brown highlight an orientation common to many realist (as opposed to the liberal) texts since the time of Thucydides: the extent to which they look back with nostalgia on an earlier period of history and view the story of their era as a *Verfallsgeschichte*, or narrative of decay. Oliver Jütersonke also acknowledges the connection between Morgenthau and Schmitt, but reminds us that Morgenthau's thinking was equally influenced by other important thinkers, notably Hans Kelsen and Hersch Lauterpacht, and legal-political debates which they animated. Nick Rengger situates Morgenthau within the Tragic tradition, and uses Michael Oakeshott's review of *Politics Among Nations* and subsequent correspondence with Morgenthau, to question that appropriateness and utility of the tragic metaphor in IR.[2] Richard Little examines the complexities of Morgenthau's understanding of the balance of power and its connections to current theoretical debates. Michael Cox interrogates Morgenthau and his theory from the vantage point of the post-Cold War era, and uses his analysis in turn to help us better understand that conflict. He shows the tensions between Morgenthau and realism on the one hand, and US Cold War foreign policy on the other, and argues that some of these tensions arise from the nature of realism itself. Drawing on his book, Campbell Craig reviews Morgenthau's evolving beliefs about a world state, and the tensions between his devastating critique of international idealism and the emergent, if not full-blown idealism, of his later writings. Michael Williams contends that Morgenthau is even more relevant today because of the framework he provides us to engage and critique the international politics of neoconservatism.

In the first section of this chapter, I examine the linkages between texts on the one hand and political and intellectual goals on the other. I lay out four ways in which texts can be used for these ends, and offer illustrations drawn from recent Morgenthau scholarship and the chapters of this volume. I then extend my argument to look at the broader question of the relationship between texts, paradigm shifts, and foreign policy. These processes are to some degree self-reinforcing because contemporary interest in texts helps to define their status, and their status in turn helps to determine which texts scholars turn to as resources. As paradigms and discourses rise and fall, the scholars who work within them receive more (or less) recognition and resources, which in turn can accelerate the shift in either direction. I conclude with some observations about what we can learn from a better understanding of the historical process of revisiting texts.

10.1. **International relations after the Cold War**

In a landmark US Supreme Court case, Associate Justice Potter Stewart wrote: 'I can't define what pornography is, but I know it when I see it.'[3] Political transformation is similar. It is difficult to define, in part because it is all in the eye of the beholder. It differs from pornography in that a consensus often emerges ex post facto that a transformation has occurred. This was true of the Cold War, whose origins, and even more its longevity, were not so obvious at the time. Bipolarity as a concept was introduced by William T. R. Fox in 1944, but not adopted by Morgenthau until 1950.[4] It only came to be regarded as a defining feature of that epoch sometime in the 1960s. The end of the Cold War came as a surprise to almost everyone, but was widely recognized as a watershed in IR even before the Soviet Union collapsed. Fools rush in where angels fear to tread, and IR theorists have not hesitated to propose definitions of system transformation. In 1979, Kenneth Waltz made it the centrepiece of his theory of international politics, and insisted that such change could only come about by war.[5] He further maintained that bipolarity was more stable than multipolarity, and certain to be with us for the foreseeable future. Events proved him wrong on both counts. The Cold War ended peacefully, and bipolarity—if it ever existed—came to an end when the Soviet Union imploded.

As Mick Cox observes, these events provided an opening for critics of neorealism, and of realism more generally, to go after them in a spate of articles and books. Most of these initial attacks focused on the failure of realists—or anyone else for that matter—to predict the end of the Cold War. Realists were held particularly responsible for this failure because their frameworks discouraged scholars from even acknowledging the possibility of a peaceful end to that conflict. It focused attention on the military balance, which really did not change markedly until the collapse of the

Soviet Union. It also downplayed the significance of internal develop-ments not directly related to material capabilities. These neglected other factors—which included the gradual disillusionment of Soviet intellectuals and *apparatchiki* with communist ideology, rising ethnic tensions, growing desires for material goods, and domestic and inter-Republic politics—that turned out to be where all the action was.

Realism was also morally compromised by the events of 1990–91. Prom-inent realist practitioners (e.g., Henry Kissinger) and academics (e.g., John Gaddis) valued stability over human rights, and had made clear their willingness to sacrifice Eastern Europe towards this end. As early as 1992, they began to regret the passing of the Cold War because of the uncertain and unpredictable nature of the world that was emerging in its place.[6] The most extreme expression of pessimism, and arguably, of amorality, was the much-criticized warnings given by John Mearsheimer to Japan and Ger-many, urging them to acquire nuclear weapons in what he insisted would be a far more threatening multipolar world. Fortunately, their leaders paid no attention to the unsolicited advice of marginal academics.[7]

The end of the Cold War provided critics of realism with both an oppor-tunity and need to go on the offensive. The need side of the equation had several terms to it. First and foremost for some was the need to dethrone realism as the reigning paradigm to make room for other approaches, and with their ascent, the possibility of directing positions and funding towards them that would otherwise have gone to realists. Critics also had political agendas. Liberals were committed to the European project and a self-regulating community of industrial powers. Constructivists favoured more far-reaching political transformations premised on the seeming success of what Karl Deutsch called pluralistic security communities.[8] As Mike Williams points out, neoconservatives were committed to a transformative agenda of a different kind, and here too, realism stood in the way. Realists of all stripes maintained that anarchy was the defining characteristic of the international system, and that it was impossible and downright dangerous to pretend that war was not the final arbiter of international disputes. Liberals and constructivists, by contrast, thought it possible to escape from, or at least, to mitigate, the worst features of anarchy through a dense network of institutions or a robust international society. The liberal posi-tion had been well developed even before the end of the Cold War, while constructivism was still an emergent paradigm. Constructivists and their fellow-travellers rallied round Alexander Wendt's timely article alleging that anarchy was what states made of it.[9] The battlelines were drawn, and the first skirmishes were taking place.

In the last decade, attacks on neorealism and realism have all but disappeared from the leading journals, indicating that critics believe the battle has been won. When the issue of realists versus critics does surface in these journals, it is because realists have gone on the attack. A recent example is John Mearsheimer's E. H. Carr Lecture at the University of Wales, Aberystwyth, in which he alleges that British academics discriminate against realists. It was printed as the lead article in the June 2005 issue of *International Relations*, and inevitably provoked a series of rejoinders by prominent British IR scholars.[10]

Critics of realism and realist critics of neorealism have displayed increasing interest in earlier realist texts, works that pre-date neorealism and the large body of contemporary realist literature that focuses on questions of material capabilities and their implications for foreign policy. There has always been interest in some of these authors, especially Thucydides, who is widely acknowledged to be the father of IR, not just of realism. Beginning in the 1980s, IR scholars critical of realism turned to his account of the Peloponnesian War to expose the weaknesses of modern realist—especially neorealist—assumptions and arguments.[11] My own contribution to this literature criticizes realists for lifting lapidary quotes out of context in support of arguments that are not supported by the text as a whole. I offer more nuanced interpretations of his understanding of the causes of the war—having more to do with Spartan identity than Athenian military power—and of the Melian Dialogue—intended as a critique, not a vindication, of power politics. I further argue that Thucydides might properly be considered the father of constructivism, given his emphasis on the importance of language and its ability in tandem with deeds to sustain or destroy civilization.[12]

The growing interest in mid twentieth century writings, including those of Hans Morgenthau, John Herz, and E. H. Carr, is a natural development as they are the foundational texts of modern realism.[13] They are also appealing because of their perspectives on IR and political science. Neorealism claimed to be a scientific theory at the system level, with testable propositions deduced from its central assumptions. Critics were able to demonstrate that it is impossible to restrict the study of IR to the system level, that Waltz's principal proposition that anarchy must produce a war-prone, self-help system did not necessarily follow. For someone who claimed that the distinguishing feature of his theory was its scientific rigour, it did not help that Waltz's key conceptual terms of anarchy, power, and polarity were not formulated in a manner that allowed their unproblematic measurement or falsification. In contrast to neorealism, mid-century foundational texts are interested in foreign policy as much as IR. They are steeped in history, acknowledge the importance of the idiosyncratic as well as the general, emphasize agents along with structures, accept the limits, if not the impossibility of prediction, and recognize the often determining influence of domestic regimes and politics on foreign policies. In contrast to Waltz, Carr, Morgenthau, and Herz all distinguish material capabilities from power and power from influence. They recognize influence as very much situation dependent, and often related to the ethical basis of the policies in question. Most fundamentally, these realists understand that their theories are products of the epoch and culture that produced them. For all of these reasons, the revisiting of foundational texts is an obvious strategy, not only for scholars who want to attack latter-day realists, but for those who want to use these texts as starting points for reformulations of realism more appropriate to contemporary circumstances and intellectual sensitivities. Several of the scholars who have contributed to this volume are committed to this goal.

The end of the Cold War is not the first major international transformation or upheaval to provoke a return to older texts with the goal of the rethinking of contemporary ideas and approaches and developing alternatives to them. In Roman times, Vergil and Ovid invoked this strategy. Machiavelli, and Hobbes did so in early modern Europe. Machiavelli wrote commentaries on the *Discourses on the First Ten Books of Titus Livius* to resurrect the concept of civic virtue as an antidote to the disorder of Italian city states, and Hobbes translated Thucydides into English in 1651 in response to the English civil war. To put this process in a broader perspective, it is useful to identify and describe the several reasons why scholars are drawn to older texts. I believe there are four such reasons, and they often, if not usually, occur in the order in which I present them.

Justification: Every new text or discourse looks for justification for its arguments or claims. One effective way to do this is to situate one's text or discourse in a tradition that is considered legitimate and respected by the intended audience. Contenders for power in Rome traced their ancestry back Aeneas, if not the gods. The gospels of Luke and Matthew buttress their claims that Jesus is the messiah by tracing his descent back through different routes to King David and through him to Adam. Political philosophers have played this game for millennia, attaching themselves and their works to particular traditions. So do IR theorists. Realists claim descent from Thucydides, Kautilya, Machiavelli, and Hobbes; liberals from Smith and Kant; Marxists from the eponymous Marx; and constructivists root their enterprise in Nietzsche and twentieth-century philosophy and anthropology. Hans Morgenthau contends that his approach to IR is based on the timeless wisdom of classical Greek and Indian writers. Lesser claims he supports with quotes from more recent authors, leading Barrington Moore in his review of *Politics Among Nations* to complain about his proclivity of 'substituting an apt quotation—preferably from an author dead at least a hundred years—for rigorous proof'.[14]

Delegitimization: If a good genealogy lends credence to texts and discourses, one way to attack and discredit them is to challenge their descent. This strategy is widely practised in contemporary scholarship. Critics of laissez-faire capitalism have gone back to the writings of Adam Smith, especially his *Theory of Moral Sentiments*, to show that he was concerned about the social consequences of unrestrained capitalism. Critics of crude neopositivism have offered alternative readings of Max Weber to offset demonstrably biased representations of his views about social science by his first English translators.[15] More recently, they have focused attention on the Vienna School to delegitimize the epistemological foundations of King, Keohane, and Verba's, *Designing Social Inquiry*. They have pointed out that the writings of Karl Popper on which King, Keohane, and Verba rely, were subsequently disavowed by Popper as both unrealistic and unnecessary.[16]

Critics of Morgenthau have engaged in a variant of this strategy. Instead of challenging his reading of the texts he cites in support of his theory, they have contested his readings of writers whom he wishes to discredit and play off against. They have shown how his characterization of Hersch Lauterpacht, Solly Zuckerman, and other international lawyers of the interwar years as 'idealists' is misleading but in keeping with his goal of setting them up as straw men.[17] Another variant is to go after a text or discourse with works they neither cite nor claim genealogy from but can nevertheless be used to discredit them. Rousseau and Nietzsche have both been mobilized to attack liberalism and neopositivism. Rengger does this with Morgenthau, by foregrounding Michael Oakeshott's critique of his reliance on tragedy as an organizing framework. Brown rightly observes that the current appeal of Carl Schmitt seems to lie in the weapon his writings offer to left-wing critics of liberalism.

Reclaiming Texts: Authors go out of style by virtue of their own views, how they have been interpreted by others and the subsequent discrediting of their projects. Friedrich Nietzsche went into decline in the West after he was appropriated by the Nazis in the 1930s, with the active support of his sister, a Nazi collaborator. In the 1960s, Walter Kaufmann wrote an intellectual biography of Nietzsche and translated many of his works to rehabilitate him. He showed that his views, especially about race, had been grossly distorted by Nazi propagandists.[18] Subsequent studies of Nietzsche have carried this project along and by the 1990s made him sufficiently respected for constructivists to find it in their interest to cite him as a forbear.

This strategy of reclaiming texts represents a combination of the first two strategies. The goal is to root one's text or preferred discourse in a text or texts that have traditionally served to legitimize opposing texts or discourses. The extraordinary attention devoted to the newly restored and translated gospel of Judas is motivated at least in part by the interest of many Western Christians to challenge the orthodox interpretation of Jesus and Christianity imposed by the Council of Nicea in 325 C.E. when it was enshrined by canonizing the gospels of Matthew, Mark, Luke, and John. Political philosophers have challenged Catholic readings of Aristotle in the writings of Thomas Aquinas, and reinterpreted his works to serve as foundations for their projects. Lang reminds us that Morgenthau attempted something similar with Aristotle, attempting to use him as a foundation for his claims about the relevance of ethics to foreign policy. Jütersonke might be described as doing the same with Morgenthau. He shows how engaged he was while still in Europe with contemporary debates over the meaning of law, the role norms and the relationship of law to foreign policy. By using Morgenthau to access these issues, he is able not only to enrich our understanding of Morgenthau, but to situate current disputes on these questions in a meaningful historical perspective.

To the extent that the field of IR has a foundational text, it is Thucydides, and it is hardly surprising that he has become the focus of scholars from competing paradigms. In *Tragic Vision of Politics*, I previously noted, one of my goals was to show that Thucydides could rightfully be claimed as a foundational text by constructivists.[19] Much of the recent interest in Morgenthau is by realists who want to use him and other mid century realists as a jumping off point for the reformulation of this paradigm. Such an effort involves not only a close reading of these texts, but emphasizing aspects of them that were neglected, misread, or simply read differently by earlier scholars.

Texts as Inspirations: Close, hermeneutical readings of texts attempt to enter into a dialogue with their authors to recreate as far as possible their understanding of their project and its meaning. Efforts to delegitimize other readings of these texts require that the readings one offers be more credible. The same is true of efforts to root one's own text or preferred discourse in a respected classic. Another, looser kind of reading is possible, and can serve an entirely different purpose. From Schelling to Hegel, Hölderlin, Nietzsche, and Heidegger, several generations of German writers and philosophers engaged in 'dialogues' with ancient Greek playwrights in their search for a discourse appropriate to their epoch.[20] Some of these readings use these texts as something akin to Rorschach inkblots on which to project their own yearnings. Hegel's reading of *Antigone*— which stresses the different ethical positions of man and woman, and how events in the tragedy unfold to reveal the need of the spirit to recognize itself in its radical individuality—offers a novel interpretation of the play that tells us a lot more about Hegel than it does about Sophocles.[21] The same is true of Nietzsche's projection of Enlightenment individualism on to aristocratic heroes, or his contention that *Antigone* and *Oedipus at Colonus* are at their core struggles between the sexes and the Apollonian and Dionysian.[22] Greek tragedy was a catalyst for Nietzsche's imagination and led him to ideas that he subsequently read back into texts. He used his interpretations to make his insights and concepts resonate more effectively with his audience. Sigmund Freud's reading of *Oedipus Tyrannus* is even more inattentive to textual detail and historical context, but nobody denies the psychoanalytic utility of the 'Oedipal complex' on the grounds that Oedipus himself clearly did not have such a complex.[23] It would not be productive to evaluate the interpretations of Hegel, Nietzsche, or Freud in terms of the tragedies they wrote about. The more appropriate yardstick is for their originality and philosophical, literary, or medical utility.

   What should we make of all of this? We might relish the irony that some of the latest efforts at originality in our field are being played out in a game that has existed for millennia. This iteration differs only in its scale and diligence, both a reflection of the large number of young scholars with political and theoretical agendas, keen to make names for themselves in the profession and for whom texts are the most obvious intellectual resource. Upon further reflection, we might acknowledge that in the social sciences and the humanities this is not only inevitable, but perhaps, a necessary strategy. Arguments depend as much on their wrapping as they do on their substance, and the purpose of all arguments is to convince. This is especially true of novel arguments, which must exploit ambiguities in existing discourses to make a wedge for themselves and to be heard. As we do with presents, let us carefully unwrap these arguments, and take pleasure in what we find, and if not, hope that they can be returned, or rewrapped and passed along to someone else for whom they are better suited. Let us also pay attention to the wrapping paper because it can be as important as the present to the extent that it offers us new insight into old texts approached and read with present-day sensitivities, interests, and understandings.

10.2. **Morgenthau and the post-Cold War world**

Every generation reads older texts from the perspective of contemporary concerns and with the benefit of knowing why previous generations turned to—or away—from these texts, what they wrote about them and how they used them to advance their projects. New readings often yield new insights. Recent books and articles about Morgenthau have lived up to this expectation.[24] They explore a set of questions that were previously neglected or considered peripheral. These works emphasize the links between his German and American writings, the debt that both owed to Weber and Nietzsche and the ways his thinking about IR evolved from the deep pessimism expressed in his early post-war writings to the more cautious optimism expressed in his later works. Considerable controversy surrounds his intellectual lineage, especially his degree of indebtedness to Carl Schmitt, the relationship of his legal to his political writings, the extent to which the understandings of politics on which he based his theory of IR were formulated before or after he emigrated from Germany, and the extent of and reasons for his advocacy of a form of transformational politics late in his career. The chapters in this volume shed new light on most of these controversies.

Let us return to the problem of transformation, made visibly problematic by the end of the Cold War. Neorealists and other realists too, differentiate systems on the basis of their polarity. System change occurs when the number of poles changes. Realists associate such with hegemonic wars, brought on, according to power transition theories, by shifts in the balance of material capabilities. Rising powers may go to war to remake the system in their interests, or status quo powers to forestall such change. For some realists, this cycle is timeless and independent of technology and learning. Others believe that nuclear weapons have revolutionized international relations by making war too destructive to be rational. In their view, this accounts for the otherwise anomalous peaceful transformation from bi- to multipolarity at the end of the Cold War.[25]

The end of the Cold War and disappearance of the Soviet Union, which are responsible for the ongoing transformation of the international system, are hard to square with these understandings. They were not the result of war. Equally anomalous is that neither Mikhail Gorbachev nor Boris Yeltsin, the Soviet leaders responsible for the changes and concessions that led to the end of the Cold War and the demise of the Soviet Union, were motivated by commitments to preserve or expand the power of the Soviet Union. Gorbachev did not foresee the consequences of his reforms, but Yelstin was fully aware that the Russian Republic's proclamation of independence would hasten the breakup of the Soviet Union.[26] The nature of the system transformation is also the subject of dispute among realists. Waltz insisted that the world remained bipolar in the immediate aftermath of the Cold War.[27] More realists describe it as multipolar, and some prominent American realists contend that it is unipolar. These disagreements reveal the essential ambiguity of the concept of polarity. There are also grounds for questioning its utility as key realist predictions based on the assumption of uni- or multipolarity have not come to pass. NATO has prospered instead of collapsing, and allies and third parties alike have looked for ways to ignore, finesse, or resist various American initiatives, but none of them give evidence of attempting to balance against it.[28]

For classical realists like Morgenthau, transformation is a broader concept and one they associate with shifts in identities, discourses, and conceptions of security. Morgenthau conceives of political systems in terms of their principles of order, and is interested in the ways in which these principles help shape the identities of actors and the framing of their interests. As Richard Little shows, in his view, the success of the balance of power for the better part of two centuries was less a function of the distribution of capabilities than it was of the existence and strength of international society that bound together the most important actors in the system. When that society broke down, as it did from the first partition of Poland through the Napoleonic Wars, the balance of power no longer functioned to preserve the peace or existence of the members of the system.[29] International society was even weaker in the twentieth century, and its decline was an underlying cause of both world wars. Morgenthau worried that its continuing absence in the immediate post-war period had removed all constraints on super-power competition. From the vantage point of the twenty-first century, Morgenthau reads as much like a proto-constructivist as he does a realist.

For classical realists like Thucydides and Morgenthau, changes in identities and interests are often the result of underlying processes like modernization, and hegemonic war is more often a consequence than a cause of such a transformation.[30] This different understanding of cause and effect has important implications for the kinds of strategies classical realists envisage as efficacious in maintaining or restoring order. They put more weight on values and ideas than they do on power.

Nick Rengger stresses that Morgenthau's understanding of modernization in *Scientific Man versus Power Politics* emphasizes its negative features. In Morgenthau's judgment, the Enlightenment promoted a misplaced faith in reason that undermined the values and norms that had restrained individual and state behaviour. In making this association, Morgenthau drew directly on Hegel and Freud. Hegel warned of the dangers of homogenization of society arising from equality and universal participation in society. It would sunder traditional communities and individual ties to them without providing an alternative source of identity.[31] Hegel wrote on the eve of the Industrial Revolution and did not envisage the modern industrial state with its large bureaucracies and modern means of communication. These developments, Morgenthau argued, allowed the power of the state to feed on itself through a process of psychological transference that made it the most exalted object of loyalty. Libidinal impulses, repressed by the society, were mobilized by the state for its own ends. By transferring these impulses to the nation, citizens achieved vicarious satisfaction of aspirations they otherwise could not attain or had to repress. Elimination of the Kulaks, forced collectivization, Stalin's purges, the Second World War, and the Holocaust were all expressions of the transference of private impulses onto the state and the absence of any limits on the state's exercise of power.[32] Writing in the aftermath of the great upheavals of the first half of the twentieth century, Morgenthau recognized that communal identity was far from an unalloyed blessing: it allowed people to fulfil their potential as human beings, but also risked turning them into 'social men' like Eichmann who lose their humanity in the course of implementing the directives of the state.[33]

For Morgenthau, the absence of external constraints on state power was *the* defining characteristic of international politics at mid century. The old normative order was in ruins and too feeble to restrain great powers.[34] Against this background, the Soviet Union and the United States were locked into an escalating conflict, made more ominous by the unrivalled destructive potential of nuclear weapons. The principal threat to peace was, however, political. Moscow and Washington were 'Imbued with the crusading spirit of the new moral force of nationalistic universalism', and confronted each other with 'inflexible opposition'.[35] The balance of power was a feeble instrument in these circumstances, and deterrence was more likely to exacerbate tensions than to alleviate them. Bipolarity could help to preserve the peace by reducing uncertainty—or push the superpowers towards war because of the putative advantage of launching a first strike. Restraint was needed more than anything else, and Morgenthau worried that neither superpower had leaders with the requisite moral courage to resist mounting pressures to engage in risky and confrontational foreign policies.[36]

Realism in the context of the Cold War was a plea for statesmen—above all, American and Soviet leaders—to recognize the need to coexist in a world of opposing interests and conflict. Their security could never be guaranteed, only approximated through a fragile balance of power and mutual compromises that might resolve, or at least defuse, the arms race and the escalatory potential of the various regional conflicts in which they had become entangled. Morgenthau insisted that restraint and partial accommodation were the most practical short-term strategies for preserving the peace. A more enduring solution to the problem of war required a fundamental transformation of the international system that made it more like well-ordered domestic societies.

For Morgenthau, the universality of the power drive meant that the balance of power was 'a general social phenomenon to be found on all levels of social interaction'.[37] Individuals, groups, and states inevitably combined to protect themselves from predators. At the international level, the balance of power had contradictory implications for peace. It might deter war if status quo powers outgunned imperialist challengers and demonstrated their resolve to go to war in defence of the status quo. But balancing could also intensify tensions and make war more likely because of the impossibility of assessing with any certainty the motives, capability, and resolve of other states. Leaders understandably aim to achieve a margin of safety, and when multiple states or opposing alliances act this way, they ratchet up international tensions. In this situation, rising powers might be tempted to go to war when they think they have an advantage, and status quo powers to launch preventive wars against rising challengers. Even when the balance of power failed to prevent war, Morgenthau reasoned, it might still limit its consequences and preserve the existence of states, small and large, that constitute the political system. He credited it with having served these ends for much of the eighteenth and nineteenth centuries.

Morgenthau wrote in the aftermath of destructive wars that undermined the communities and conventions that had previously sustained order at home and abroad. He did not think it feasible to restore the old way of life, aspects of which had become highly problematic even before the onset of war. Nor, Craig Campbell tells us, was he attracted to liberal, international projects that aspired to impose limits on state sovereignty. He searched instead for some combination of the old and the new that could accommodate the benefits of modernity while limiting its destructive potential. By 1962, the émigré scholar who twenty years earlier had considered the aspirations of internationalists dangerous would now insist that the well-being of the human race required 'a principle of political organization transcending the nation-state'.[38] By the 1970s, he had become more optimistic about the prospects for peace. In his view, détente, explicit recognition of the territorial status quo in Europe, a corresponding decline in ideological confrontation, the emergence of Japan, China, West Germany as possible third forces, and the effects of Vietnam on American power had made both superpowers more cautious and tolerant of the status quo.[39] Of equal importance, their daily contacts, negotiations, and occasional agreements had gone some way towards normalizing their relations and creating the basis for a renewed sense of international community.

Morgenthau's belief in the need for some form of supranational authority also deepened in the 1970s. Beyond the threat of nuclear holocaust, humanity was also threatened by the population explosion, world hunger, and environmental degradation. He had no faith in the ability of nation states to ameliorate any of these problems.[40] If leaders and peoples were so zealous about safeguarding their sovereignty, there was little hope of moving them towards acceptance of a new order. Progress would only occur when enough national leaders became convinced that it was in their respective national interests. The series of steps Europeans had taken towards integration illustrated the apparent paradox that 'what is historically conditioned in the idea of the national interest can be overcome only through the promotion in concert of the national interest of a number of nations'.[41] Paradoxically, if slyly, he envisaged realism, with its emphasis on state interests, as a means of ultimately transcending the nation state.

In the best tradition of the Greeks, Lang observes, Morgenthau aspired to develop a framework that actors can use to work their way through contemporary problems. He insisted that 'All lasting contributions to political science, from Plato, Aristotle, and Augustine to the *Federalist*, Marx and Calhoun, have been responses to challenges arising from political reality. They have not been self-sufficient theoretical developments pursuing theoretical concerns for their own sake.'[42] Great political thinkers confronted problems that could not be solved with the tools on hand, and developed new ways of thinking to use past experience to illuminate the present. Beyond this, Morgenthau sought to stimulate the kind of reflection that leads to wisdom and with it, appreciation of the need for self-restraint, especially on the part of great powers. He remains a man for all seasons.

10.3. **Texts as resources**

Almost contemporaneous with the invention of writing, political authorities recognized the importance of texts and their need to control them. The Old Testament was codified with this end in mind, and for over a millennia the Roman Catholic church forbade translations of the Bible into the vernacular. At its core, the Enlightenment was an attempt to use reason to destroy tradition and free the individual, and its proponents envisaged texts as powerful weapons in this struggle. Christian and Muslim fundamentalists offer striking contemporary examples of how radical discourses and the interpretations of texts they enable can be used to mobilize political support against the religious and political establishment.[43] Their readings certainly treat the Bible and Koran as Rorschach inkblots, but their inventive readings of these texts have not prevented them from gaining numerous adherents.

Any examination of the relationship between texts and politics must differentiate between authoritarian and open societies. Texts play a somewhat different role in both kinds of societies, are controlled much more closely in the former and accordingly require different strategies for reinterpreting or discrediting them. Successful decentreing of texts in authoritarian societies is also likely to have more immediate and far-reaching implications.

The Soviet Union provides a good illustration of how texts function in authoritarian societies. The writings of Marx and Engels, and then of Stalin became required reading. Stalin's *Short Course of the History of the All-Russian Communist Party*—known everywhere as the *Short Course*—was published in 1938 and considered the encyclopaedia of Marxism. In 1956, when Khrushchev denounced Stalin's 'Cult of the Personality' at the Twentieth Party Congress, over 42 million copies of the book had been printed and distributed in 67 languages. Intellectuals and writers often had to make ritual genuflections to this work and the Marxist–Leninist canon more generally to have any chance of getting their own works published. Works of fiction had to adhere to the party line, and even when they did, their authors were still at risk when that line changed. In periods of thaw, some experimentation becomes possible, and artists, journalists, and publishers usually pushed against the limits of expression. Judging from the Soviet and Chinese experiences, thaws are frequently followed by periods of renewed repression. In this environment, producers and consumers of texts resort to two quite different strategies. They rely on illegal means of communication, which include *samizdat* (mimeo texts passed from hand to hand), wall posters hung furtively at night, underground performances, foreign radio broadcasts, and uncontrolled Internet websites and chat rooms. They also rely on 'double discourse', which uses plot lines and dialogue with hidden references or double meanings, unrecognized or tolerated by the authorities, to satirize the regime and its policies. This is a time-honoured practice that has occasionally resulted in great works of literature, philosophy, or art, such as Montesquieu's *Persian Letters* and Kasimir Malevich's painting *Red Cavalry*.

Authoritarian regimes on the wane, especially ones whose ruling elites have lost faith in their ideology, find it increasingly difficult to maintain control over texts. Periods of thaw and repression become more frequent, with overall, if slow, movement towards greater freedom of expression. This has been the pattern in China. A period of thaw can also spin out of control, as in Gorbachev's Soviet Union, leaving leaders little choice but to make whatever accommodation they can with a fast-changing reality. Regime survival in these circumstances is difficult because long-suppressed antagonism towards the regime and between different components of the society (i.e., classes, ethnic, and religious groups) can become pronounced.

In more open societies, texts also play an important role, and there are likely to be multiple texts sustaining multiple discourses. Control over them is much less certain, especially if it is exercised by government, and criticism and reformulation of texts is more open. Discourses shift more quickly without disrupting the political order, and their implications for the society, while ultimately profound, are not necessarily evident at the time. Indeed, the reasons why interpretations change, the ways in which they affect the appeal of discourses, and the routes by which changing discourses influence politics remain mysterious, undertheorized, and relatively unexplored empirically.

The academic community is all about texts. Reputations are made from producing, interpreting, and critiquing them. Unless we view this activity as an elaborate *jeu d'esprit*, like games of chess played for their own sake or the reputations and other benefits they confer on those who excel, the production and reading of texts must have substantive implications for the real world. Most academics believe they do influence society, and I know from conversations with colleagues that this belief is especially widespread among scholars of IR. We can all point to books about IR that we believe have had significant impact on foreign policy. Morgenthau's *Politics Among Nations* (1948) would probably head the list. E. H. Carr's *Twenty Year's Crisis* (1939) might come next. If we relax our criteria to include books not specifically in the field of IR we might add, among others, Carl von Clausewitz, *On War* (1832–37), Alfred Thayer Mahan, *The Influence of Sea Power Upon History* (1890), Houston Stewart Chamberlain, *The Foundations of the Nineteenth Century* (1907), V. I. Lenin, *On Imperialism* (1916), John Maynard Keynes, *The Economic Consequences of the Peace* (1919) and Bernard Brodie, *The Absolute Weapon* (1946). The most recent contender for this august list is arguably, Samuel Huntington's *Clash of Civilizations* (1996). I use the words 'might' and 'arguably' because there is no rigorous way to determine the influence of books on the thinking of people in general, on leaders in particular and on the policies that either the public or leaders support or adopt. Sales of books are at best an imperfect indicator of influence. Many non-fiction books that make best-seller lists may be purchased but not read, as seems to be the case most recently with Bill Clinton's memoirs. Leaders' sometimes identify books that had an enormous influence on them; for Field Marshal Moltke the Elder it was Clausewitz, and for George Marshall, Thucydides. There is, of course, no way of knowing it this was really the case, or if they were drawn to these books because they justified policies they already favoured.

Assuming for the sake of argument that my list is a reasonable, if by no means an exclusive one, it suggests that scholarship in the most direct sense has only a limited influence on the practice of international relations. Ten plus books in more than a century-and-a-half is not very many. And only one of them was published since 1950 (not counting new editions), and it does not have an unambiguous claim to the list. The three books published at the beginning of the Second World War or in its aftermath had more diffuse influence. They helped to shape how a generation of students and influential people thought about the post-war world and problems of security. Thomas Schelling's *Arms and Influence* (1966) might recommend itself to the list for the same reason.

Most of the books fit into two categories: they pertain to war and weapons, or tap and play on primordial fears of their readers. Clausewitz, Mahan, Lenin, and Brodie all fit into the first category, and Chamberlain and Huntington into the second. Clausewitz—misread by Germans and French alike—helped to justify offensive strategies and decisive battles. Mahan provided the logic and justification for America and Germany's naval build-ups in the latter part of the nineteenth century. Lenin's views had a direct influence on Soviet and Chinese foreign policies. Brodie provided the logic and justification for deterrence and mutual assured destruction. Chamberlain's book combined social Darwinism with racism, propagated the idea of an Aryan race, and was widely read in Europe. It was the inspiration for Gobineau's equally racist book in France, and had a major impact upon Richard Wagner. Chamberlain was invited to court by Kaiser Wilhelm and was acknowledged by Adolf Hitler as having been instrumental in his racist thinking.

There is a paucity of books on the list that have peace as their principal message or are devoted to strategies for conflict management and resolution. There are many fine studies of this kind, but only one—Keynes, *Economic Consequences of the Peace*—has become a best seller, and its author almost a household name. Keynes's book encouraged widespread disenchantment with reparations in Britain and the US, and was instrumental in bringing about the Dawes Plan (1923) and the Young Plan (1930). Another work on conflict management that achieved a lesser degree of influence in the policymaking community is David Mitrany, *The Road to Security* (1944), which advocated functionalism as a strategy of conflict management. Academic writing on strategic arms control and the relationship between economic development and peace was also important, but there are no one or two books that stand out above all others in this connection.

Another disturbing finding is that the seeming influence of a book bears little relationship to its quality. In the first instance, this is due to the market; scholarly books lack commercial appeal. What publishers bring before the public is what they think will sell, and in the non-fiction category, this is most often simple books with simple messages. Huntington is appealing for precisely this reason. The publishing playing field is far from even. Books that praise a country's leaders (when they are popular) and build or support its myths are far more likely to get published and sell than those that are critical. In most countries, media outlets are controlled by large corporations, some of whose leaders have political agendas and support and publicize books advancing their points of view. The success of the neocons is at least in part due to their ready access to conservative magazines, publishing houses, and television networks. Other forums for publicity rarely feature serious works. How often have you seen a professor interviewed by Oprah Winfrey?[44] Reading as a pastime is declining, as witnessed by the shrinking number of quality newspapers and their readerships. The net effect is to marginalize books in general, and serious books in particular.

There are alternative networks for selling books, and these sometimes achieve phenomenal success. The multiple volumes of Rev. Tim LaHaye's and Jerry Jenkin's *Left Behind Series* have generally grabbed the number one position on the *New York Times* best-seller list their first week of release. As of September 2005, *Harry Potter* books had sold 30 million copies worldwide, while the *Left Behind* series sold twice that number in the United States alone. *Left Behind* peddles a primitive, parochial, and retributive version of morality: good and evil is sharply delineated; those who embrace Jesus go to heaven and everyone else suffers eternal damnation.[45] The books are very much about international politics. Their plots revolve around a conflict between Jesus and the anti-Christ (a Romanian Secretary General of the United Nations), which reaches its climax at the Battle of Armageddon. The books offer a thinly veiled policy agenda, which is frequently reinforced at church meetings where the *Left Behind* books are discussed and sold. Measured in terms of the number of people they reach in the United States, and increasingly abroad as well, they undoubtedly are having more influence than any book or books produced by any scholar or community of them.

When scholarly or otherwise weighty books achieve influence they generally address newsworthy problems, are published at an opportune moment, and often have prominent sponsors. Brodie's book offered a useful conceptual framework for thinking about nuclear weapons, a problem on the mind of every military officer, foreign policy official, and much of the educated public in the aftermath of Hiroshima and Nagasaki. Brodie and Morgenthau both benefited from the enormous public interest in America's pre-eminent role in the world after the Second World War, the onset of the Cold War, and the search for ways of dealing with the Soviet Union short of destructive war. Clausewitz's *On War* was neither newsworthy nor published at a good time, but had a very prominent sponsor. The posthumous publication of Clausewitz's works in 1832–37 made little impact until Germany's stunning triumphs over Austria in 1866 and France in 1870–71. When Field Marshal Helmuth von Moltke, the architect of those victories, told the press that *On War* had been his campaign bible, Clausewitz became an overnight sensation and his work was translated into a score of European languages.[46]

Even this cursory review of the world of IR scholarship and its public and policy impact suggests a sharp disconnect between the practices expected to govern the world of scholarship and those that are in fact operative in publishing and politics. The norms of scholarship are those of science: data and research should be shared and subject to critique, good scholarship is evaluated in terms of an ever-evolving set of practices, and good scholarship is expected to drive out the bad.

This expectation rests on two rarely articulated and untested underlying assumptions. The first is that the appeal and legitimacy of any scholarly discourse within the academy depends on its intellectual rigour. If so, texts can be expected to lose favour and decline in perceived importance to the degree that they can be shown to be inconsistent, at odds with the evidence or based on weak conceptual foundations. Texts and discourses come and go, but rarely, it seems, on the basis of their demonstrated excellence or lack of it. Neorealism took enough hits to sink the *Bismarck*, but still it stayed afloat, if not always able to proceed at full steam, until the end of the Cold War. External developments finally made it list dangerously, and primarily because they foregrounded a new set of problems for theorists to which neorealism did not seem relevant. Marxism confronted all kinds of intellectual difficulties but remained an important paradigm in Western scholarship until the collapse of communism in Eastern Europe and the Soviet Union, regimes that were arguably communist in name only. Deterrence theory remains alive and well despite compelling empirical critiques that immediate deterrence rarely succeeds. Rational choice positively prospers despite its inability to account for the so-called voting paradox, or much of anything else.

The second assumption is that there is some connection between academic and policy discourses. If the former exist in a hermetically sealed world of their own, there is little incentive for someone ultimately interested in policy to engage them. For the most part, I think it fair to say that elite and mass discourses exist on parallel tracks with few cross switches. There are times when they intersect, and with powerful consequences. Thucydides and Plato wrote at such a moment in fifth-century Greece. Tocqueville describes a similar development on the eve of the French Revolution, which he attributes to the influence of Enlightenment writers and propagandists.[47] Elites are at least as ignorant of mass discourses. My informal survey of academic colleagues at a recent meeting of the International Studies Association revealed that hardly any of them have ever heard of, let alone read, any of the volumes of the *Left Behind* series. Only four Ivy League libraries have any of the volumes.[48]

Elite-academic intercourse is more common. In Europe, the elite press reviews serious books and reports on key academic debates. In Germany, the so-called *Historikerstreit* over the Third Reich and the singularity of the Holocaust received wide coverage.[49] In the United States, there is considerable movement of people between the academe and Washington, but much less traffic in texts and ideas. Few academic books are found in governmental offices or on the night tables of top officials. In the 1980s, every IR scholar and graduate student was familiar with Waltz's *Theory of International Politics*. For better or worse, it was largely unknown to policymakers. To the extent that policymakers and their advisors have any time or inclination to read, they are likely to turn to history and biography, not to political science. Prominent academic historians and presidential biographers like Arthur Schlesinger, Jr., Robert Dallek, and Ron Chernow sell widely, and are not infrequently cited, even quoted, by officials.

The uphill struggle IR scholars face in presenting their research to a wider audience should make us respectful of those few members of our profession who have succeeded. Morgenthau, Carr, George Kennan, and Raymond Aron all reached beyond the academy, but only Morgenthau was a political scientist. Carr and Kennan were historians, and Aron, a sociologist. Morgenthau had additional handicaps. He was a foreigner who spoke with a strong accent, wrote theory, not biography or historical narratives, and was generally critical of administration policy, especially during the Vietnam War. Viewed in this light the success he had in finding fora from which he could speak truth to power is all the more impressive.

10.4. **Conclusions**

To this point in my argument I have written about the external benefits of revisiting texts, that is about their instrumental ability to influence contemporary theoretical debates and foreign policy decisions. There are internal benefits as well, and I would like to conclude my chapter and our book by directing our attention to them. This provides a more upbeat ending because unlike the external benefits, which while real, are difficult to achieve, the internal benefits are within the grasp of each of us.

Scholarship differs from journalism in its emphasis on theoretical underpinnings, strivings for conceptual rigour and terminological precision, and adherence to sophisticated rules for the selection and evaluation of evidence. Scholars hold themselves to different, some would say, higher standards than journalism, and certainly of the kind of writer that engages in partisan advocacy. On one level, the practice of science, and scholarship more generally, is dependent on an ever-evolving set of protocols that we use to conduct and evaluate research. At a deeper level, science and good scholarship in any discipline or field depend on the ethical commitments of practitioners. These commitments not only make us aspire to play by the rules, they encourage us to improve our ability to conduct good scholarship. And here is where the reading of texts comes into the picture. They teach us by example, by their quality, enduring appeal and, in the cases of great texts, the normative commitments that drove their authors and can still motivate us.

Revisiting texts, especially when they represent different traditions, can teach us humility while widening our intellectual perspectives. We learn that even the greatest works—especially in our field, but in all social science—have serious weaknesses, become rapidly dated in some ways, and incorporate ideas, perspectives, or approaches to problems that have subsequently lost legitimacy. Contributors to this volume tell us that Aristotle is an important figure for Morgenthau, but that his reading of him is at times superficial. They point out that Morgenthau's treatment of the concept of the balance of power is confusing, if not contradictory, that he never reconciles thermonuclear weapons and his resulting support for supranational authority with his fundamental principles of realism, and that from our perspective, his discussion of alliances and balancing appears overly mechanical. We can denigrate Morgenthau and any other respected text of the past for their incompleteness, inconsistencies, occasional superficiality, and even downright errors, or we can recognize that works greater than any we are likely to write have serious flaws. This is a particularly important lesson for graduate students, who are taught from their first day in class to bring to light all the conceptual and empirical shortcomings of everything they read. They are rarely instructed to appreciate the difficulties and limitations under which scholars work, and may develop unrealistically high and possibly crippling expectations about what they might be able to achieve.

Even though most of us know better, it is easy to slip into the mindset that we have some privileged vantage point outside of history that provides us a timeless perspective on politics. Revisiting texts can expose this pretension—particularly prevalent among those IR scholars from quantitative and modelling traditions who characterize what they do as 'normal science'. Revisiting texts, even the greatest of them like Thucydides, Plato, and Aristotle, reveals how culture- and time-bound they are, even if some of their insights appear to have withstood the test of history. These works, of necessity, reflect the contemporary interests of their authors, usually embody concepts and categories common to their era as well as modes of expression and language. The older they are, or the further away their culture from ours, the more work we must put in to understand these texts in any way approaching the intentions of their authors. Not only their framing of problems, but their solutions may strike us as wrong or simply anachronistic. Here too we need to look into the mirror and recognize the extent to which our publications reflect parochial perspectives and forms, and have 'use by' dates of much shorter duration than the classics we so much admire.

Revisiting texts broadens our horizons by demonstrating that no text, no matter how great, has a monopoly on the truth. We learn that the best of texts convey partial truths, and that to develop a more holistic understanding of the politics of any period, or of the subject of politics more generally, we need to read and assimilate the insights of multiple, often competing texts and perspectives. Recognition of this truth should teach us tolerance, respect for people and works in differing traditions, and encourage us to learn from them.

For all of these reasons, Morgenthau, who speaks to us across the abyss of Weimar, the Nazi era, the Second World War, and the Cold War, still has much to teach us.

☐ NOTES

1. Richard Ned Lebow, *The Tragic Vision of Politics* (Cambridge: Cambridge University Press, 2004), Chs. 5 and 7.
2. Lebow, *Tragic Vision of Politics*, offers a defense of tragedy, as Rengger recognizes. See Toni Erskine and Richard Ned Lebow (eds.), *Tragedy and International Relations* (forthcoming), for a more thorough evaluation of the concept of tragedy as applied to international relations.
3. *Jacobellis v. Ohio*, 378 U.S. 184, 84 S. Ct. 1676, 12 L. Ed. 2d 793 [1964].
4. William T. R. Fox, *The Super-Powers* (New York: Harcourt, Brace, 1944); Morgenthau, *Politics Among Nations*, 270–8. For Morgenthau's uses of the term bipolarity,

see *In Defense of the National Interest* (New York: Knopf, 1951), 45; *Politics Among Nations*, 2nd edn. (New York: Knopf, 1954), Table of Contents and 325.

5. Kenneth N. Waltz, *Theory of International Politics* (Boston, MA: Addison-Wesley, 1979), 165–70.

6. John Lewis Gaddis, 'Toward the Post-Cold World', *Foreign Affairs*, 70 (1991), 102–22.

7. Kenneth N. Waltz, 'The Emerging Structure of International Politics', *International Security*, 18: 2 (1993), 5–43; John J. Mearsheimer, 'Back to the Future: Instability in Europe After the Cold War', *International Security*, 15: 4 (1990), 5–56; Mearsheimer, 'The Case for Ukrainian Nuclear Deterrent', *Foreign Affairs*, 72: 3 (1993), 50–66.

8. Karl W. Deutsch, et al., *Political Community and the North Atlantic Area: International Organization in the Light of Historical Experience* (Princeton, NJ: Princeton University Press, 1957).

9. Alexander E. Wendt, 'Anarchy Is What States Make of It: The Social Construction of Power Politics', *International Organization*, 46: 2 (1992), 391–425.

10. John J. Mearsheimer, 'E.H. Carr vs. Idealism: The Battle Rages On', *International Relations*, 19 (2005), 139–52; John J. Mearsheimer, Paul Rogers, Richard Little, Christopher Hill, Chris Brown, and Ken Booth, 'Roundtable: The Battle Rages On', *International Relations*, 19 (2005), 337–60.

11. Daniel Garst, 'Thucydides and Neorealism', *International Studies Quarterly*, 33: 1 (1989), 469–97; Clifford Orwin, *The Humanity of Thucydides* (Princeton, NJ: Princeton University Press, 1994); Paul A. Rahe, 'Thucydides Critique of Realpolitik', in Benjamin Frankel, *Roots of Realism* (Portland, OR: Frank Cass, 1996), 105–41.

12. Richard Ned Lebow, 'Thucydides the Constructivist', *American Political Science Review*, 95 (2001), 547–60.

13. E. H. Carr, *The Twenty Years' Crisis: An Introduction to the Study of International Relations* (London: Macmillan, 1951); John Herz, *Political Realism and Political Idealism: A Study in Theories and Realities* (Chicago, IL: University of Chicago Press, 1951); and *International Politics in the Nuclear Age* (New York: Columbia University Press, 1959).

14. Barrington Moore, Jr., 'Review of *Politics Among Nations*', *American Sociological Review*, 14 (April 1949), 326.

15. The first attempt to do this took the form of a biography with extensive excerpts from Weber's work. Reinhard Bendix, *Max Weber: An Intellectual Portrait* (Berkeley, CA: University of California Press, 1960).

16. Richard Ned Lebow and Mark Lichbach (eds.), *Theory and Evidence in Comparative Politics and International Relations* (New York: Palgrave-Macmillan, 2007).

17. Brian C. Schmidt, 'Anarchy, World Politics and the Birth of a Discipline: American International Relations, Pluralist Theory and the Myth of Interwar Idealism', *International Relations*, 16: 1 (2002), 9–31; Lucian M. Ashworth, 'Did the Realist–Idealist Great Debate Really Happen? A Revisionist History of International Relations', *International Relations*, 16, 1 (2002), 33–51.

18. Walter Kaufmann, *Tragedy and Philosophy* (Princeton, NJ: Princeton University Press, 1968).

19. Lebow, *The Tragic Vision of Politics*, Chs. 2–3.

20. Dennis J. Schmidt, *On Germans and Other Greeks: Tragedy and Ethical Life* (Bloomington, IN: University of Indiana Press, 2001), 192–3.

21. Georg Wilhelm Friedrich Hegel, *The Phenomenology of Mind*, trans. by J. B. Baillie, ed. George Lichtheim (New York: Harper & Row [1967]), paras. 457, 463–6.

22. Friedrich Nietzsche, *The Birth of Tragedy*, trans. by Walter Kaufmann (Mineola, NY: Dover, 1995), Sections 1 and 3.

23. Sigmund Freud, *The Interpretation of Dreams*, trans. and ed. James Strachey, 3rd edn. (New York: Basic Books, 1955), 'Dostoevsky and Parricide', in James E. Strachey (ed.), *The Standard Edition of the Complete Psychological Works of Sigmund Freud* (London: Hogarth Press, 1961), vol. 21, 188; and *A General Introduction to Psychoanalysis*, trans. Joan Riviere (New York: Liverwright, 1935), 291, for Freud's evolving understanding of the Oedipal complex and the play.

24. Andreas Sollner, 'German Conservatism in America: Morgenthau's Political Realism', *Telos*, 72 (1987), 161–77; Greg Russell, *Hans Morgenthau and the Ethics of American Statecraft* (Baton Rouge, LA: Louisiana State University Press, 1990); Joel Rosenthal, *Righteous Realists: Political Realism, Responsible Power and American Culture in the Nuclear Age* ((Baton Rouge, LA: Louisiana State University Press, 1991); Christoph Frei, *Hans J. Morgenthau: An Intellectual Biography* (Baton Rouge, LA: Louisiana State University Press, [1994] 2001); Tarak Barkawi, 'Strategy as Vocation: Weber, Morgenthau and Modern Strategic Studies', *Review of International Studies*, 24: 2 (1998), 159–4; Jan Wilhelm Honig, 'Totalitarianism and Realism: Hans Morgenthau's German Years', *Security Studies*, 5: 2 (1995–96), 283–313; Martti Koskenniemi, *The Gentle Civilizer of Nations: The Rise and Fall of International Law 1870–1960* (Cambridge: Cambridge University Press, 2002); Benjamin Mollov, *Power and Transcendence: Hans J. Morgenthau and the Jewish Experience* (Lanham, MD: Lexington, 2002); Campbell Craig, *Glimmer of a New Leviathan: Total War in the Realism of Niebuhr, Morgenthau and Waltz* (New York: Columbia University Press, 2003); Anthony F. Lang, Jr. (ed.), *Political Theory and International Affairs: Hans J. Morgenthau on Aristotle's Politics* (Westport, CT: Praeger, 2005).

25. Waltz, *Theory of International Politics*, and 'The Emerging Structure of International Politics'; Mearsheimer, 'Back to the Future'; William C. Wohlforth, 'Realism and the End of the Cold War', *International Security*, 19 (1994–95), 91–129; Kenneth A. Oye, 'Explaining the End of the Cold War: Morphological and Behavioral Adaptations to the Nuclear Peace?', in Richard Ned Lebow and Thomas Risse-Kappen (eds.), *International Relations Theory and the End of the Cold War* (New York: Columbia University Press, 1995), 57–84.

26. Robert D. English, *Russia and the Idea of the West: Gorbachev, Intellectuals, and the End of the Cold War* (New York: Columbia University Press, 2000); Archie Brown, *The Gorbachev Factor* (Oxford: Oxford University Press, 1996); Richard

K. Herrmann and Richard Ned Lebow (eds.), *Ending the Cold War* (New York: Palgrave-Macmillan, 2004); George Breslauer, *Gorbachev and Yeltsin as Leaders* (New York: Cambridge University Press, 2002).

27. Waltz, 'The Emerging Structure of International Politics'.
28. For a review of this literature and the fuzziness of the concepts on which these debates are based, see Richard Ned Lebow, *Rethinking International Relations Theory* (Oxford: Oxford University Press, forthcoming).
29. Hans J. Morgenthau, *Politics Among Nations; the Struggle for Power and Peace*, 3rd. edn. (New York: Knopf, 1960), 160–6; *In Defense of the National Interest*, 60. Paul W. Schroeder, 'A. J. P. Taylor's International System', *International History Review*, 23 (2001), 3–27, makes the same point.
30. Lebow, *Tragic Vision of Politics*, Ch. 7 for further development of this argument.
31. G. W. F. Hegel, *Phenomenology of Spirit* (1807) and *Philosophy of Right* (1821). Charles Taylor, *Hegel* (Cambridge: Cambridge University Press, 1975), 403–21.
32. Morgenthau, *Politics Among Nations*, 169. The psychological component of this analysis relied heavily on the earlier work of Morgenthau's Chicago colleague, Harold Lasswell, *World Politics and Personal Insecurity* (New York: McGraw-Hill, 1935). Morgenthau also drew on Hegel.
33. Hannah Arendt, *Eichmann in Jerusalem: A Report on the Banality of Evil* (New York: Viking, 1964).
34. Hans J. Morgenthau, *The Decline of Democratic Politics* (Chicago, IL: University of Chicago Press, 1958), 60.
35. Hans J. Morgenthau, *Politics Among Nations*, 1st edn. (New York: Knopf, 1948), 430.
36. Morgenthau, *Politics Among Nations*, 1st edn., 169; *Decline of Democratic Politics*, 80; Letter to the *New York Times*, 19 June 1969.
37. Morgenthau, *Decline of Democratic Politics*, 49, 81.
38. Ibid. 75–6.
39. Morgenthau, *Politics Among Nations*, 5th edn. (1972), preface. Pages 355–6 still reflect the pessimism of earlier editions.
40. Kenneth W. Thompson, 'Introduction', *In Defense of the National Interest* (Lanham, MD: University Press of America, 1982), v; personal communications with Hans Morgenthau.
41. Morgenthau, *Decline of Democratic Politics*, 93.
42. Hans J. Morgenthau, 'The Purpose of Political Science', in James C. Charlesworth (ed.), *A Design for Political Science: Scope, Objectives and Methods* (Philadelphia, PA: American Academy of Political and Social Science, 1966), 77.
43. Susan Friend Harding, *The Book of Jerry Falwell: Fundamentalist Language and Politics* (Princeton, NJ: Princeton University Press, 2000), shows how fundamentalists use the Bible as a generative text to create new cultural forms. They invoke the Holy Spirit as a unifying interpretive convention that allows ongoing creation. Fundamentalist language is therefore the opposite of a sceptic's literalist reading that searches for contradictions: rather it seeks to integrate, reconcile, and generate, to create hybrid cultural forms rather than separatist ones.

44. http://www.oprah.com/tows/booksseen/tows_booksseen_main.jhtml (last accessed 27 April 2006) for a list of books discussed on her show.

45. LaHaye and Jenkins, *Left Behind*, 12 volume series.

46. Eberhard Kessel, *Moltke* (Stuttgart: K. F. Koehler, 1957), 108.

47. Alexis de Tocqueville, *The Old Régime and the French Revolution*, trans. Stuart Gilbert (Garden City, NY: Doubleday, 1955), Part 3, Chs. 1–2, 138–57.

48. 'Borrow Direct', Ivy League Library search, November 2005.

49. Richard Ned Lebow, Wulf Kansteiner and Claudio Fogu (eds.), *The Politics of Memory in Postwar Europe* (Durham: Duke University Press, 2006) for a more general discussion of the intersection of academic and elite discourses in Europe.

☐ INDEX

Items from notes are indexed in bold letters e.g. 164n.

Kersten, Jens 115n
Kessel, Eberhard 268n
Keynes, John Maynard 258, 259
King, Gary 247
Kissinger, Henry 122, 135n, 228, 238n, 244
Klingerman, H. D. 189n
Klusmyer, Douglas 40n
Koskenniemi, Martti 16n, 87n, 96, 97, 107,
    113n, 114n, 115n, 117n, 190n, 238n,
    239n, 266n
    From Apology to Utopia 99
Krauthammer, Charles 228, 238n
Kriskol, Irving 217, 218, 219, 220, 222, 223,
    225, 227, 236n, 237n, 238n
Kunz, Joseph L. 103

LaHaye, Tim 260, 268n
Landon, Harold R. 192n
Lang, Anthony F. 9, 10, 38n, 191n, 241, 248,
    255, 266n
Latin America 55, 71, 73, 75, 76
Lauterpacht, Sir Hirsch 11, 94, 95, 97, 98, 99,
    100, 110, 113n, 114n, 115n, 242n, 247
law 11, 108, 110, 248
    and politics 7–8, 11
    pure theory of 103
    see also international law
leadership 31, 33, 233, 234
    Soviet 168
    USA 81, 176, 224
    world 226
League of Nations 49, 55, 68, 73, 77, 83, 84,
    172
Lebow, Richard Ned 5, 13, 15n, 17n, 61n,
    91n, 92n, 112n, 123, 134n, 135n,
    189n, 191n, 193n, 213n, 238n, 264n,
    265n, 266n, 267n, 268n
    The Tragic Vision of Politics 119, 241, 249
Ledeen, Michael 237n
legalism 2, 83, 124–5
legality 65, 67, 68, 69
legislation 23, 108
Legro, Jeffrey W. 14n, 189n
Lenin, V. I. 258
liberalism 4, 31, 47, 49, 68, 76, 77, 82, 110,
    118, 149, 171, 173, 218, 219, 221, 227,
    234, 244, 246, 248, 254
    modernity in 13, 217, 220, 221, 223, 224,
    227, 229, 232, 233
    Morgenthau on 123, 124, 176, 180, 181–2,
    187, 229

Schmitt on 94, 124
    in USA 71, 73, 172
    see also politics, in opposition to
Lichbach, Mark 265n
Lieven, Anatol 40n
Lincoln, Abraham 70, 83, 230
Lind, Michael 236n
Linklater, Andrew 15n, 119
Lippmann, Walter 122, 173
Little, Richard 12, 187, 190n, 242n, 252
Lo, Chih-Cheng 162n
Luttwak, Edward 60n

McCormick, John 16n, 113n, 239n
Machiavelli, Niccolo 6, 26, 108, 246, 247
Mahan, Alfred Thayer 257–8
Marshall Plan (1947) 182
Marx, Karl 247, 255, 256, 261
Mastny, Vojtech 193n
materialism 187, 225, 244
Mayers, Robert J. 189n, 190n
Mazur, G. O. 16n
Mearsheimer, John 14, 17n, 134n, 139, 160n,
    167, 188, 189n, 190n, 193n, 235n, 244,
    245, 265n
    The Tragedy of Great Power Politics 119
Meier, Heinrich 86n, 91n, 239n
Meinecke, Friedrich 4
Mercer, Johnathan 17n
Merkl, Adolf Julius 104
Merriam, Charles E. 111, 117n
Métall, Rudolf Alasdár 116n
Meyer, Karl E. 194n
Middle East 176, 201
Mill, John Stuart 198
Milton, Giles 60n
Mitrany, David 215n, 259
    A Working Peace System 212
Mollov, Benjamin 14n, 25, 39n, 266n
Molloy, Sean 15n, 189n
monarchies 147, 150
    Europe 142, 148, 149
monistic systems 103–4, 109
Monroe, President James 151
Monroe Doctrine (1823) 11, 48–9, 55, 72–7,
    80, 151
Montaigne, Michel de 130, 131
Moore, Barrington 247, 265n
moral judgments 20, 48
moral philosophy 21, 22
moral standards 19, 30